DATE DUE

MAY 18 2006	

DELINQUENCY and CRIME: Cross-Cultural Perspectives

Ruth Shonle Cavan
Northern Illinois University

Jordan T. Cavan
Emeritus, Rockford College

J. B. Lippincott Company
Philadelphia & New York

Library of Congress Catalogue Card Number: 68-15721
Printed in the United States of America

Preface

This book, planned for general reading by college students and interested laymen, was undertaken out of an interest in widening the perspective on delinquency and crime. It is not a survey of delinquency and crime around the world, but an intensive study of such behavior in 14 societies, with attention given to village and urban contrasts, to the effects of massive social change, and to such social aberrations as criminal societies. We, the authors, asked ourselves such questions as these: Do all countries have as much delinquency and crime as the United States? We found that some societies, for example Eskimos and the remote villages of Mexico and India, had little or no delinquency and in some instances little adult crime. But we also found that large cities in Mexico and India had their share of both delinquency and crime. We asked whether all countries placed the same types of conduct in the category of delinquency and crime. We found that acts punished as delinquency or crime in some countries were approved in others. We felt it was necessary to dig beneath the surface and study the whole society: What are the important values; how are families organized and how do they raise their children; what effect has the growth of cities, the development of impersonal industries, and the crushing weight of war had on the behavior of people? We do not feel that we have found firm answers to these and similar questions; we hope we have clarified some.

As with many cross-cultural studies, this one rests on published accounts rather than first-hand research. We have spent short periods of time in most of the European countries discussed, attended international criminological conferences that covered non-European as well as European countries, talked informally with representative criminologists from these countries, and visited numerous correctional schools and prisons. Nevertheless, the detailed information was derived primarily from published materials. The task of selecting societies to be included and assembling data was complicated by a number of factors: lack of available published material; differences of concepts in the various countries which, with the nonuniformity of statistical reports, made comparisons dubious, and the defensive and occasionally propagandistic slant of some reports.

We finished the task with a list of questions, hunches, and hypotheses, to some of which we hope to be able to turn our attention in the future. If the readers find even part of the stimulation and interest in reading the book that we found in writing it, we shall be content.

Ruth Shonle Cavan

Jordan True Cavan

DeKalb, Illinois.

Contents

1/ A Cross-Cultural View of Delinquency and Crime

This book presents to college students and general readers, in nontechnical terms, a description of delinquency and crime in selected countries. In the present state of collaboration and interdependence among countries, no country may further its cultural growth and well-being apart from the growth and well-being of other countries. Economic cooperation and cultural exchange are examples of trends toward bringing the development of all countries into line with the attainments of the most fully developed countries. Problems that once were regarded as being of national interest alone are now within the realm of international concern.

Two crucial problems of international interest are juvenile delinquency and crime, neither of which is strictly self-contained within national boundaries. For example, criminal philosophies and behavior are carried by migrants from one country to another. The Chinese introduced tong wars to the United States, Sicilian immigrants followed a Mafia-like type of crime, and the Spanish carried pickpocketing to Mexico. The most striking importation of crime came when England transported minor offenders and criminals into America and Australia. Such crimes infiltrate into the host society, sometimes generating bitter conflicts between an intrusive group and the indigenous society. An example is found when European countries have conquered and colonized less developed or less aggressive countries. Not only were crimes and criminals sometimes carried to the colony, but the conquerors imposed their legal criminal codes, system of courts, and methods of punishment, which often were contrary to and deeply resented by the conquered people. The natives of a country often were punished by foreign powers for following their own values, even those with religious significance.

International understanding of crime is called for when temporary residents in a foreign country are accused of a criminal act that may not be a crime at all in their own country, or may be a minor offense. Such temporary residents include businessmen, students, tourists, military men, and, sometimes, diplomats and their families. Differences in laws, court procedures, and penalties come into sharp focus, as witness the predicament of some tourists in Communist countries who face long prison terms for offenses that are serious under Communist law but would be considered trivial in the United States.

Finally, knowledge of only one society creates the impression that the social structure found there is inevitable, fixed for all time. Acquaintance with a number of societies breaks through these preconceptions and places delinquency and crime in a cultural setting that increases understanding of one's own society.

These and other reasons point to the desirability of international understanding of differences among societies, and of the conflicts and changes that evolve when nations with greatly different criminal systems meet. An international exchange of knowledge on a voluntary basis has existed for some time and is increasing constantly. In the late eighteenth and early nineteenth centuries, when prison reform centered on correctional schools, jails, and prisons, officials and social reformers freely traveled about Europe and the United States, following up reports of new types of construction. International prison congresses were held in London (1872) and Stockholm (1878), and later an intergovernmental penitentiary commission was formed which held several such congresses until it was dissolved in 1951 and its functions continued by the United Nations, which has held world congresses "on the prevention of crime and the treatment of offenders" in 1955, 1960 and 1965, and sponsors regional conferences.

Other international and regional societies are also active. Understanding and prevention of delinquency and crime call for a world view.

Point of view

Delinquency and crime are defined by every society in terms of its own cultural values. No two societies have quite the same line-up of offenses, although there are strong resemblances. Basically, delinquency and crime are negative concepts; they are violations of values. Each society, no matter how primitive, seeks to socialize its children into positive values and approved behavior supporting those values, a corollary being avoidance of behavior that weakens or corrupts the values. For example, if the right to own private property is a positive value, children are taught that certain things belong to them for their own use. The corollary is that they must avoid taking or disposing of the private property of other people. Where communal property is the value held, children are taught that they may use only their share of the property and may not otherwise appropriate any of it.

From this point of view, delinquency and crime are the result of the failure of a society to completely socialize children into the values and behavior deemed important for the preservation of the society. Delinquency and crime indicate a failure of the educational mechanisms of society rather than a shortcoming of the individual. The noncriminal, or nondelinquent, is the one who has been successfully socialized to accept the values, to fit into the approved patterns of behavior, and to find his personal satisfactions within the prescribed limits. The socialized person, steeped in the social values and their coordinated behavior patterns from childhood, accepts the values of the society as his own. He has internalized them; he has identified with his society; his concept of his self unquestioningly reflects the values of his society. He and his society are one, two faces of the same coin.

The criminal or delinquent is the person whom the society has somehow failed to socialize into the prevailing values and customs. Rather than a self-propelled deviant or rebel, he is society's failure. As such, he is a threat to his society, which may already have developed weaknesses or splits that prevent a high degree of socialization.

Complete conformity often places unbearable strains on some people, who then act contrary to the approved norms of behavior or, in more extreme cases, violate the basic values. Sometimes these violations, especially of the norms, become so widespread that they are tolerated though disapproved. For example, in Mexico City a "Thieves' Market" caters to the needs of the thief who brings in his stolen goods, and also to the needs of the poor person who buys them at less than the market price. Crime and delinquency are nurtured in type and frequency by the society in which they are found; they are part of the cultural pattern of the society and are integrated into the social structure. A psychological element exists, best shown perhaps by the fact that only a minority of persons in a society becomes delinquent or criminal. Also, a few people deviate from the customary crime pattern of a society to commit irrational and often heinous crimes, condemned by all. A discussion of psychological elements is not within the scope of this book, however, which is limited to cultural and social aspects.

It is also part of the thesis that a stable society with a small amount of slow cultural change and little disturbance of the social structure controls delinquency and crime at a moderate level. As a corollary, vast or sudden changes are accompanied by corresponding changes in culture and social organization. Usually an increase of crime and delinquency follows, often with the introduction of new types of crime, not as the automatic result of rapid change, but because of the inability of the society itself to cope with change and, hence, its inability to control deviant behavior of all kinds. Few societies are without continuous or periodic change.

The plan of this book is to describe delinquency and, where necessary for an understanding of delinquency, crime in a fairly stable social situation and as affected by social change.

Five types of change appear in the societies selected for discussion: the normal changes of countries already industrialized; changes attendant upon internal migrations from simple villages or rural communities into industrialized or industrializing cities; the effect of intrusions of one, usually powerful, society into a simpler, relatively defenseless society; disruption that comes with ideological revolution; and acute changes occasioned by war. In some instances, more than one type of change occurs in a given society.

Delinquency as a corollary of crime

The chief focus of the book is juvenile delinquency. Nevertheless, in certain chapters a discussion of crime is included.

Crime is an old concept; juvenile delinquency a very new one. Crime has been a part of organized society since at least the time of the first written records and, no doubt, long before. The first use of the term juvenile delinquency was toward the end of the eighteenth century, and another century passed before the term became embodied in law.

In several chapters a discussion of crime is included as a foundation for the discussion of juvenile delinquency. There are several reasons for this:

1. In some societies it is difficult to separate juveniles from adults. Boys and girls at an early age pass from childhood into adulthood without an intervening period of adolescence—the period that in western societies is sometimes referred to as the "delinquency age." Youth either play the role of children, under the control of the family elders, or abruptly they are held responsible for their behavior and are treated as adults whose misdeeds are controlled or punished by community action. There is no concept of juvenile delinquency. There are misbehaving children or adult criminals. Many young persons who would be considered juvenile in the United States are adults in some other societies.
2. In some societies a major emphasis of adult life is well-organized aggressions against outsiders, for example, the criminal tribes of India or the traditional Mafia of Sicily. Children are reared in a culture regarded by the society as justified but by the victims as criminal. Parents and other adults are the teachers.
3. In certain segments of some societies almost the only adult career which is open to children is a criminal one. Children are drawn into association with adult criminals in a relationship that suggests an apprenticeship.

Definition of crime

Crime will be defined first, since it represents a more clearly accepted and historically earlier concept than does delinquency. A preliminary question requiring a working answer is how crime can be defined to fit the great diversity of culture in different countries. Formal, written laws are not the answer in view of the great number of nonliterate societies. In many tribal and folk communities the definitions of crime lie in the memories of the inhabitants, and the treatment of crime is imbedded in customary procedures without formal courts or penal institutions.

The definition cannot be in terms of specific acts, since what is a crime in one nation may be a laudatory act in another. Even in the United States, criminal laws differ among the states, and still more and greater differences appear among nations. For example, killing an aged person for the sake of survival of the village was formerly approved in some Eskimo communities; by contrast, in India, where the extended family owns farm land jointly, the elders have status and authority. Even when an act is regarded as criminal in a number of nations, as stealing is, interpretation differs: what is stolen and the meaning of the theft differ from one society to another. Various primitive tribes, including the Eskimo, traditionally regard theft from a fellow-tribesman as a serious crime, but felt no compunction about stealing from another tribe or from traders or hunters who intruded into their territory.

The act itself does not make the crime. The act becomes criminal when it threatens highly regarded social values and is most heinous when those values are sacred in nature.

In many societies a distinction must be made between private and public offenses. For instance, quarrels and feuds, even of a murderous nature, may be regarded as private, to be settled between individuals or their families, whereas wanton killing may be a public crime to be settled by third parties not involved in the criminal act. In the United States these disinterested third parties are police officers and judges. In less well-organized societies, formal officers may not be provided, but all know that men in certain positions of status have the duty and authority to deal with public criminals.

Based on the above discussion, a working definition of crime, applicable to both simple and complex, literate and nonliterate, societies may be formulated as follows:

Typically, a crime is an act that violates the values held or professed by the dominant stratum of a society and considered necessary for its survival. *Survival* refers either to physical survival or to survival of the specific system of morals and approved behavior held at a given time. *Dominant* refers to the controlling group within a society: in a democratic society, the majority of the people; in a dictatorship, the controlling person in the state; in other societies, the ruling clique or "party leaders."

It may be argued that many acts violate values but are not serious enough to be considered crimes. A further statement then may be added to the definition:

Characteristically, the violating act must be specifically defined or generally accepted as dangerous — that is, a societal threat. This specification may be in written legal codes or, in societies without written codes, may exist in the values that are disseminated orally to the young of each succeeding generation along with the corresponding patterns of behavior. Any violation of these laws or codes results in penalties or deterrents already established in law or in custom, or embodied in precedents. The judgment of violation is made and the penalties applied by officials or certain categories of persons designated by the society.

In brief, then, a crime is an act that violates a value considered vital for physical or cultural survival of a society, is recognized by that society as a violation, and is officially enforced by established penalties.[1]

By this definition, crime is not merely an individual act that some other individual may refer to as "a crime." Nor is it an act that one society may classify as a crime when it occurs in another society. Crime is related to the values of the society in which it occurs. It is part of the internal social organization of that society and takes its meanings from the belief in the damage that it would do to that society. Its control through repression or punishment is part of the internal social organization.

Adolescence and juvenile delinquency

The abrupt transition in some societies from childhood to adulthood has been noted. In these societies the concept of juvenile delinquency is lacking.

The concept of juvenile delinquency rests upon a prior concept of an intermediate stage of development when the person is no longer a young child but not yet an adult — a period when it is thought he should not be held fully accountable for crimes and should have less serious offenses treated as due to shortcomings in his training rather than as willful offenses. In western societies this period is given the cultural definition of adolescence. Not all countries recognize a period of adolescence; they rarely have a concept of juvenile delinquency.

[1] For comparison, Hoebel's definition of law (without regard to crime) follows: "A social norm is legal if its neglect or infraction is regularly met, in threat or in fact, by the application of physical force by an individual or group possessing the socially recognized privilege of so acting." E. Adamson Hoebel, *The Law of Primitive Man, A Study in Comparative Legal Dynamics,* Harvard University Press, 1954, p. 28; also, Hoebel, *Men in the Primitive World,* McGraw-Hill, 1958, Chapter 27.

The shortening or omission of adolescence as a recognized stage in human development seems to occur when certain social conditions are present: well organized family, with some hierarchy of status that places children in subordinate roles to specified adults, generally older males; control by the family elders of means of livelihood, which usually call for simple skills; political participation by family representatives rather than by individuals; few outside agencies for child training or social control that compete with the family; pervasion of all phases of life by religious beliefs and sanctions; and isolation of the family from outside cultures. The roles into which each boy or girl is destined to fit are well established. He is allocated to certain roles with little choice. Therefore the child can be socialized specifically for his ascribed roles and transferred to these roles at the appropriate age. Since skills are simple and family control relatively total in nature, little occasion arises for choice of roles or for long-drawn-out preparation for them. The boy or girl becomes an adult psychologically and socially near the time when he is physically mature. He has no need for an intermediate period of adolescence and none is granted him. He has little opportunity for a public display of delinquency.

In contrast is the situation in western industrialized societies, where both a period of adolescence and a concept of juvenile delinquency exist. The family does not operate as a social, economic, or political unit. A child, at an early age, enters specialized agencies that compete for his loyalty and open many choices to him for present or future aspirations and goals. The passage from childhood to adulthood is not clearly and almost inevitably channeled toward a specific adult role. In the transition from early childhood in his family to later childhood in organized agencies, the child may escape incorporation into any conventional, organized group and become a kind of "free lance" in his behavior, lacking in self-discipline or clear orientation toward a goal. Also, full entrance into adulthood calls for a prolonged period of training in vocational or professional knowledge, and exercise in self-discipline and the ability to make rational decisions. This period of slow transition, lasting perhaps six or more years, is adolescence. It has been variously deplored as a wasted period or accepted as a needed period for youth to explore life and, with little guidance, find his own way into adulthood, a period when his most influential companions are his similarly seeking peers, a period when a distinct youth culture develops, with the possibility for a delinquent subculture.

The lack of a period of adolescence and a concept of juvenile delinquency without full criminal responsibility in some societies complicates the formulation of a definition of juvenile delinquency that will transcend specific individual cultures. In fact, a formal definition is most applicable to western and westernized societies. Its pertinence for the simple societies rests in the need to explain the nonexistence of juvenile delinquency combined with the existence of adult crime.

Juvenile delinquency defined

Juvenile delinquency is basically conduct that violates criminal laws or codes as defined for adults; it also includes other acts that are considered to be detrimental to youth. The age period may be stated in law or by custom. In societies where it is not, for this book the period is considered to end with entrance into adult activities and status, such as entrance into men's societies, assumption of adult family or societal activities, marriage, or initiation rites into adulthood. When not specifically stated, delinquencies will be considered to be misbehavior that leads to formal or customary penalties predetermined in the culture of the society and dealt out by persons appointed officially or by custom. The punishing person may be a judge, the leader of a men's cult, or the father in a patriarchal society, who, as the chief disciplinarian figure, metes out punishment according to law or custom and not according to his individual feelings in the situation.

The formal legal concept of juvenile delinquency usually is detailed and elaborate. The United States is used as an example. Only the general outlines can be given, as each state has its own laws.

After a long period of recognition of crime among children as of a different quality than crime among adults, juvenile delinquency was legally defined in 1899 in Illinois. Laws were passed that not only defined juvenile delinquency but established a special court to handle the cases. Other states passed similar laws. Meanwhile European countries were going through a similar process of singling out youthful offenders and making special provisions for them. Countries with colonies in Africa and Asia transplanted their provisions for juvenile delinquents to their colonies, supplanting in the cities the traditional indigenous methods of handling such offenders. In the folk or tribal areas of the colonies the old ways prevailed, and sometimes among recent migrants to the cities the old ways persist under a thin veneer of westernization.

Generally speaking, in the United States juvenile delinquency, as distinct from crime, rests on three points:

1. Definitions of what constitutes youthful offenses. The laws of the various states include, as delinquency, acts harmful to other people that would constitute crimes if committed by older persons, and, in addition, a long and varied list of types of misconduct thought to be harmful to the developing and maturing child or youth. The latter acts are not defined as legal offenses for adults, for example, being on the streets late at night, drinking before a certain age, or being truant from school (the adult equivalent would be absenteeism from work).
2. Age limits for the delinquency period are set by each state. Usually, children below a certain age, perhaps seven, are not regarded as responsible for their acts, no matter how heinous. Through a period of 10 or 12 years (often between the ages of seven and 18) the child is held responsible but deserving of special treatment, the intent of which is the child's own welfare as well as the safety of society. Above the upper age limit, the child is regarded as an adult and no longer has the protection of special laws.
3. Segregation of delinquents from adult criminals from the time of arrest, through trial, to final probation or confinement of the delinquent in a training school. However, for serious crimes of the adult type, some states permit offending juveniles above a certain age to be handled in the same way as adult criminals. Thus the chronic school truant may be treated as a juvenile delinquent up to the upper age of compulsory school attendance (usually 16 or 18), whereas the young teenager who has committed murder may be transferred to the adult system of criminal procedures (jail, trial, imprisonment, even the death penalty) and denied the protection and retraining facilities provided by the juvenile court system.

In some countries only adult-type crimes, committed by juveniles, are considered juvenile delinquencies, with minor offenses being handled by social welfare or educational agencies. Other nations do not recognize the concept of juvenile delinquency and disregard the age of the offender when a crime is committed.

Scope of this book

This book identifies criminal and delinquent behavior in selected societies according to the definitions already given. It goes on to relate such deviating behavior to the strengths and weaknesses of the society in which it occurs. For many reasons the discussion can only be tentative and suggestive of relationships rather than definitive and positive. The book draws upon a variety of published materials, some of which are carefully documented official reports, some limited research studies, others observational and descriptive in nature. Accounts and reports have been checked carefully against one another in order to avoid fantastic imaginings of casual observers.

In considering delinquency and crime in a number of countries, the temptation is strong to compare them with each other as to types or frequency of offenses. A valid comparison is not feasible since each country has its own conception of delinquency and crime. For example, public drunkenness, which leads to thousands of arrests in the United States, is not regarded as a legal offense in many European countries; prostitution stands in somewhat the same position. Gambling, illegal over much of the United States, is not only a legal activity in many countries, but may be operated or fostered by the government for its own financial benefit (as in Nevada also). Penalties may differ—most European countries do not have the death penalty, but much of the United States still has it on the statute books. The age limits for juvenile delinquency differ widely. For these reasons virtually the only comparisons that are made refer to general direction of trends without regard to degree of change or types of offenses.

Certain questions have been held in mind in assembling material:

1. What are the chief characteristics of the society?
2. What are the types of behavior regarded by the society as breaking the rules in such a way as to endanger the society?
3. How is this behavior related to the total culture and social organization, both under stable conditions and during periods of change?

4. What means, especially in the training of children, are used to prevent this behavior?
5. What reaction does the society make to crime or delinquency?

No attempt has been made to "cover the subject" in the sense of a world survey. The societies were selected for variety rather than for representativeness of different cultural types. A deliberate effort was made to include a number of different kinds of cultural change. The countries and their main interests for this book are:

Chapter 2. Eskimos, the primitive tribal community and contacts between Eskimos and modern civilization

Chapter 3. Mexico, contrast of the folk village, the village in transition, and Mexico City with its many village migrants

Chapter 4. India, four different types of community: tribes; criminal tribes; peasant villages; large cities with migrations of villagers into the complex urban culture

Chapter 5. Soviet Union, the effect of a radical change in ideology on crime and delinquency

Chapter 6. Mafia in Sicily, a criminal society as the disastrous result of weak government

Chapter 7. England, changing concepts and the development of delinquency; the war

Chapter 8. Eight European countries, primary emphasis on the period of World War II and since

The final chapter points out similarities among the societies.

2 / The Eskimos: Delinquency and Crime in a Primitive Society

The Eskimos have one of the least complex tribal societies, in many places still living in traditional simplicity. They are an extreme example of a nonliterate, isolated, small community with virtually no delinquency and a minimum of crime. One task is to search out the reasons for the lack of delinquency. The Eskimos also illustrate the processes that come about when a simple society comes into contact with a sophisticated, highly organized, technological society, including the effect on deviant behavior.

From islands off the Alaskan Coast, across some 6,000 miles of the Arctic and sub-Arctic region of North America to Greenland lies the inhospitable land where for centuries the Eskimos have built their crude huts from whatever material was provided by nature—blocks of ice, wood, stone, or skins. They are seasonally nomadic, with each small community moving in an annual cycle, calculated to intercept their major source of food—the caribou inland, the walrus and seal along the coast.

Some 20,000 Eskimos have occupied these lands for centuries, unfriendly toward northwest American Indians and in most places only recently disturbed by the encroachments of Europeans, Americans, or Canadians. In this state of isolation, Eskimos have developed a distinctive culture, much of which still remains, especially in the isolated inland or frigid areas that have not attracted men of modern culture.

THE TRADITIONAL CULTURE

To avoid complicated explanations of regional differences, the so-called "classic" Canadian Eskimo is used as the basis of discussion with attention given to regional differences where they contribute to the subject of the chapter (5, 10, 12, 14, 18, 19, 20).* In spite of differences in detail certain elements of basic culture are discernible, for example in the general type of religious beliefs and the reaction to the rigorous physical environment. Most important for this discussion, the social organization differs little from coast to coast. The Eskimos are discussed here as a basically uniform culture group, with distinctions noted when they are pertinent to the purposes of this chapter.

Juvenile delinquency and crime in the traditional culture

No reference to juvenile delinquency was found in the researches for this book—no runaway children; no predatory gangs exploiting, stealing, or injuring people; no incorrigibles; and no school dropouts—or the equivalent in a land without formal schooling. Among adults, stealing—our most prevalent crime—occurred only rarely. Violence occasionally erupted, almost always in the context of personal conflicts and regarded as part of a private altercation, to be settled between the individuals concerned or their families. This lack of delinquency and scarcity of crime cannot be attributed to rigid laws, strict police control, efficient courts, or excellent correctional schools or prisons. None of these agencies of social control had even been thought of, much less established, in the native Eskimo villages or nomadic groups.

Eskimos did not live in a state of anarchy, however. They had a simple but orderly life. Built into the culture through past generations were many features whose chief function was physical survival in a very unfavorable environment. A side effect of this organization for survival was the avoidance of delinquency among the young, and a minimum of adult crime. Delinquency and crime in and of themselves were not problems. But any disturbance of the carefully balanced culture might spell physical disaster and starvation.

Enclosure of the individual by the family

Each Eskimo was a member of a family group. There was literally no place for a detached individual. Orphans, widows, and widowers became members of some relative's family. The ideal was the nuclear family of husband, wife, and their children. But this nuclear family

* Numbers in parentheses refer to the references at the end of the chapters.

was incorporated within an extended family, organized around the oldest male. When a young man married, he brought his wife to his father's house. When the group became too large for a single snow house, hut, or tent—all limited in size by the type and scarcity of building material—adjacent dwellings were built for segments of the family. Under these circumstances, the different households still considered themselves members of the same family, sharing duties and privileges.

The integration of the household group was not only functional in that hunting, preparation of food, making of clothing, and other necessary activities were shared, but life was also shared in a physical sense. The ten or twelve persons constituting one household lived in one room. Especially in the winter, housekeeping, personal physical functions, and social contacts were all carried on in this common room. An exception was found in a few areas, where skins divided the sleeping space according to families. In spite of the virtual absence of privacy, decorum was observed and the privileges and obligations of nuclear family units were respected.

In utilitarian matters, the household operated as a unit, with specialized tasks and roles assigned on the basis of age and sex. Preparation of food might be in the hands of one person; making skin clothing belonged to the women; the men hunted for the entire household. Through these shared functions the needs of the household were met.

In such a tightly organized household, each person had to adapt himself to the needs of the whole group. There was no place for the unruly or incorrigible child. There was also no place in the family organization for neglect of children. While the rearing of children was primarily the duty of parents, older children and other adults took a hand; the child was never unattended or left to his own resources.

This tight incorporation into a functioning family with a place for everyone and the ready availability of child care eliminated some of the tensions that we tend to think of as contributing to delinquency. Uncontrolled emotions on the one hand and emotional deprivation on the other were incompatible with the demands of Eskimo life.

The integrated community

The extended family in its turn was part of a small community of such families, often with some degree of relationship tying them together. Rarely did the whole community number as many as a hundred persons. Each community was independently organized, but in a loose and flexible fashion. There were no elected officials. The leaders had earned their status. The acknowledged best hunter was the secular leader. He was a "natural" leader of competence in the field of hunting, technically skilled and respected for his ability to plan and organize. The only other leader was the shaman or *angakok,* the man who was versed in the religious beliefs and in ways to manipulate the spirits for the welfare of the community. The skills of the secular and spiritual leaders were passed on to younger members of the community; as the older men failed with age or died, new natural leaders were ready to take their places, all by common consent and acceptance by the community.

It has often been said that the Eskimos had no political organization and no government. This was true so far as formal organization was concerned. But a body of beliefs, values, and customs developed that provided the framework within which Eskimo public life functioned. Children grew up within this body of beliefs and skills. They accepted them without question.

Decisions regarding moving to a new location with better food supply, when to start on a hunt, how to control the occasional miscreant were achieved by consensus of the adult males, sometimes after consultation with the women. They were not the result of formal legal or official authority. Even though the consensus was bounded by tradition, custom, and religious beliefs, a degree of flexibility and democracy prevailed. If the decision proved a poor one, it was at least the result of shared opinion and discussion. Thus resentments were reduced to a minimum and rebellions were unheard of.

Both the family and the small community were intimate personal groups. Everyone knew everyone else. To incur displeasure or disapproval of family or community was a cruel punishment, one that a child could not withstand and that sometimes drove an adult or family to move on to a nearby settlement.

Uniformity of culture

The uniformity of Eskimo culture prevented many of the situations related to delinquency and crime that arise in modern complex societies. Among most Eskimo groups there were no social classes with unequal distribution of wealth and inherited status that placed one family above another. Hence there tended to be neither envy nor frustration, nor adoption of the values of a higher class combined with inability to achieve those values. Individuals or families gained a position of prestige by individual skill in the common process of meeting needs. Such a position was regarded as earned and justified.

Moreover, each Eskimo community resembled nearby communities in degree of cultural development and standard of living. Most Eskimos did not travel far except for the nomadic groups; they usually met only members of neighboring communities very like their own. There were no cultural conflicts of values and standards of behavior, no group that might give approval to behavior stigmatized as beyond toleration in the home community. The Eskimo had little choice but to conform: he knew of no alternative forms of culture and he could not escape the pressures of his own community.

Pressure-reducing mechanisms

In a community with such close personal contacts and such demand for cooperation and conformity, it might seem that tensions would rise to such heights that outbursts would necessarily result. Several tension-reducing mechanisms were part of the culture.

The crowded households were not a year-round arrangement. In the relatively warm summer months, extended families tended to separate into their nuclear units. With all their household goods stacked on dog sleds or—if the melting snow would not permit the use of sleds—on the backs of men, women, children, and dogs, small family units moved in all directions. They traveled only short distances and eventually returned to some customary or prearranged place for the winter months. Thus for several months each year the small nuclear family might be free from the physical crowding and constant supervision of other family members and neighbors. Children were released from the indoor life and could play in the open and explore the nearby area. Few daily demands were made on the children except when a large project was underway, such as moving, or hunting caribou. Adults also were freed from personal irritations arising from overcrowding and had more opportunity for individual initiative.

Marriage created special problems and had its own means for solving them. Marriage was arranged by the parents and apparently accepted without objections. The girl wanted a man who was a good hunter, and the man wanted a wife to satisfy his needs and produce children. Various tensions might arise after the marriage. The wife might not be able to fulfill her functions, such as accompanying her husband on a long hunting trip to look after his needs, and preparing the skins or carcasses for transportation home, especially when she was ill, pregnant, or nursing a baby. To resolve this potential difficulty, it was customary for the hunter and a man who remained in the village to exchange wives for the duration of the hunt. The wives, reared in a society where such exchanges were customary, apparently did not object.

A permanent arrangement for sharing of wives was also followed in some groups and served to reduce several types of tension. On St. Lawrence Island two men who were partners but members of different clans sometimes entered into a permanent relationship for intermittent exchange of wives. The arrangement was not clandestine but was made known in connection with certain community ceremonies, which ended in a random temporary pairing of men and women for sexual relations. In the permanent exchange relationship, all children born to the woman were considered the children of her husband. In fact, one motivation for the arrangement seems to have been the desire for children—or a male child—when husband and wife had no children. The visiting male might be the biological father, but the child was considered to be the child of the husband. In addition to this function, the relationship served the usual utilitarian functions of wife exchange, and also provided a means of variation in sexual gratification.[1] Another reason was to extend the kinship group and provide friendly relatives to greet the traveler.

Polygyny, or the system whereby a man has exclusive possession of more than one wife, was not common but might occur, especially when the number of women exceeded the number of men. Marriage was a way of incorporating the extra women into the social organization and making them useful in a family group.

Divorce was a frequently used method of reducing marital tensions. Either husband or wife might divorce the other. The divorce was accomplished by separation with consent, a method just as informal as the marriage, which in some groups had been formed simply by sexual consummation and the establishment of joint living quarters.

[1] Charles C. Hughes, *An Eskimo Village in the Modern World,* Cornell University Press, 1960, pp. 267-69. By 1954 this practice had been discontinued.

In these ways, marriage had many socially approved adaptations to take care of tensions or hardships without loss of the essential principle of family continuity. These various methods (except divorce) were all initiated by the husband and were part of the cultural pattern of marriage.

Another accepted method of reducing tensions was in the approved killing of members of the community who were not self-supporting as judged by the amount of work they could do. These persons were the very old whose days of usefulness were over, and babies born under circumstances that made it impossible for the parents to provide for them. The killing of the old had no sacred connotations; it was a practical expedient, practiced in only some of the Eskimo tribes. Where it was customary, the son who took his parent to a remote place and left him (or her) with a small amount of food, soon to die from the cold, was regarded as having performed a meritorious act.

Only under certain circumstances was a baby put to death, and then only within a few hours after birth before the child had been accepted as either a human being or a member of the family. The circumstances justifying infanticide were the death of the mother; birth of twins, only one of which could be nursed adequately; defectiveness of the baby; the birth of a child when the preceding child was still dependent on nursing for food; or any other situation that might preclude the survival of the child. If anyone wished to "adopt" the unwanted baby, it was gladly surrendered to that person. As with the abandonment of the old, infanticide was a practical expedient. The continued existence of the child threatened the survival of the cooperative community.

Another means of reducing tensions was in the system of religion. The spirits were held accountable for many mishaps, especially those of a widespread nature that affected the food supply. The Eskimos did not sit helplessly by waiting for a change of weather or for the seal or caribou to appear before supplies were at an end. The *angakok* by various magical devices sought to propitiate the spirits and induce them to change the weather or send the animals. The belief in the power of the *angakok* directed resentments, hostilities, and also hope toward the spirits.

Sometimes an individual was accused of injuring another person or making him ill. Instead of attributing this circumstance to the accused person as a malicious act, the person was thought to be in the power of an evil spirit. The *angakok* then, through magical means, exorcised the evil spirit, with the result that the accused person was restored to the good graces of the community—and presumably the ill or injured person recovered. Under some circumstances a person accused of being a sorcerer was killed.

The *angakok* was thus a powerful person in social life, who mediated between the people and misfortune, and in terms of their religious beliefs could turn aside evil influences and bring the promise if not the actual accomplishment of good fortune.

By these many social mechanisms, tensions that might have led to crime were prevented. It is important to note the controls placed on the use of the mechanisms; individuals could not kill the old or babies, seduce a wife, or make use of spirits for their own wanton desires. The mechanisms could be applied only for the regulation and good of the community.

Training of children for the integrated community

Children were specifically trained to fit into the primary family and the cooperative integrated community. The little child began to learn the routines of daily life by imitative play, with toy bows and arrows, kayaks, and household objects. The little girl learned the household tasks through association with her mother and other adult women, including preparation of food for immediate use and preservation of it for winter, and working with skins and shaping them skillfully into clothing that would keep the person dry and warm in bitterly cold weather. By the age of six, little girls were given the care and supervision of a younger child. The little boy was similarly occupied. At first he helped his mother, but as soon as possible he went with his father and other men to fish and hunt. He learned to manage the dogs and to maneuver the kayak, to fish for seals in the freezing cold of winter, and to make the intricate tools, weapons, and household equipment needed for survival. He was expected to be physically hardy, strong, self-confident.

It is significant that the children learned the skills needed as adults by participating with adults in the daily performance of work. Education and daily life were not separated. Teachers and parents were one and the same. Children saw the relationship of what they did to the total family life, and they used and saw others use the results of their labor. The practical training tied them closely to the family and the community.

As children learned the skills in the family, so also did they learn the religious beliefs and the coordinated attitudes that held the community together and laid the basis for social control within both the family and community. Myths, legends, and songs contained both the history and the values of the Eskimos; children learned these from infancy.

Mother and child

The relationship between mother and small child was physically close and emotionally warm. An infant lived in a pouch sewed into the mother's upper garment. Here he was safe, warm, and nearby for nursing or other care. The mother worked, traveled, fished, visited, and danced in the community dances with the baby on her back. When, on occasion, she laid him on the sleeping platform, she watched over him carefully, for a hungry sled-dog might injure or kill the baby. When he was old enough to walk he was placed in the care of an older child. The mother nursed the child until he was two or three years old, as other suitable food was not available.

The mother's treatment of the child was soothing, considerate, and nonaggressive. There was little or no physical punishment, perhaps because the child was named after an ancestor who would become angry if the child were thus punished. When a child transgressed the rules of good behavior he was quietly reprimanded or gently restrained; he learned that such behavior displeased the mother and would cause other people to avoid him. Harsh scolding, rough handling, and physical punishment that might arouse hostility and break the bond between mother and child were not used. The child was taught to modify his behavior to conform to the community expectations. He was not held to unnecessary rigid rules or ones that he was not ready to obey. Training (toilet training, for instance) was gradual and lapses did not become an issue or crisis. The house of the Eskimo was simply furnished and outside there were no flower beds or precious shrubs; there were few don'ts for the child to observe.

Most of the care of the little child was in the hands of the mother. Between child and father, the relationship was one of unquestioning obedience on the part of the child and respect for the father. This "father" might actually be the grandfather of the children in the family, to whom grown sons paid respect and obedience. As one adult Eskimo stated in the 1950's, "There is no age limit. It's not like the 21 age limit, when the person becomes an adult."[2] The discussions of child training do not include a discussion of how this respect was instilled in the child. Since the extended family was based on a hierarchical system and each generation owed obedience and respect to the next older, it may be assumed that the child accepted this system as the natural order. There is no indication in various accounts of Eskimo life of harsh authoritarian treatment on the part of the father or grandfather.

The treatment of the Eskimo child developed compliance, for which he was rewarded by the approval of parents and other adults. He adapted to the close family and community life without aggressive resistance. It has been suggested that this compliance to established culture reduces initiative on the part of the adult Eskimo, but this might be debatable. Although the Eskimo functions within a framework of seasonal changes and of religious taboos, individuals, families, and small communities must take the initiative, in all they do, to remain alive.

The procedure and surroundings of child rearing were very different from those in the United States, where rigid rules are typical, often of a nature that the small child does not understand. Harsh treatment and physical punishment often arouse hostility on the part of the child, matched by equal feelings in the parent; the aggressive behavior of the scolding, punishing parent is often matched by equal aggressiveness on the part of the child. The training of the Eskimo child did not call forth such reactions. At present in the United States, some juvenile delinquency is attributed to family conflicts, unloving parents, and harsh parental treatment. To the extent that this relationship is valid, it did not exist among Eskimos.

No place for adolescence

The lack of a long period of social adolescence in some societies has already been discussed in Chapter 1, and it was noted that in these societies there was little juvenile delinquency. The traditional Eskimo society lacked both adolescence and delinquency. The child

---

[2] Hughes, *op. cit.*, p. 236.

and youth was never physically separated from his family, either on a daily basis for education, employment, or recreation, or on a yearly basis at college or for a prolonged journey. There were no hangouts or lighted street corners where youth might gather. As adult skills were learned, the child's status increased and in some groups special recognition was given as each new stage was reached. A special step toward adulthood was reached when a boy was given his own kayak, usually at about age eight or nine, or when, inland, he brought down his first caribou at about age 11 or 12. In some groups, the killing of the first major meat animal called for special celebration. As soon as the youth had killed at least one of each such animal he was considered ready for marriage. Thus step by step, the boy made his way from childhood to adulthood, always living within and participating in the activities of family and community. With perhaps less group recognition of progress, the girl also learned step by step how to fill the adult role.

The girl was ready for marriage at about age 14, the male at about age 17. Prior to marriage, sex relations on a personal basis were permitted, but after several short affairs the boy or girl was expected to settle down and assume the responsibilities of marriage. Too long a period of sexual dalliance was disapproved. Marriage did not bring independence from the family, although it signified adulthood. The groom brought his bride to his father's (or grandfather's) home; they were given a special sleeping place. The young man continued his participation in the family hunting and fishing expeditions. The young wife transferred her relationship of respect for her own father and of shared activities with her mother to her new parents-in-law. If, as occasionally happened, the marriage did not work out satisfactorily, the impasse was ended by divorce and the return of the wife to her parents.

Why little or no juvenile delinquency?

Eskimo mores are not oriented to prevention of delinquency. They are positively related to training for conforming behavior, which automatically precludes delinquency. These factors include:

1. Complete incorporation of each child in an extended family.
2. Integration of these families into a compact community.
3. The need for adaptation to avoid conflict in these tightly bound groups.

4. Uniformity of culture and the absence of social classes.
5. High degree of cooperation necessary for physical survival.
6. Control of the community by consensus rather than autocratic authority.
7. Presence of pressure-reducing mechanisms that prevented the building up of hostilities.
8. Methods of child-training that produced compliance to the guidance of the mother, acceptance of the authority of the father, and willing cooperativeness.
9. Absence of a period, between childhood and adulthood, when the child might escape from incorporation in adult groups.

ADULT CRIME

The compliance and adaptability built into the child's personality did not serve for a lifetime (1, 5, 12, 13, 16). Adult crime was not rife in the Eskimo society, but it existed, was recognized as such, and was combatted by specific customary methods beyond the scope of family control. Since children came early into adult status, young offenders would be subjected to public social control at an age when in most parts of the United States they would still be classified as juvenile delinquents.

Threats to survival

A crime was behavior that constituted a threat to the welfare or survival of the community, primarily on a physical level. Chief among such crimes was stealing. Opportunities for theft were limited. The land and the sea where a village customarily hunted belonged to the community as a whole. Personal possessions, clothing, tools, weapons were privately made and belonged to the individual. The tools and weapons could be borrowed with the permission of the owners, thus reducing the temptation to steal. If a theft did occur, it was severely punished. Animals, individually killed, belonged to the hunter. However, much hunting was a group enterprise, the meat being distributed according to fixed rules. Private ownership was also limited by the axiom that no one might have more possessions or food than he could use. Generosity and gift-giving were ways of sharing that enhanced the giver's prestige. Hoarding was thus discouraged, and since all shared equally, theft was also automatically discouraged. Taking or keeping food beyond one's share was regarded as stealing and as a community threat since in extreme cases the survival of the entire village was at stake. A person guilty of creating conditions of starvation was considered a murderer.

Lying was also identified as a crime, apparently as a violation of the trust that the community felt it must be able to place in each individual. Abuse of one person by another was also a crime.

Killing another person was not necessarily a crime. The destruction of an old parent or a new-born baby, as discussed earlier, was not a crime. Nor was it a crime for a man to kill the seducer of his wife. But unprovoked killing or a chain of murders that threatened to deplete the supply of men in a community and therefore endanger the food supply was a serious crime and called for community action.

Private quarrels and wrongs

Distinct from public crimes were private wrongs, one of the most serious of which was adultery or, still worse, persuasion of a wife to leave her husband. The ease with which husbands passed their wives back and forth should not be misunderstood. So long as the husband made the arrangements, extramarital sex relations were not a cause for hostility. When the wife stepped out of her subservient role, however, and on her own initiative engaged in sexual relations with another man or went to live with him without a previous divorce, a grievous wrong had been committed against her husband. A still greater offense against the husband came if another man raped his wife. In any case, the wrong was not committed by his wife, but by the man who lured her away or took her by force. The seduction of a wife was the greatest insult that one man could impose on another. It was an attack upon his status as proprietor of his wife and as a man. To restore respect in his own eyes and in the eyes of the community, the husband had to recognize the offense and challenge the offending male. He might assault the man or challenge him to a test of physical strength or to a song contest, which will be discussed later. If the second male actually induced the wife to leave her husband and live with him, the husband might kill him without punishment from the community. Such murders were not regarded as offenses against the community, that is, as crimes. They grew out of a private altercation and conflict and hence were to be settled privately, even to the extent of killing. Sometimes such a murder led to a feud with a chain of killings which were often then defined as crimes, that is, as an offense against the community. Incidentally, an adulterous husband was not regarded as having wronged his wife and she took no action against him or his paramour.

The killing of an offender in a private wrong might leave behind a chain of responsibilities. The man who avenged an insult to him by killing the offender was responsible for the care of the widow and her children. In some cases it was the duty of a murdered man's son to avenge him when the son reached a suitable age. One account cites the case of a boy whose father was killed when he was a baby. He was reared with the knowledge that it was his duty to destroy his father's murderer. When he was 14, his kin told him the time had come and he killed the man who had taken his father's life. For this act he was not censured or punished.

Although blood vengeance was recognized as justified, it had unfortunate repercussions in the community. It set one family or kin group against another and disrupted the established pattern of co-operation upon which the community depended for survival. A latent feud might continue for several generations, bursting into violence from time to time. Therefore various devices were used to prevent a feud and at the same time save face. A man with a respected status in the community whose kin had been killed might go unarmed to the murderer and ask him to kill him also. When the killer refused the matter was closed without loss of face. Or the murderer might present himself unarmed to the kin of his victim and give them an opportunity to dispose of him. Again, their refusal closed the matter.

From sin to crime

The Eskimo's daily life was circumscribed with numerous taboos or prohibitions against certain behavior. The taboos were closely linked with the belief in powerful spirits of animals and in gods. To violate a taboo was to sin, to offend the spirits or gods, who then retaliated by sending illness, an inadequate food supply, or some other calamity. It was then the task of the *angakok* to set in motion long involved procedures through which the offender would be identified: he might confess or might simply be accused. Since the offense was against supernatural powers, presumably they would punish the offender. Actually, the *angakok* sometimes constituted himself a judge and assigned earthly punishment, such as abstention from specified foods or separation of husband and wife.

Sometimes the distinction between a sin and a crime was blurred. Hoebel distinguished between a sin and a crime as follows: the violation of a taboo was a sin supernaturally sanctioned; willful and repeated sinning became a crime legally (or in custom) punished.[3] The transition from sin (offensive to the spirits) to crime (harmful to the community) is clearly seen when the broken taboo actually (and not simply symbolically) threatened the community. Many taboos were related to hunting and the use of food. Strict rules, governed by supernatural taboos, controlled the hunt, the distribution of meat and other products from the animals killed, and the consumption of food. Violation of the taboos not only offended the spirits but hampered the community in its struggle for survival. For repeated offenses of this kind, the *angakok* might assign a severe penalty. An incident related about the Labrador Eskimos is illustrative. A girl who had violated certain food taboos and thus had offended the animals and also threatened the food supply was exiled by the *angakok* from the village during the winter cold. Her fate was to freeze to death.[4]

Penalties

Penalties for the various types of public crimes were compatible with Eskimo culture. Eskimos were less concerned with making the offender suffer for his crime, deterring others, or reforming the criminal than with ridding the village of a dangerous person and hence preserving the routines of life necessary for survival. Exile from the village, especially in the winter, was a severe penalty. It rid the village of a menace—and the village was not much concerned with the fate of the offender.

Execution of the offender by common consent of the village heads of family was the most drastic action and permanently disposed of the offender. This publicly approved execution must not be confused with the killing of one man by another whose wife he had stolen. The killing in a private quarrel was a matter between two men and their kin. Wanton killing or a succession of murders by one man was a threat to the entire society since it was unpredictable, deprived the community of a hunter, and left a widow and children to be cared for

[3] E. Adamson Hoebel, *The Law of Primitive Man, A Study in Comparative Legal Dynamics,* Harvard University Press, 1954, pp. 73-74.

[4] Diamond Jenness, *People of the Twilight,* University of Chicago Press, 1959, pp. 85-89.

by others. The decision to execute was arrived at in some such manner as the following: the leader of the community went from one male head of a family to another. If all agreed on the offender's guilt and the necessity of disposing of him for the benefit of the community, either the leader killed him or this task was assigned to a member of the offender's own family. In either case, the matter was then closed; no reprisal against the executioner was allowed. The executioner temporarily played the role of the hangman in American society or the man who pulls the switch for the electric chair. He was not acting for himself but as the representative of society.

Another less drastic but effective way of penalizing an offender was to make him feel the displeasure of the community through social ostracism or ridicule. Social ostracism was a severe handicap. Others might continue to work with the offender, but otherwise avoid him. In the small village the offender had no choice of another group to which to attach himself. Sometimes the offender moved to another village, usually one in which he had relatives.

Sometimes the victim of a minor theft would ignore it as a misfortune. Or if he mentioned the theft in public he did it in a humorous manner to make the thief appear ridiculous to the villagers. This was a common means of punishment and strongly disliked as it caused the object of the ridicule to lose face in the small community where everyone soon knew about his loss of status.

Some Eskimo communities had a system of settling conflicts by song duels and tests of strength, held publicly and much enjoyed by the audience. The purpose was to clear the air of tension and to establish the relative status of the contestants, although the victim did not always come out the victor. Buffeting and head-butting were formalized tests of strength. In buffeting, the opponents alternately struck each other's heads with stiffened arms. The one who first toppled was the loser, and the respect of the crowd went to the winner, regardless of his position in the original quarrel. In butting, one contestant butted the head of the other with his head, the one receiving the blow moving his head to intercept it. The one who fell was the loser. In some areas, wrestling served a similar purpose.

Song duels, sometimes combined with the physical contests, were a way to settle disputes of all types. Even a murder might be settled in this way instead of by blood revenge, if the avenger felt that he was not in a position to avenge the death of a relative. Traditional songs were interspersed with references to the current dispute or to the frailties or idiosyncrasies of the opponent. The applause of the audience determined the winner, whose prestige then rose. It would then be possible for the original offender to gain in status, the original victim to sink in status.

The accounts of these customary, permissible ways of settling private disputes and wrongs and the ways of controlling or eliminating a publicly acknowledged criminal all apply to adults. The accounts contain nothing about serious misconduct among children. The tight incorporation of children and youth in the family either prevented serious misconduct or that which occurred was handled as a family affair. It was true that adulthood came early among the Eskimos.

The accounts deal almost exclusively with men. Only occasionally is a woman mentioned as an offender who is dealt with as a public criminal; the case of the young woman who had taken food and been exiled has been mentioned. Women's lives were circumscribed by the family to a much greater extent than men's, and, also, they were under the control of their husbands. Men had a wider life in the village, on the hunt, and in sealing operations. There was more opportunity for conflict with other men over the rights accorded to each man in the cooperative process of these operations. Also, since men "owned" their wives, it is they who were personally outraged if a wife was seduced or was induced to leave her husband to live with another man.

Reasons for adult crime

In view of the absence of juvenile delinquency, some consideration should be given to the occurrence of adult crime. As long as the boy (or girl) played the role of child, he was docile and repressed hostile impulses. However, the background for violence was present, especially among males. Boys were taught to kill animals and often to exert tremendous strength in a close struggle with a large animal. They were prepared for physical violence. The cooperative and conciliatory attitude toward human beings and the physical violence toward animals might easily create ambivalent attitudes.

When a quarrel or conflict arose between two Eskimos there was no means of recourse to an outside agency, such as police. The controls exerted by kin groups or the community came after a crime had been committed—they were not preventive of the initial crime, although they might prevent a blood feud or retaliatory series of murders.

There were few ways in which a man might demonstrate his superior status—not by property or political success. Civic leadership and the status of *angakok* came to few. But the possession of a wife was common to all, and seduction of another man's wife was a way to increase the status of the seducer and reduce the status of the husband. It seems possible that much rivalry, which in another society drains off through economic or political competition, among Eskimos was concentrated in the sexual area.

Marriage did not call for love or inter-personal attraction; it was on a utilitarian level with low emotional content. Personal attraction might very well develop outside marriage. To satisfy the pull of a man toward a woman, however, entailed an insult to the woman's husband. The husband was not forced to try to keep his wife. He might relinquish his claim—in effect, divorce her. But if he felt strongly about his right to his wife, violence might result.

Women seemed uninvolved in crime, and even when they betrayed their husbands sexually were not regarded as having wronged the husband. The difference between regarding the man as culpable and the woman as guiltless for the same sexual act is related to the cultural definition of sex as a physical need for men but simply as a means of serving a man for the woman. The woman was expected to be placid, docile, and unemotional. Her conception of herself as a woman did not involve sex, whereas a man's masculine conception included sexual possession of a woman. The only references to crime among women found in the reports were to occasional thefts.

CONTACTS WITH EUROPEAN-AMERICAN CULTURE

At present, Eskimo families and villages are found in the traditional culture and in all stages of transition to the urban, industrialized culture of Americans and Canadians as found in Alaska and Arctic Canada (2, 6, 7, 8, 10, 11, 15, 17). The degree of change of culture depends primarily upon the frequency, continuity, and depth of contact with Caucasians. The contacts at first were intermittent, beginning when some parts of the Arctic were explored in the sixteenth century, and continuing through long-spaced trading visits of whalers in the nineteenth century. Explorers, trappers, traders, miners seeking gold, and scientific groups came and went, each group making some impact on the Eskimo culture, each seeking more often to take from the Eskimos than to contribute to their welfare.

Effect of intermittent contacts

The early intermittent contacts were all made by the intrusion of Caucasians into the well-organized and long-established Eskimo culture. They were not sought by the Eskimos, but were not repulsed. Through trading ivory walrus tusks, whale baleen, and sealskins for guns, knives, small household items, and rum or whiskey, the Eskimos regarded the contacts as advantageous. The use of alcohol was learned, but the supply was intermittent. Some of the intruders sought and secured sexual relations, apparently without protest from the Eskimos. The traditional custom of wife-lending with the consent of the husband or in some cases the father made these contacts acceptable. If a baby was born it was absorbed into the mother's family. Certain diseases were also brought in, but it seems doubtful whether the Eskimos connected the diseases with the intruders. Their customary explanation was that displeased or evil spirits brought disasters.

From an outsider's point of view the results of the contacts were not always favorable. But the Eskimos valued the material objects that they secured, and used them to lighten their hunting and household tasks. The intermittent contacts did not disturb the basic Eskimo culture directly—certainly not the religion, family organization, or cooperative and self-sustaining economic system.

Settlements by Caucasians

Another and more pervasive type of contact with whites came in the latter part of the nineteenth century and continues to the present: the semi-permanent or permanent introduction of white settlements, usually for some specific purpose and often including a primary or secondary interest in the welfare of the Eskimos as conceived by the whites. A typical settlement of this type has a religious mission, a school (formerly run by the mission, now often by the government), a police agency, a native village council instituted by the whites, a trading post, and more recently a few governmental representatives. A limited number of Eskimos secure employment for wages in these settlements. Officially the settlements are operated by the whites. Eskimos cluster in and near the settlements, adapting superficially to the white culture but remaining essentially "Eskimo" in family organization and system of values. One objective of the white settlement is partly to fulfill the purpose of its establishment, for example, trade for skins that Eskimos are encouraged to bring in, maintain a military post, or carry on some other type of governmental operation. The whites at the settlement usually are under contract to remain a limited number of years; hence the white population is impermanent and contacts with the Eskimos are impersonal. Some of the white agencies are primarily for the benefit of the Eskimos, for example, the mission, school, and governmental welfare services. Although there is some variation of attitude, in general the white attitude is that the Eskimos should be converted culturally into whites. The result often leads to the breakdown in the family and village way of life and methods of social control; however, it also results in improved health and in limited education to fit Eskimos for available jobs.

More diversified white settlements draw in many Eskimos for employment in manual labor. In Canada, Eskimos may be resettled in newly developed white towns by the Canadian government to offset actual starvation that causes many deaths.[5] Other Eskimos, singly or in families, move into open areas in or on the edge of towns and erect their huts or "tent cities." Some of these families go out on the land in the summer to hunt or fish. Others cling to the city, working when they can find employment. Eskimos who have steady employment live in better housing, sometimes provided by the government or the industry for which they work. These neighborhoods usually are segregated and have their own social life and churches. The Eskimos on the fringe of the white towns are in a beginning stage of transition to white culture, marked primarily by confusion between Eskimo and white standards and customs. Those in the settled

[5] In many parts of the Arctic the natural sources of food and material products have decreased to a point where they are no longer adequate to sustain the Eskimos. The delicate balance between Eskimo population and food animals was upset with the introduction of guns to replace arrows, lances, and harpoons, and the encouragement of traders to kill animals not alone for life-needs but for trade. In 1919, a hundred Eskimos died of starvation in the Baker Lake region northwest of Hudson Bay, and in the same area between 1949 and 1958 starvation was the third most frequent cause of death, the first two being pulmonary diseases and infant mortality. F. G. Vallee, *Kabloona and Eskimo in the Central Keewatin.* Northern Coordination and Research Centre, Department of Northern Affairs and National Resources, Ottawa, Ontario, May, 1962, pp. 14, 40-41.

neighborhoods are well on the way to complete acculturation to Caucasian culture or to some form of integration of Eskimo and white beliefs and customs.

At the present time the process of acculturation is a continuous one, as Eskimos on the open land drift into cities or are encouraged to come in for schooling, jobs, or health measures.

Redefinition of Eskimo concepts of crime

Whites came into Eskimo territory with preconceived ideas of sin and crime that they held very strongly. With little consideration for the Eskimo concepts or the relation of their definitions to the total system of beliefs or the social organization, a rather peremptory attempt was made to impose white definitions on the Eskimos. The results varied.

Catholic and Protestant missionaries sought to induce the Eskimos to substitute the Christian religious faith for the traditional systematic belief in spirits and myths, to dispense with taboos, and to substitute the Christian clergyman for the *angakok*. Eskimos did not fight against the Christian religion; some simply added the Christian god to their traditional array of spirits; some followed the Christian rituals in the mission and their own at home. The acceptance of Christianity was facilitated by the fact that it was introduced at the time that the food supply was becoming uncertain and the *angakok* was no longer able to guarantee the supply of food. At present, town Eskimos follow the Christian religion with some private intermixture of the old religion.

Missionaries redefined some of the Eskimo's ways of reducing life tensions as sinful, and police and other government officials defined the same acts as illegal or criminal. These acts, functional in the Eskimo way of life, but strongly disapproved in the white culture, included the various forms of killing: infanticide, killing of the helpless old, killing to avenge a private wrong, and the informal way of obtaining community approval of the execution of a criminal. As various forms of cash relief were developed in the United States and Canada and extended to the Eskimos, some of these old ways of eliminating problems did become useless. In fact, when old people and children began to receive financial aid, their status was reversed. From a burden in the past they now became an important source of income. Private killings and public executions were brought within the framework of the laws of the whites, to be handled by trials and legal punishments. This process was not accomplished with ease, since Eskimos clung to their traditional concepts and methods and did not readily seek the aid of the police or trust their affairs to remote courts and prisons which they did not understand.

Thefts by Eskimos increased with frequency of contact with whites. Since Eskimos regarded only thefts from their own village as a crime, they had no feeling of guilt about stealing from the intruding whites or from white homes or institutions in the settlements. Moreover, the whites did not follow the Eskimo custom of freely lending articles or sharing food. Stealing was a forced kind of sharing. The whites, however, regarded these acts as thefts.

From the point of view of the missionaries and other whites, the Eskimos had many immoral customs, such as the informal methods of marriage and divorce and the customs of wife-lending. Government authorities sought to have the Eskimos obtain a marriage license and secure a divorce through the courts, which might be a long distance from some Eskimo villages. Missionaries also sought to bring Eskimos within this framework, to provide a Christian wedding, and to discourage divorce. All the forms of wife-lending were defined morally and legally as adultery. Children born of irregular unions were legally illegitimate.

The breakdown of family control

The traditional means of social control among the Eskimos loses effectiveness as contacts with whites increase. Police replace the family, trials the disapproval of elders, jail the village ostracism, parole or probation the close family supervision. These are all impersonal city methods of control. They are resented by the Eskimos and bypassed when possible. The crux of the problem of control is not, however, the cities or the presence of police, but the inability of the family, oriented to subsistence living on the land, to accommodate to normal urban strains and demands.

The old, tight family organization was admirably fitted to the stringent life where physical subsistence was the primary objective. The shift to wage employment brings in elements that run counter to the old ways. Employment is on an individual basis; hence family cooperation is not necessary. Employed children still typically live at home and share their wages, but this is on a voluntary basis. The counsel of the competent male head of the family is no longer "law." The hierarchy of status has changed. The formerly dependent old person has gained status, while the status of parents has declined.

Many parents, newly come into contact with white towns, are unfamiliar with white concepts, laws, and skills. They are unable to socialize their children into compliance with the white culture in which the children at least are destined to live. Schools, churches, community centers, and the police have assumed the functions of child-training. The taverns and street corner groups give socialization of another kind, into deviant behavior. Eskimo culture is neglected. The adherence of the older people to Eskimo culture and the socialization of children into white culture makes a rift between the generations and reduces the effectiveness of parental control.

Rise of youthful male delinquency

Town Eskimos on the whole are eager to have steady jobs, earn money, and live with at least some of the amenities of whites (3). A small portion conform to neither the traditional Eskimo nor the white standards. Their behavior seems to have several interrelated features. The members of this category are primarily young males in the late teens and early twenties, who are unmarried and whose work experience has been intermittent. A minority of girls is included. Many of these young people live with their parents, who are only partially aware of what goes on, are confused in their attitudes toward the behavior, and are unable to swing their sons and daughters back to an Eskimo pattern or help them to move more completely into the white pattern. However, the relationship between parents and youth tends to be friendly.

In many ways these young people are experiencing for the first time in Eskimo life a period of poorly controlled adolescence with the defining boundaries not being childhood and adulthood as in American society but emergence from Eskimo culture and incomplete acceptance in white culture.

The deviant behavior of this culturally detached group takes several forms, often of a disorganizing nature and rarely extending into serious crime. Typical behavior includes loitering on the streets, drinking in taverns, frequenting dance halls, a certain amount of rowdiness, and gambling. Thefts from white establishments and assaults are also common. Much of the behavior is carried out by more than one person and therefore is social in nature. Some acts bring the Eskimo to the attention of the police and lead to arrest, often with marked physical resistance.

Excessive use of alcohol is central to such misconduct as public rowdiness, fighting, and sexual exploits. Eskimos in both Alaska and Canada have known the use of alcohol since early traders came, but only in more recent years has a regular supply been possible. In Canada, for example, the ban against the sale of alcoholic beverages to Eskimos was in force until 1960. One study suggests that as Eskimos become more accustomed to its use and more familiar with moderate types of consumption, the excessive use will decline.[6] It was noted that employed, married men bought more at the bottled goods store and less in the tavern for immediate consumption than did the younger unmarried men. The employed men voluntarily controlled their drinking and often limited it to special occasions. They drank to become "happy," but not to the point of drunkenness. They had much to gain by this control—retention of their jobs, respect of white people and of nondrinking Eskimos, and self-respect as they sought to emulate the higher-status whites. Excessive use and public drunkenness were more common among the young unmarried males.

A study of two Canadian towns, one with and the other without a liquor store, noted that the first town drew many young men from the other. These young men arrived with all their money which they freely spent in a binge that lasted as long as the money did. Assaults were common and gambling was a nightly event in the "tent city" where they usually stayed. Heavy drinking was regarded as a sign of masculinity and gambling as a favored recreation. The author of the study found police records difficult to interpret because of the number of out-of-towners and the marked tendency of Eskimos not to report crimes to the police. It was the general impression of officials that thefts and vandalism were increasing.[7]

Sexual deviance of girls

The seeming looseness of Eskimo marital and sex customs played

[6] John J. and Irma Honigmann, "How Baffin Island Eskimo Have Learned to Use Alcohol," *Social Forces,* 44 (September, 1965), pp. 74-83.

[7] D. H. J. Clairmont. *Deviance among Indians and Eskimos in Aklavik, North West Territory.* Northern Coordination and Research Centre, Department of Northern Affairs and National Resources, Ottawa, Ontario, October, 1963, pp. 54-61.

into the hands of the detached white men who were usually the first whites to pass through or settle in an area. The girl was not disgraced by intimacy or pregnancy and later was able to marry an Eskimo.

With more sustained contacts with whites, the concept of illegitimacy—unknown among traditional Eskimos—has become a part of the town Eskimo's changing array of concepts, without, however, adequate means of prevention or control. Eskimo teenaged girls from the fringe villages are no longer content to remain at home and at an early age marry a man of their parent's choice. They are drawn to the tavern, the dance hall, or simply the street corner where they make unsupervised contacts with white youths. The girls admire the whites, their style of dancing, and their ready cash to pay for a drink. They understand that in return they are expected to give sexual favors. The white men are unconcerned if the girls become pregnant. The girl and her baby may still live with her parents. However, the Eskimo attitude is changing. Older Eskimos refer to the girl who becomes pregnant without probability of marriage as silly or stupid; younger Eskimos refer to her as "loose" or a "whore." Young male Eskimos, already angry because Eskimo girls prefer white youths to themselves, declare they will not marry an Eskimo girl with an illegitimate child. Girls themselves are beginning to accept these definitions of their behavior. If the girl's behavior includes rowdiness or public drunkenness or if she seems to be courting unfavorable attention from men, she is very likely to be picked up by the police.[8]

INTERPRETATIONS OF THE CURRENT STATUS OF ESKIMOS

Various interpretations have been made of the current status of Eskimos, including their delinquent and criminal behavior.

1. The traditional family and village control of behavior has broken down among Eskimos who live in or adjacent to white towns. The old type of family and village organization that

[8] In addition to the touch and go sexual contacts described above, many white men "married" Eskimo women, especially in the early days of settlement simply by living with and supporting them and establishing permanent homes. Others had semi-permanent liaisons during the period of a few years that they might stay in the North on a government or business assignment. These temporary wives were not regarded as whores. Clairmont, *op. cit.*, pp. 3-11; R. W. Dunning, "An Aspect of Recent Polygyny and Wife-lending in the Eastern Arctic," *Human Organization*, 21 (1962), pp. 17-22.

enclosed the individual as child and adult is not applicable in a town form of economy where individual jobs make family and village cooperation unnecessary.

2. Eskimos, especially younger ones, turn to the white society for their model of behavior and way of life, first with reference to material possessions, later with reference to values and personal aspirations. Unfortunately, white society offers a variety of models. Eskimos who secure steady employment are able to enter into white society at least in secondary relationships and often are given a certain amount of protection and stability by the industry where they are employed, for example, housing.
3. Eskimos who fail to make a stable contact with whites often find a model among unstable whites who are themselves not incorporated into the middle-class stratum that sets the standards for conformity. These Eskimos most often are young, unmarried males with an intermixture of females. At the same time that they find deviant white models, they are aware of the middle-class standards that give greater prestige but which they are unable to achieve.
4. Marriage often stabilizes the males. With family responsibilities they are drawn into a conforming pattern, either Eskimo or white or more likely a combination of the two. Job stability improves. There are new motives for the control of behavior.
5. One writer sees in the social aspect of alcoholism, gambling, and other deviant activities the beginning of a delinquent subculture, as elaborated by Cohen for American youth.[9] Cohen views the typical delinquent as a lower-class boy who is a member of a gang which sets standards for status that are in opposition to the prevailing middle-class standards which the gang members are unable to reach. Out of their frustration they become defiant and hostile toward the middle class and create their own little social world with its own standards of success. Among the Eskimos, these status-giving behaviors would include drinking, gambling, fighting, and sexual prowess. However, gangs have not formed among the Eskimo youth and their goals are ambivalent. After marriage they often become affiliated with a church and active in community affairs.

[9] Clairmont, *op. cit.*, pp. 67-72; Albert K. Cohen, *Delinquent Boys, the Culture of the Gang*, Free Press, 1955.

Other writers, not specifically concerned with delinquency and crime, also point out the recent trend for Eskimos to move beyond adoption of material objects from the whites, to a stage where they formulate their values and self-concepts on white models.[10] This trend involves rejection of the Eskimo culture without guaranteeing the assimilation of Eskimos into white culture. An intermediate step would be acceptance of Eskimos into white impersonal associations, with complete assimilation delayed until Eskimos are accepted into intimate social groups of whites.

6. Comparisons have been made between the transition of Eskimos to American or Canadian culture and the transition of immigrants. The present status of town Eskimos resembles that of the second generation immigrants, where the young are caught between the outmoded cooperative rural culture of their parents and the individualized urban culture which calls for self-discipline and integration into competitive industrial and institutional life—qualities that the second generation does not possess. Most descendants of immigrants become well-adjusted; some never do; a few pass into major crime in metropolitan cities.
7. Vallee foresees that Canadian Eskimos will form an Eskimo-Canadian ethnic group, similar to the French-Canadian ethnic group.[11] Some Eskimos will become assimilated into white groups and forsake the Eskimo culture. Many will identify with elements of the traditional culture and become an ethnic group which as a group will become integrated into modern Canadian life while still retaining many Eskimo characteristics.

REFERENCES

1. BIRKET-SMITH, KAJ. *The Eskimos.* London: Methuen and Co., Ltd., 1936, revised 1959.
2. CHANCE, NORMAN A. "Culture Change and Integration: An Eskimo Example." *American Anthropologist,* 62 (December, 1960), pp. 1028-44.
3. CLAIRMONT, D. H. J. *Deviance among Indians and Eskimos in Aklavik, N.W.T.* Ottawa, Ontario: Northern Coordination and

[10] Hughes, *op. cit.,* pp. 339-346; Vallee, *op. cit.,* Ch. 10.

[11] Vallee, *op. cit.,* pp. 211-212.

Research Centre, Department of Northern Affairs and National Resources, October, 1963.

4. Dunning, R. W. "An Aspect of Recent Eskimo Polygyny and Wife-lending in the Eastern Arctic." *Human Organization*, 21 (1962) pp. 17-22.
5. Hoebel, E. Adamson. *The Law of Primitive Man, A Study in Comparative Legal Dynamics.* Cambridge: Harvard University Press, 1954, Ch. 5.
6. Honigmann, John J. "Arctic Town Life as a Stimulus to Eskimo Culture Change." Paper delivered at the Central States Anthropological Society, Lexington, Kentucky, April 16, 1965.
7. Honigmann, John J. "Community Organization and Patterns of Change among North Canadian and Alaskan Indians and Eskimos." *Anthropologica,* N. S. 5, No. 1 (1963), pp. 3-8.
8. Honigmann, John J. and Irma. *Eskimo Townsman.* Ottawa, Ontario: University of Ottawa Press, 1965.
9. Honigmann, John J. and Irma. "How Baffin Island Eskimo Have Learned to Use Alcohol," *Social Forces,* 44 (September, 1965), pp. 73-83.
10. Hughes, Charles C. *An Eskimo Village in the Modern World.* Ithaca: Cornell University Press, 1960.
11. Hughes, Charles C. "The Patterning of Recent Cultural Change in a Siberian Eskimo Village." *Journal of Social Issues,* 14, No. 4 (1958), pp. 25-35.
12. Jenness, Diamond. *People of the Twilight.* Chicago: University of Chicago Press, 1959.
13. Lantis, Margaret. "Social Culture of the Nunivak Eskimo." *Transactions of the American Philosophical Society,* N. S. 35 (1946), Part III.
14. Moore, Riley D. "Social Life of the Eskimo of St. Lawrence Island." *American Anthropologist,* 25 (1923), pp. 339-75.
15. Murdoch, John. *Ethnological Results of the Point Barrow Expedition.* Ninth Annual Report of the Bureau of American Ethnology. Washington, D.C.: Government Printing Office, 1892.
16. Nelson, E. W. *The Eskimo about Bering Strait.* Eighteenth Annual Report of the Bureau of American Ethnology, 1896-97, Part I. Washington, D.C.: Government Printing Office, 1899.
17. Parker, Seymour. "Ethnic Identity and Acculturation in Two Eskimo Villages." *American Anthropologist,* 66 (1964), pp. 325-40.
18. Spencer, Robert F. *The North Alaskan Eskimo, A Study in Ecology and Society.* Smithsonian Institution, Bureau of American Ethnology, Bulletin 171. Washington, D.C.: Government Printing Office, 1959.
19. Thalbitzer, William. *The Amassalik Eskimo, Contributions to the*

Ethnology of the East Greenland Natives, Second Part. Copenhagen, Denmark: C. A. Reitzels Forlag, 1941.

20. VALLEE, F. G. *Kabloona and Eskimo in the Central Keewatin.* Ottawa, Ontario: Northern Coordination and Research Centre, Department of Northern Affairs and National Resources, May, 1962.

3 / Mexico: Folk, Village, and Transplanted People

At first glance, juvenile delinquency in Mexico might seem to follow the same lines as among the Eskimo. Masses of people live in small villages in near-primitive conditions, other people in transition from primitiveness to urbanization, and still others struggling to snatch the glitter of the large city. However, in Mexico this process takes place on a level of social, political, and economic development above that of the Eskimos, although below that of some other societies. It also takes place within a fairly uniform basic culture.

The first and most pervasive foreign contacts of the indigenous Indians in what is now Mexico began some 450 years ago when Hernán Cortés overthrew the Aztec emperor and took possession of his capital city (now Mexico City), which housed some 250,000 to 500,000 people (2). Radiating out from this center, Spanish armies conquered the native peoples, priests established missions and churches, and the Spanish crown instituted a system of land grants to army officers and settlers, who soon reduced the Indians to serfdom. Spanish colonialism brought in many elements of Spanish culture, equipment, dress, language, village customs, and religion. Although Mexico achieved independence from Spain in 1810, today the native culture is a mixture of the original Indian and the colonial Spanish culture.

Biologically, mixture also took place. Few Spanish women came to the New World in the early period and Spanish men lived with Indian women, often without the formality of marriage. The children were reared in the mixed culture. Later, small numbers of Negroes were brought in as slaves and their biological heritage was added to the population, as well as that of Caucasians other than Spaniards. So complex is the intermixture of races that in 1921 the census of Mexico abandoned the earlier practice of trying to classify the population into Indian, Caucasian, and *Mestizo* (mixed).

Within the same general cultural and racial framework gradations appear that affect social customs and processes, including those related to delinquency and crime. At one extreme are small tribal groups, more Indian than Spanish biologically and culturally; at the other is Mexico City, more Spanish than Indian and moving from colonial Spanish into a more generalized urban culture. Three types have been selected for discussion in this chapter: the most "Indian" of the neighborhoods in a small village; a village in transition from Indian to modern culture; and Mexico City.

JUVENILE DELINQUENCY IN MEXICO

A number of writers have stated rather bluntly that the rate of juvenile delinquency in Mexico is low, certainly lower than in the United States, although there are not adequate statistics to support such a statement. Two psychologists write ". . . all who know both cultures agree that there is far less juvenile delinquency in Mexico, far less juvenile vandalism and destruction, and practically never a juvenile gang attack upon adults. Traditionally, adolescent gangs fight gangs but not adults; they might also attack police, who are not respected by either young men or adults."[1]

The lack of delinquency in Mexico is clearer for the peasant village than for the city. Norman S. Hayner, a sociological criminologist, who has studied Mexico for many years, states that in agricultural countries, such as Mexico, "juvenile delinquency seldom occurs outside the large cities. Where family and community controls are effective, formal agencies such as the courts are not needed." In Mexico, he says, "Parents are strict and family discipline strong in all classes."[2]

Beard writes that juvenile delinquency is a term heard only in Mexican cities.[3] In rural Mexico there are "bad boys" and "wayward girls." They are not referred to as headed for adult criminal careers,

[1] A. H. Maslow and R. Diaz-Guerrero, "Delinquency as a Value Disturbance," in J. G. Peatman and E. L. Hartley, editors, *Festschrift for Gardner Murphy,* Harper and Row, 1960, p. 229.

[2] Norman S. Hayner, *New Patterns in Old Mexico,* College and University Press, 1966, pp. 170-71.

[3] B. B. Beard, "Mexico's Way with Children," *Journal of the American Association of University Women,* 38 (1944), pp. 15-18.

and no special legal machinery is set up for them.

THE MEXICAN FOLK VILLAGE

Mexico, an agricultural land, is dotted with small folk villages, loosely related to small market towns. Typically, a village consists of several neighborhoods or *barrios* that cluster around a town square where the administrative buildings, Catholic church, post office, school, market place, and several small stores are located.[4] The barrios may differ in the degree to which they adhere to the Indian traditions in contrast to Spanish patterns. In the most primitive Indian barrios juvenile delinquency is virtually nonexistent. The problem here, as with the Eskimos, is to discover how almost complete conformity is attained.

An Indian barrio

Juxtlahuaca, located in the state of Oaxaca in southern Mexico, is a typical folk village. With a population of 3,600 it is divided into four barrios, grouped around the town square (12). The barrios fall into a hierarchy based on the degree of their daily use of Spanish, which all can speak, and the typical length of time since they left the outlying areas. The barrio of Santo Domingo with 600 people is the lowest in the social hierarchy, the most "Indian" of the barrios. This barrio has been thoroughly studied by a husband-wife team of specialists who spent a year there.[5]

For most of the year, the entire village is a closed community, so far as outside personal contacts are concerned. It is physically isolated. A dirt road, impassable during the rainy season—May to September—connects the village with a town on the Pan American Highway, 65 miles away. During the rest of the year, a jeep or large truck can cover the distance in 14 hours. Small aircraft can land on a cleared field in the dry season but are handicapped by winds.

---

[4] This village structure was introduced by the Spanish, who gathered in the surrounding Indians and placed them under Spanish control.

[5] Kimball and Romaine Romney, "The Mixtecans of Juxtlahuaca, Mexico," in Beatrice Whiting, editor, *Six Cultures, Studies in Child Rearing,* John Wiley and Sons, 1963, pp. 541-691. A briefer description of a village of 700 people, Lachigoló, of Zapotec background, is given by Hayner, *op. cit.,* pp. 108-10. The same type of physical living conditions is noted. Between 1940 and 1950 almost no changes occurred, aside from some reduction of illiteracy. In these rural villages, change comes slowly, in contrast to more rapid movement toward modern techniques and attitudes in larger towns and especially those near or in communication with Mexico City.

The barrio of Santo Domingo consists of clusters of houses built around courtyards and occupied by related groups of nuclear families. The houses consist of one small main room and a cook shack. The floor is of tamped earth. Life is lived primarily on the ground. Woven mats called *petates* are used instead of beds and chairs. When a family has a few chairs they stand low to the ground. Almost the only furniture is a chest or trunk in which clothing is kept, a simple altar, and a wall bench where the men sit. The stove is a crude circle of rocks or broken pots around a small fire in the middle of the cook shack. Dishes and cooking utensils are made in villages in the mountains. Water must be carried in from the river or wells. The fields, the riverbank, or a corner of the courtyard serve as a toilet. These simple homes are kept neat and clean. There is no accumulation of possessions not actually needed for daily life.

The men work their fields, typically walking from a half hour to an hour and a half each way. Work is with hand tools or oxen. Women keep the house neat, grind corn by hand on a *metate* (or, more recently, carry it to the local corn mill), care for their children, and keep their men well fed.

The people of the barrio dress and live in a style that is identified as "Indian" by residents of the other barrios. The men wear homemade trousers of white cotton material (*calzones*), a long-sleeved collarless shirt, *huaraches* locally made, a sombrero, and a wool blanket, or *serape,* used both as a protection against the cold in the daytime and as a blanket at night. Women wear a homemade long full skirt, and a hand-embroidered blouse. Around their heads and shoulders they wear a long cotton shawl, or *rebozo,* not only for warmth when it is cold but to support the baby who rides in it on the mother's back. Women do not wear shoes.

The other barrios in the village are less "Indian" and not only exhibit more influence from the early Spanish culture (language, for instance) but also are more influenced by modern trends in style of clothing, types of houses and furnishings, and school attendance of children.

The closed society of the barrio

The authors of the report on Santo Domingo gave special attention to the conforming, nonaggressive behavior of both children and adults and their ability to adjust to minor differences without recourse to the court located in the center of the village, to which residents of other barrios more often referred their problems. The statement is made that really serious crimes committed by barrio adults, such as homicide, would be referred to the courts. Such crimes rarely occur. During the year of residence, no one from the barrio was in court, no thefts nor accusations of thefts were known, and the investigators themselves who lived in the barrio lost no goods although these were not well protected.

A number of factors may be suggested to account for this almost totally nondelinquent and noncriminal situation:

The barrio maintains a high degree of isolation from the remainder of the village. Physically, it is set apart by a river. The barrio is also socially isolated. The farming activities of the men do not take them to the center of the village, but away from the village into the fields. When work is heavy the men help each other on a reciprocal basis, without pay. However, when a barrio man assists a farmer from the village proper, the arrangement is more formal and the man is paid.

Women have few village contacts, except for trips to the market or to the corn mill. Children leave the barrio only for specific purposes. An older child may be sent to market, and children must leave the barrio to attend school. Many go irregularly and some not at all.

The barrio carries on the essentials of group life within its boundaries. It has its own church to which a priest comes for mass, confessions, and a class in catechism. The barrio has its own fiestas; people typically attend only three fiestas annually outside the barrio. Politically, the barrio has a *regidor,* who manages public finances and is appointed by the village president. Barrio men show little interest in the government of the village and few vote in the election for president.

The social isolation of the barrio is accentuated by the rejecting attitude of villagers toward the barrio people, whom they regard as "Indian," uncultured, and basically inferior. In school, teachers often favor the village children. These children often attack barrio children verbally or physically by throwing stones. When barrio people attend a village religious observance or fiesta, they must walk at the end of the procession and are served last in the feast. Barrio people seem to accept these punitive discriminations without protest;

their response is to avoid contacts.

The family and the socialization of children

When considered in relation to the village as a whole, the barrio is a unit to which its residents give loyalty and with which they identify. Within the barrio, there is a division into family groups, with related families living in houses built around a patio that provides some privacy from other housing units but does not shut off social contacts within the barrio. Each family thus forms its own social group where traditional culture is passed on from parents to children. The family is artificially extended through the close association between parents and the godparent of each child.

Children are desired and are carefully supervised. Each age level seemingly has a feeling of responsibility for younger age levels. Although children are loved and cared for, they are not tied closely to their parents. The close attachment of the baby to its mother, when it still nurses and sleeps with the mother, ends with weaning at about age two. The child then begins to sleep with other children and much of its care is passed on to a slightly older sister who is made responsible for its care. Soon the child is assigned small tasks, performed with brothers and sisters. As the child grows, its tasks are increased, and it is expected to grow in self-reliance. Soon it may in its turn have a younger sibling to watch over.

The girl's tasks center around the home, and the mother consciously trains her daughters for their future roles as wives and mothers. The boy is given minor tasks outside the home and by the age of 12 is accompanying his father to the fields, where he learns the tasks of his future roles. Formal schooling is regarded as a secondary, and often not very useful, form of training.

The training of children is thus specifically oriented toward certain adult roles. Children have little opportunity to choose roles, and their knowledge of the world is so limited that they do not aspire to roles above those that their parents and grandparents fill. They are saved from the conflicts of choice and the frustrations of possible failure.

Intimacy between parents and children is not usual. Fathers rarely play with their children, although they are concerned that they should be well trained. Mothers expect children to learn early to take care of themselves, although children are never without supervision by some older person, child or adult.

Children are not harshly disciplined. The authors give examples where young children were told by an adult in the family to do something but neglected to follow instructions. No issue was made of the disobedience. However, mothers scold their children or whip them on occasion. Fathers are more disciplinary in their reactions to disobedience than are the mothers. The general impression gained from the account is of a minimum of conflict between parents and children.

The simplicity of life in the barrio should be noted. The possible occasions for conflict are greatly diminished as compared with modern styles of living. Barrio people typically do not undress at night; the morning dressing routine for a woman consists of shaking out her *reboso* which she has used for a blanket and putting it around her shoulders. Sleeping mats on the floor do not have to be "made" or have sheets to be changed or laundered. There is no heavy emphasis on washing, bathing, or laundering. Toilet training is casual. While cooking may be time-consuming if meal is ground at home, the menus are simple and the cooking and eating equipment held to a minimum. There are only one or two rooms to be swept and made neat. Thus many conditions leading to parent-child conflicts in a more modern household do not exist.

Children are taught to be compliant and nonaggressive. They are taught not to fight and, in case of an argument with other children and a potential fight, they are expected to withdraw and return home. Fighting is an occasion for the parent to scold or possibly hit the child. Parents also scold children for ordering other children about. Competitiveness is discouraged.

Children grow up to conform to the simple life of the barrio and to avoid situations where aggression is called for. They are group-minded and group-adjusted within the social world of the barrio. Here their roles and aspirations are set and here they find their major satisfactions.

Adult crimes

Adults are also relatively nonaggressive. For one thing, they have a background of childhood training in compliance and avoidance of aggression. When aggression does break out it usually concerns women, politics, or land disputes. However, there is relative tolerance over infidelity of either husband or wife. Occasional fights occur between barrio men and men from the village over political differences, especially in an election year. Barrio men, however, have little interest in local politics. The year in which the Romneys' study was made was an election year, but there were no fights.

The authors of the study attribute the absence of adult aggression to the feeling of identification with the barrio, loyalty to the barrio, and pride in belonging to it. Social control is maintained through these feelings and by the possibility of social ostracism for the nonconformer. The authors cite the ritualistic drinking by barrio men at certain fiestas that goes on for many hours, interspersed with speeches. No man may refuse to drink if he wishes to be considered a member of the group and to function in group activities. Not only is this ritual drinking a means of identification with the barrio but also a representation of mutual but controlled aggression. Other barrios in the village do not have this pattern of drinking. Between fiestas, barrio men seldom drink.

Another type of control of aggression is cited by the authors—the firmly held belief that strong emotions, such as anger, jealousy, and aggressiveness cause illness and eventually death. Barrio members related various incidents where extreme emotional displays were followed by illness and death. Apparently this belief and the fear of illness and death act as a deterrent to uncontrolled display of violent emotions.

Emergence from the barrio

Although barrio people tend to live their lives within the social world of the barrio, some emerge. There is occasional attendance at markets or fiestas at some nearby village within walking distance. The hold of the barrio is not weakened by these brief visits. Some people, chiefly young people of both sexes, go to the cities to work, but they tend to return to the barrio to marry and settle down. Some men have worked intermittently as laborers in the United States, and others have their experience broadened through compulsory military service. In addition to the many who return home to resume barrio life, are others who remain in the cities where they must adjust to a very different pattern of life in which the old rules do not always apply.

THE VILLAGE IN TRANSITION

Tepoztlán, a village of 4,000 south of Mexico City, is in transition from the traditional Indian-Spanish village to a more urbanized modern small town (7, 8, 9, 11). In contrast to the folk barrio described above, Tepoztlán is not physically isolated from the main streams of communication. There is a railroad along the mountain above the town built in 1900. The city has an asphalt road connecting it with a highway to Mexico City, two bus lines since the late 1930's, daily mail service since 1926, and telephone and telegraph connections. Trade relations with Mexico City are necessary and important. The village also has close relationships with many nearby villages and towns.

Social isolation is also breaking down. The knowledge of Tepoztecans is chiefly limited to their region; they are, however, slowly developing a feeling of identification with the state of Morelas and the nation. Children receive more schooling than their parents had and a few leave the village for further education. An occasional movie and a traveling cultural mission as well as agency-sponsored annual visits to other parts of Mexico further widen the viewpoint of adults and children.

Differences between the barrios of Tepoztlán are not marked. The Revolution of 1910-21 broke down the old class system and redistributed the use of the land in a more equable manner. According to a study made in 1943-48, 60 per cent of the families may be classified as very low on a scale of wealth, 22 per cent as low, 14 per cent as in a middle position, and 4 per cent as wealthy, all by local standards.[6] As one ascends the scale of wealth, houses and clothing become somewhat more modern, there is more education, land, and income. However, there is not a complete break with the typical Indian culture, as described for Juxtlahuaca. All men are primarily farmers (a high status occupation) and all go to the fields clothed in the typical peasant garb of white *calzones.*

Family controls

Family controls in the barrio of Santa Domingo and in Tepoztlán are in sharp contrast, with more severity of punishment in Tepoztlán. The basic framework of family structure found in the barrio is evi-

[6] Oscar Lewis, *Life in a Mexican Village, Tepoztlán Restudied,* University of Illinois Press, 1963, p. 174. Hayner, *op. cit.,* p. 45 quotes a lawyer in Oaxaca (population about 78,000) as estimating that 69 per cent of the population lived in misery, 28 per cent in poverty, and 3 per cent in riches. These and other sources indicate the prevalence of poverty in Mexico.

dent, but the almost complete isolation of the barrio is replaced in Tepoztlán by various outside contacts and conflicts between parents and children.

The father achieves respect and obedience through his aloofness, status as chief supporter of the family, direct training by the mother, and punishments, often severe. Children are beaten for disobedience by either parent, with a stick or rope. The wife also may be beaten by her husband, treatment that she rarely protests. The mother frequently punishes children by slapping or spanking, or by denying privileges. The policy is to treat little children kindly, give severe punishment to those between the ages of five and twelve, and scold those who are still disobedient after the age of twelve. Upon occasion these older children may also be beaten by the father or mother.

Related families live close together and create a circle of control beyond that of the nuclear family, sometimes protecting a member of the family when other members are too harsh, sometimes bringing pressure on a deviating member to conform. This larger kin group feels pride or shame at the behavior of kin members.

Socialization of children

Children early imitate their parents in play. By the age of twelve a girl is able to fulfill the role of the typical peasant woman, and a boy is helping his father in the fields. Since farming is an occupation with status, most boys like their entrance into the man's world in the fields.

Children are positively taught to suppress aggression. They are taught not only to respect their parents and accept punishment without protest, but to be quiet physically and vocally, especially in public.

Children are not given sex education directly, although the custom whereby all members of the family sleep in the same room as well as observance of farm animals breeding undoubtedly gives some knowledge. Boys, who have much greater freedom than girls as they come into adolescence, experiment with girls who escape close supervision at home or, when older, with some widow or married woman.

Socialization tends to extend beyond the family and the barrio to school and church. This passage of training from the family to outside agencies creates tensions for parents. Boys and girls, but especially girls, are discouraged from spending much time away from the barrio.

Some parents are uneasy about school attendance because it takes children away from their personal supervision. Only the few higher-level families value education or provide for their children to attend school elsewhere after they have completed the local educational offerings. Many parents do not approve of recreation recently provided by the school or the Church, especially when it includes social dancing.

The beginning of a period of adolescence

Social adolescence is developing in Tepoztlán and constitutes a major difference from the barrio of Santo Domingo. It is related to the intrusion of outside influences, such as emphasis on education and recreation for youth, a break in the strict control by the family, and the increased opportunities for deviant behavior.

Until recently a special period of adolescence did not exist. Roles were firmly fixed by age and sex, without a relatively undefined period between childhood and adulthood. To the age of 12, girls were regarded as children, then from 12 to 14 as *señoritas.*[7] At this time girls were provided with new clothing that distinguished them from children, and before long they were married. Some girls passed directly from childhood to marriage. Girls who were not married by midteens were regarded as *solteras.* Parents chose the mate and arranged for the marriage. Boys were regarded as juveniles until about age 17 or 18, then as youths; marriage for boys came any time from 16 to 30. Both boys and girls were withdrawn from school at age 12 or earlier to assume an adult work status. In this system of fixed roles and uninterrupted parental control there was little opportunity for choice of activity by the child or teenager.

In the 1940's when Lewis made his major study of Tepoztlán, the above pattern of roles and controls had begun to loosen. Girls still were usually withdrawn from school at age 12 but were considered to be children until age 15 and then as *señoritas* from 15 to 20, and as *solteras* only after age 20. Marriage occurred in the mid-teens. Therefore in the 1940's girls had a long period between termination of schooling and marriage—a period of later childhood and adolescence. During this period they worked at home—occasionally outside—and were expected to give up childhood friends but not to make

[7] Oscar Lewis, *Tepoztlán, Village in Mexico,* Holt, Rinehart and Winston, 1960, pp. 77-83.

friends among boys.

In the 1940's, boys went to work for their fathers at age 15 instead of 12, thus having their childhood period prolonged. Most boys were married at 19 or 20.

In the 1950's, when Lewis again visited Tepoztlán, changes whose beginnings were evident in the 1940's continued—longer period of schooling, more freedom for girls as well as boys, some tolerance of boys and girls associating with each other in public, recreation in the form of sports and social affairs, and changes in attitudes especially among the better educated middle class. The lower class (82 per cent of the people) remained much as it was in the 1940's.

Juvenile delinquency and deviancy of youth

The studies of Tepoztlán, detailed in other respects, do not mention juvenile delinquency, except to note its absence. Whatever misbehavior occurs apparently is defined as disobedience to the parents and is punished by them.

A certain amount of deviancy from this rigid pattern is permitted to young unmarried men, although it does not take the form of serious delinquency or crime. On Sundays groups of young men take the bus to Cuernavaca, 15 miles away. They spend the day walking about, drinking in *cantinas,* playing pool, or visiting prostitutes, all behavior disapproved by village standards. Other men, often married, go to this city for secret meetings with widows or married women from Tepoztlán. The days spent in the city are more in the nature of escape from possible criticism in the village than a search for delinquent behavior.

Some girls and women go to the city to buy or sell in the market, to window-shop, or to buy a few things. Girls who are more sophisticated (who have perhaps been away at school or who have worked for a time in a city) may go to see a motion picture or buy fashion magazines.

The diversions of Cuernavaca supplement the meager offerings in Tepoztlán, where a number of efforts at similar diversions have perished for want of patronage and with disapproval of parents. Modern recreation is often regarded as the opening wedge to drunkenness, gambling, or illicit sex relations, especially for the girls.

Along with these changes has come the beginning of courtship on the part of youth. The former selection of the mate by the parents had weakened by the 1940's to approval by parents of agreements made by a boy and girl. By the 1950's, individual mate selection had become customary. However, since girls were not supposed to meet boys in private, the process of selection went on by writing notes secretly delivered by friends, supposedly chance meetings in public, and occasional secret meetings with sex relations. The last often led to elopement, belated approval by parents, and entrance into a free union (locally recognized as marriage), or civil marriage, but rarely a church wedding.

Since parents and future husband alike expect a girl to be a virgin at marriage, premarital sex relations not followed by marriage constitute a grievous moral lapse. The girl is moving toward promiscuity and a loss of status. Similar behavior by the boy or man is not disapproved, as sexual pleasures are regarded as a natural right of males and their early fulfillment adds to the male self-concept of virility.

Adult deviancy and crime in the village

At some poorly defined age the boy becomes a man and his misdeeds take on a more serious character. Police and courts may become part of the proceedings. People who know of legal offenses do not always report them to the police, as there is a code other than the legal one. The local code phrases lapses in terms of sin rather than crime, as a few examples will illustrate.

Excessive drinking is disapproved. In general drinking is restrained among men; few women drink. Drinking in itself is not considered bad but is criticized because it dissipates money needed for necessities and also interferes with a man's work. Men customarily take a drink after their day's work is finished. More extensive drinking is reserved for fiestas or holidays, but at none of these is excessive drinking a customary part of the festivities.

Stealing is not always regarded as sinful. Carrying away movable parts of a temporarily vacant house (roof tiles or hearthstone) is not regarded as sinful. If a domestic animal is accidentally killed, it is not thought necessary to inform the owner so that he may make use of the carcass; anyone may take meat. People who are without means of support sometimes make a practice of stealing animals from a distant place and selling them; this may be known and is regarded as justifiable. But it is wrong to steal corn or money, and especially so from other villagers. Acceptance of bribes by local officials is regarded as one of the natural rewards of holding office.

Homicide may also be regarded as justified under certain conditions. The killing of a known enemy is a form of self-defense, since it forestalls death at the hands of the enemy. Shooting of a thief or suspected thief on sight is not condemned. Many family feuds spill over into killings. Private disputes over land, water usage, cattle, or women are often settled at first hand without recourse to the courts.

When these or other legal offenses come to public attention, the first official who hears the complaints is the president of the *municipio* (similar to a New England town or a county). These complaints are of a minor nature, such as quarrels between neighbors over such things as property matters, accusations of stealing, assault, or immorality. When the president is unable to settle the case, it is passed on to the local judge, who conducts trials of more serious offenses. Lewis lists the criminal offenses for six years, occurring intermittently from 1927 to 1943. A total of 808 recorded crimes may be grouped as in Table 1, or an average of 135 per year for a population of about 6,000 in 1940.

TABLE 1
Criminal Offenses, during Six Selected Years in the Municipio of Tepoztlán

Offense	*Number*	*Percentage*	*Average Number Per Year*
Assaults and homicides (Homicide 10 cases)	418	51.8	69
Thefts of various sorts	143	17.7	24
Damages, plunder, trespassing, arson	102	12.6	17
Calumny, defamation, scandal	62	7.7	10
Sex offenses	48	5.9	8
Abandonment	18	2.2	3
Frauds, falsifying documents	11	1.4	2
Miscellaneous	6	0.7	1
Total	808	100.0	135

Based on Lewis, *Life in a Mexican Village: Tepoztlán Restudied,* University of Illinois Press, 1963, p. 227.

A preponderant proportion of the offenses are types of assault, although only 10 cases are homicides. The other types fall primarily under two headings, physical injuries and blows (192 cases) and injuries and threats (200 cases). In a discussion of interpersonal relationships, Lewis says that affection and trustfulness are not well developed. People tend to be suspicious and distrustful of each other. The numerous assaults may be an expression of this basic hostility. At the same time, Lewis discusses many types of indirect expression of hostility in the form of malicious gossip, stealing, secretive destruction of property, ridicule, deprecation and envy, and sorcery.[8] It should be recalled also that direct expression outside the criminal range is possible: beating of wife, child, younger sibling, or animals; throwing things—rocks at offending persons, or the plate of unliked food on the floor; temper tantrums or fighting among boys. Not all direct assaults are reported to the police.

The intermediate position of Tepoztlán

The village of Tepoztlán shares with Santo Domingo many old customs and beliefs. But it also seems in a state of tension over the intrusion of outside influences, especially those that draw children and young people away from the family. A period of social adolescence has developed. The adolescents usually live at home and economically are part of the family group. The trend is toward more education and the village is beginning to offer other types of work than farming. Young men who return from military service or from work as agricultural laborers in the United States bring in new ideas. The direct line of transportation with Mexico City brings a movement back and forth of individuals or families who go to the city to work or live.

As the old patterns and controls lose their effectiveness, deviant behavior that borders on delinquency and crime increases.

MEXICO CITY

The political, commercial, and cultural center of Mexico is Mexico City, located in the Federal District (legally comparable to the District of Columbia). Mexico City has a population of about four million and the Federal District about six million (3, 4, 5, 6, 13). Old families of Spanish or Spanish-Indian stock go back for many gener-

[8] Lewis, *op. cit.*, pp. 227, 293-297.

ations and are the carriers of the intellectual and cultural life. Much of the population growth is supplied by the in-migration of peasants from racial and cultural backgrounds similar to those found in the folk and transitional villages already described. Their first place of urban settlement usually is in one of the many large slums, from which they hopefully aspire to move, but in which many families are permanently trapped. One third of the population lives in the slum housing or *vecindades*.[9]

Life in the vecindad

Lewis refers to the style of life in the vecindad as "the culture of poverty."[10] In physical structure, the vecindad resembles the poorest of the village barrios. The one-room, one-story apartments, sometimes expanded by a makeshift cook shack, are built along long outdoor corridors, which are sometimes closed off from the public by a wall at each end and a door that is locked at night. In the better vecindades the floors of the houses are of cement, but in the poorer ones they are of dirt. The flat roof of the cook shack may be reached by a ladder and is used for hanging laundry, keeping chickens, growing herbs and flowers, or holding a gas tank for the cook stove.

The vecindad differs from the barrio in that it has some traces of urban influence. There is a flush toilet either in a corner of the house or in the patio, often out of order, and often poorly protected from common view by a half-door or a curtain. Some vecindades have electricity and some families use a gas stove. An occasional family has a radio or a television set. Water is drawn from a faucet instead of the river or a well. As the family is able through the pooled earnings of its members, a few items of furniture are added to the already crowded rooms. Ready-made clothing is worn instead of the peasant-style, homemade clothing of the village. Women and girls visit the beauty parlor when they have enough money. The family is strictly on a money economy, as there is no place to raise food. Money is

---

[9] Hayner, *op. cit.*, p. 287. The term *casa de vecindad* means neighborhood house and refers to old large residences in deteriorated neighborhoods that have been subdivided into one-room apartments for the poor. The term *vecindad* is also used for the one-room, one-story apartments built around a common courtyard where many poor families live. In a few areas these old structures have been replaced by low-rental housing projects.

[10] Oscar Lewis, *Five Families: Mexican Case Studies in the Culture of Poverty*, Basic Books, 1959.

always scarce and buying on the installment plan tends to keep all earning members at subsistence level.

The vecindad is less of a unit than the village barrio. In one large vecindad the population of 700 came from 24 of the 32 states of Mexico. In a small vecindad of 54 people, the heads of families came from six states. There is, therefore, some cultural diversity among the families, although all share peasant background and current poverty. The population is remarkably stable. The inability to rise above the poverty level is indicated by the length of residence, for some families from 10 to 20 years.

Family life is a mixture of peasant-Indian and urban ways. Up to 10 or 12 persons continue to sleep in one room and at least some members sleep on *petates* on the floor, even though a bed may be used by others. The diet is very much the same as in the village. The father attempts to retain his headship of the family and continues to enforce his will by physical punishment, even at times beating his wife and older children, who accept this treatment as submissively as they or their relatives did in the village. An attempt is made to supervise girls closely, with age 15 being the dividing line between childhood and the status of *señorita* when marriage may be anticipated. The family tends to remain together, with sons often bringing their brides into the already crowded apartment, either in free union or a civil marriage.

Clusters of related people cling together. In a large vecindad, over a third of the families had blood relatives, and about a fourth were related by marriage or *compadrazgo*. These families give mutual aid in time of emergency. In addition, neighbors enter into group enterprises, such as raffles and the celebration of religious festivals and holidays. These are temporary affiliations on an impersonal level in contrast to the personal family ties. Among the young people, groups form, not necessarily on the basis of kinship ties, but usually within the vecindad. These young people have attended the same schools, dance together in the patio, and often marry vecindad members.

Aside from family life and close friendships, activities spread beyond the vecindad with accompanying decrease in family control and increase in exposure to urban, nonfamily patterns of recreation and money making. Although some men operate small shops within the vecindad, many leave each day for work, manual or semi-skilled, in the city. Girls and women less often work in the city although they may peddle on the city streets. The school attended by the children is outside the vecindad. Some youth break away entirely, living in rented rooms or, in some cases, on the streets.

Through such contacts the life and customs of the city enter into the vecindad. Status depends upon urban possessions—beds to sleep in, cooking utensils, a table and chairs, a radio or television set, ready-made clothes. Status also depends upon urban customs, the permanent wave and the dance in the patio which parents reluctantly permit their young daughters to attend.

Life in the vecindad is hard—for the least educated and trained because they cannot secure good jobs; for the better prepared and ambitious because more money than they earn is needed to buy the material symbols of the social status they desire. Youth and adults alike have found ways to release tensions and to add to their income illegally.

Juvenile delinquency

The Federal District has an institutional setup to handle delinquency similar to that in the United States. The equivalent of a juvenile court is staffed with a lawyer, psychiatrist, and teacher; there is provision for psychiatric treatment, a detention home, and training schools. The bad boys and wayward girls of the peasant villages have become the delinquents of the city.[11] Enough of the peasant philosophy carries over that parents in the vecindad try, with varying success, to control their children, especially the daughters. Many marginal types of behavior are tolerated, and many victims do not report delinquents or criminals to the police.[12]

Few of the children referred to the juvenile court are in school. Children of the poor drop out of school early, to save the expenditures for school supplies and to help their mothers in various kinds of low-paid employment, such as peddling candy, fruit, newspapers, or lottery tickets on the street.

Much of the stealing by both children and adults is of a petty nature. It may be thought of as stealing at subsistence level to supplement less than subsistence earnings. In addition to outright thefts are many types of dishonest conniving to gain an advantage or to get money beyond what can be earned by work. These activities are

[11] Beard, *op. cit.*
[12] See Table 2 for offenses referred to the courts.

carried on without much concealment and are rationalized in the name of necessity or as common custom. Children become familiar with these practices on the part of their parents or kinfolk and may participate in them. The culture of poverty is also the culture of getting by and making a little on the side.

Delinquencies tend to take place in the areas of the vecindades although not necessarily within them. Shoplifting is from nearby markets. Older boys and adults range over the city and penetrate the affluent neighborhoods to steal from cars and to burglarize. So entrenched in Mexican city life is the practice of supplementing income by thefts that one of the large city markets is nicknamed the "Thieves' Market." Here thieves come to sell their stolen goods or a small merchant buys from thieves without asking questions and then sells at a price that gives him a profit but undercuts the normal price. Poor people especially buy in this market.

The exposure of children in the vecindad to dishonesty may be illustrated by the following list of attempts by one man to get ahead. By vecindad standards he was not a criminal. With a partner he opened a bicycle shop by buying about 50 unclaimed, damaged, or stolen bicycles. The business thrived, but the partner gradually stole bicycles from the shop and opened his own business. The man was thus driven out of business. Later, trouble was caused by police who sought to reduce bicycle thefts.

The man then invested small sums of money in unclaimed jewelry from pawnshops or stolen articles, for resale at a profit. On one occasion he secured gravel from a construction project by paying the overseer three pesos for each load; he then sold the gravel at a profit within the vecindad.

When this man was younger he was employed in a bicycle factory, where he and the foreman reported certain parts missing from incoming shipments and then secretly carried off the parts and sold them to stores. The man, in relating this exploit said, "We gave them a good buy for their money because I've always been a stickler for honest dealings."[13]

When this man joined a union he discovered that the union paid the full salary for illness, and 900 pesos for an operation. By simulating illness, he collected his daily salary without working. Finally after trying to injure himself and have an operation he was operated

[13] Lewis, *op. cit.*, pp. 125-209.

on for appendicitis and received the 900 pesos. He then attempted to give himself a permanent injury on the machine he operated, but was discovered in the act.

Whether or not boys form gangs depends to some extent on the definition of gang. Writers already cited seem to agree that the fighting gang found in the United States does not appear in Mexico City. A delinquent subculture that grants status on the basis of violence and hostility has not developed. Children and youth respect their elders and support the same values. They do not fight against adults. However, boys belong to small peer groups which sometimes come into conflict with each other. This struggle or contest between juvenile gangs is regarded as of a different character from wanton attacks on adults.[14]

Occasionally, loosely formed groups of boys may cause disturbances. In 1959, a Mexican newspaper, *Excelsior,* stated, "Youth has become fond . . . of the belief that the adolescent has to be daring, virile, irresponsible, and a gypsy."[15] The reference is to groups of adolescents that destroy furniture in motion picture theatres, attack women, organize thefts, and sometimes attack other adolescents. One theater was seriously damaged when an Elvis Presley film was being shown. The account notes that in some cases the youths were from well-to-do families. Such events have occurred only three or four times in the history of Mexico.

Physical violence occurs among both juveniles and adults much more often than in the United States, where assaults and homicides account for only 9 per cent of adult crimes and a still lower percentage of juvenile offenses. Violence varies, however, from one part of Mexico to another, according to court statistics. Differences in reporting cannot be ruled out. Statistics already cited state that in the municipio of Tepoztlán slightly over half of court cases (adults) are assaults of some type (but few homicides). In Oaxaca (Table 4) adults have a high percentage of both homicides and physical injuries. Minors in Oaxaca (Table 3) commit few homicides, but are guilty of inflicting many physical injuries. For Mexico City in 1965, however, among offenders brought before the court, only 10 per cent of boys and 7 per cent of girls were guilty of homicide, blows, or

[14] Maslow and Diaz-Guerrero, *op. cit.*, p. 229.
[15] *Ibid.*

physical injuries.[16]

Various accounts agree on the custom of knife-carrying by male youth and adults. Carrying a knife at all times or equipping oneself with a knife when going into a dangerous area of the city or entering a gang fight is a common custom in slum neighborhoods. The knife comes out quickly in a controversy, first as a threat and then as a dangerous weapon.

Sex customs and offenses

The dividing line between what is regarded as normal sex partnerships and exploitative, abusive, or commercialized relations is narrow. As in the village, sex experience is regarded as a sign of masculinity that the teen-age boy seeks early. The ideal for the girl is still to be a virgin at the time of marriage; in the city slum, however, it is difficult for parents to isolate the girl, supervise her activities, prevent early social contact with boys, and select a marriage partner for her. In higher social levels, close family supervision of girls is the custom. In the vecindad when a boy and girl are attracted to each other, they agree to be *novios,* a relationship similar to "steady dating" or even an engagement in the United States. Parents may try to interfere, emphasizing the defects of the partner. Eventually marriage is agreed upon by a boy and girl, usually in free union. They spend a night together and then go to the home of the boy or of a relative. An extra *petate* is spread on an unused floor space and the couple become a part of the boy's family, sharing their expenses, hardships, or good fortune. These unions arranged by the boy and girl rest upon personal attractiveness, with little consideration for qualities that the parents consider important—the housekeeping ability of the girl or the earning power of the boy.

Since the free union is not a legal relationship, a divorce is not needed to effect a separation, and one free union may follow another, with a child or two from each union. When such a marriage breaks up, the girl typically takes her children and returns to the home of her father or some other older relative until she enters into another free union. The free union which is relatively permanent in the village becomes extremely loose in the city, fraught with insecurity for the woman and irresponsibility for the man. The system, however, is accepted among the lower class as a form of marriage. It is

[16] See Table 2.

not regarded as immoral or illegal. It does not lead to arrests, trials, or accusations of nonsupport.

Some teen-aged girls or young women detach themselves from their parental family, work outside the vecindad, and rent a room for independent living. They are then open to many approaches by men, some of whom they accept sexually on very short acquaintance. Such relationships easily lead into promiscuity, often without commitments on either side. The woman continues to support herself and any children who are born. Legal complaints or arrests sometimes follow, but in general the woman accepts the situation or returns to the home of her father.[17]

The opportunity for freedom from family control may be used by a girl as a way to achieve the luxuries of middle-class status, which she is not able to afford from her earnings. Lewis cites in detail the autobiography of a girl, born in a vecindad, whose father was able to pay for her training at a commercial school.[18] She became an office worker, desirous of full middle-class status but spending most of her wages in trying to help her brothers and sisters and their children to leave the slum, which to them was still home. She was approached by various middle-class men—sometimes by her employer—not for marriage as they already were married, but as a sexual companion. After much soul searching, she tried various types of relationship, none of which led to the legal marriage that she craved. She eventually solved her problems by cutting herself off from her relatives, stopping work, and becoming the mistress of a middle-class man. The relationship of mistress differed from that of free union in that the man was already married; his allegiance lay with his wife and children. The man supported her but did not acknowledge her as his wife. She was repudiated by her family.

The status of mistress is regarded as demeaning to the woman and she is usually scorned by her family, to whom poverty and the unstable free union are valued higher than the position of mistress with middle-class possessions but nonacceptance in the middle class.

[17] Lewis gives the case of a girl who was sent by her father from a village to a city to be trained as a teacher. She became a teacher but also formed a liaison with a man by whom she had a child. She returned to the father's home, where she was beaten by him but permitted to remain. Eventually she sank back into the peasant life and married a local man. Oscar Lewis, *Pedro Martinez,* Random House, 1964, pp. 470-73.

[18] Oscar Lewis, *Children of Sanchez,* Random House, 1961, pp. 88-132, 234-86, 403-42.

Hayner states that it is common for a man of wealth to have a recognized wife and children in a large house (*casa grande*) and a mistress with perhaps another family of children in a little house (*casa chiquita*). He may take the mistress for sexual pleasure after he and his wife have all the children they wish.[19] Although the mistress does not have legal status, the relationship is recognized by public welfare provisions. In case of sickness or death of the man, her children as well as the children of the legal wife receive public benefits. The mistress herself may not receive benefits, which go to the legal wife only; but if the man is not legally married (that is, has a free union only), the mistress may receive benefits.

In contrast to these diverse and unstable sex relations stands the great care taken by middle- and upper-class parents to preserve the virginity of their daughters until marriage, through close supervision, restrictions on public activities, and chaperonage. After marriage, these women are expected to close their eyes to the extramarital activities of their husbands, for whom extensive sex relations are regarded as in keeping with masculine virility.

Thus the irregular sex relations that are common throughout the city are accepted as normal, not only by the lower class but by middle and upper classes as well. Although these various types of sexual relations are not considered in the category of delinquency and crime, solicitation by a prostitute is illegal.

Prostitution

Prostitution goes on openly (4). Formerly two "zones of tolerance" or "red-light districts" were in existence in Mexico City. These have been abolished, but prostitutes openly solicit customers on certain streets. A study in 1943 of a crowded slum area revealed the following provisions for prostitution: 21 hotels, three houses of assignation, two boarding houses, one tavern selling beer, one private home, and an entire block used for prostitutes. Prostitutes were expected to register and report periodically for a physical examination. If they were found to have a venereal infection they were expected to enter a hospital for treatment. These regulations were circumvented by one woman taking the cards belonging to a number of prostitutes to the office of the medical examiner, where for a small payment the cards were all stamped without an examination.

[19] Hayner, *op. cit.*, pp. 128-29.

Since many prostitutes depend on street solicitation for their customers the legal ban on soliciting creates a problem. It is solved in characteristic fashion: to avoid arrest, the prostitute pays the policeman a proportion of her fee from each customer.

Professional crimes

Boys who are proficient in thefts and deception may move on into professional criminality, and become skilled in the arts of burglary or picking pockets. Burglary, usually carried out by two men, is the most frequently practiced form of professional theft; the skills have been known in Mexico City for at least two hundred years. Swindling, counterfeiting, smuggling in goods from the United States, and shipping opium and marijuana out of the country are other types of crime. Youth have their specific kinds of crime. Young men, called "coyotes," may arrange a social affair with American women students in order to steal their purses. Stealing from cars may net the thieves hundreds of dollars worth of goods.

Stealing is not limited to the slums. Officials often syphon off public funds or accept bribes to do a favor for some individual or organization. Several accounts indicate that such fattening of the individual's purse is regarded as normal and that the honest public official is regarded as foolish or stupid.

The police

People lack confidence in the honesty and efficiency of the police. They often do not report thefts or even assaults to the police. They believe that dishonest policemen will warn a thief as soon as the crime is reported to headquarters, or that the detective who investigates the case may make further thefts from them. The failure to report crimes is true for both adult and juvenile offenses.

Police readily work out a system of small bribes whereby violators of minor regulations may avoid arrest. Not only the prostitute but the street peddler as well may avoid arrest by regular payments of small bribes, called *mordida* or "the bite." More serious offenders may sometimes secure release by paying a *mordida*.

Variety and frequency of offenses, Federal District and Oaxaca

From the court in the Federal District that handles juvenile cases of a serious nature it is possible to make some comparisons (Table

2). Considering the population of the Federal District, the number of cases is very small. As is true in most countries that keep statistics, boys exceed girls. There are 6.5 boys for each girl. For every offense except prostitution, boys exceed girls in number of offenses. However, when each offense is computed as a percentage of the total number of offenses for boys and girls, girls exceed boys in sex offenses, disorderly conduct, and minor offenses. Boys exceed girls in stealing, homicide and physical injuries, and a few infrequent offenses. For both boys and girls, stealing of various types overshadows other offenses.

Tables 3 and 4 are based on records of the criminal court in Oaxaca, a state of 1,750,000 in southern Mexico. The capital, Oaxaca, had a population of 31,839 in 1940, slightly before the first date shown in the tables, and of 74,765 in 1960. People not living in the capital city are distributed over a wide area, in small towns and rural villages, often isolated from the larger cities. It will be recalled that the rural village of Juxtlahuaca, described early in this chapter, is in the state of Oaxaca. Many such villages abound in the state, more Indian than Spanish, more traditional than modern.

The state of Oaxaca has no juvenile courts. Tables 3 and 4 are based on cases of children under 16 and adults over 16, respectively, who appeared before a criminal court. Table 3, for minors, refers to cases primarily from the city of Oaxaca, while Table 4, for adults, covers the entire state. The lawyer who compiled the statistics stated that offenses similar to those of minors in Oaxaca occurred also in smaller urban centers and "could" occur in the rural areas, such as Juxtlahuaca, which was found by the Romneys to be free of delinquency during the year they spent there.

The number of delinquencies has increased from 1946 to 1959 more than the population has. In contrast the number of adult crimes (over 16 years old) has shown a decided decrease between 1946 and 1956, regardless of the population increase. Homicides have increased slightly for juveniles, but decreased for adults. Other offenses have also increased for juveniles, but a large part would be due to population increase.

The most frequent crimes differ as between juveniles and adults. By numbers, adults exceed juveniles for all offenses, but as percentages of the total number of crimes, adults commit homicide more than juveniles; they are about equal in inflicting physical injuries. Juveniles are far more guilty of stealing than are adults.

Explanations for changes and comparisons are not available.

TABLE 2

Summary of admissions of minors to Center for Observation and Investigation, of the Courts of the Federal District, from the Statistical Section, 1965

Reason for admission	*Males*		*Females*	
	No.	*Per cent*	*No.*	*Per cent*
Thefts, robbery, housebreaking, etc.	1,714	43.3	200	32.7
Homicide and physical injuries	390	9.9	42	6.9
There are only 58 homicides for males and 7 females				
Sexual offenses, rape, carnal knowledge, prostitution	200	5.1	73	11.9
Intoxication, disorderly conduct	594	14.9	122	20.0
Primarily disorderly conduct				
Minor offenses	782	19.8	164	26.9
Other	279	7.0	10	1.6
Total	3,959	100.00	611	100.0

Secured by Norman Hayner through Gilberto Bolanos Cacho, Administrator, Tribunal Para Menores, Obrero Mundial 76, Mexico, Federal District, Mexico. Edited and arranged by Hayner and the author.

TABLE 3

Summary, by classes of crimes, of cases of minors less than 16 years old, subject to penal process, in the State of Oaxaca, Mexico, 1946-1959

Year	*No. of cases*	*Homicide*	*Physical injuries*	*Sexual offenses*	*Damage to another's property*	*Stealing*	*Abuse of confidence*	*Fraud*	*Other*
1946	15	0	4	1	1	8	0	1	0
1947	4	2	0	0	0	2	0	0	0

TABLE 3 (continued)

1948	13	1	4	0	2	5	0	0	1
1949	14	4	3	0	0	5	0	1	1
1950	19	1	8	2	0	8	0	0	0
1951	22	2	7	0	0	12	0	0	1
1952	16	0	4	1	0	11	0	0	0
1953	18	1	8	2	0	6	0	1	0
1954	36	2	13	1	1	17	0	0	2
1955	20	1	4	3	1	11	0	0	0
1956	25	3	10	0	0	9	0	2	1
1957	28	1	10	2	1	13	0	0	1
1958	31	3	7	1	5	13	0	0	2
1959	41	2	9	5	1	20	1	0	3
**Total*	302	23	91	18	12	140	1	5	12
Percentage	100	7.6	30.1	6.0	4.0	46.4	0.3	1.6	4.0

* Some of the cases include more than one individual.
Secured by Norman Hayner from Pedro Yescas Peralta, attorney of Oaxaca from a manuscript entitled *Delinquency of Minors.*

TABLE 4

Summary, by classes of crimes, of cases more than sixteen years old, subject to penal process, in the State of Oaxaca, Mexico, 1946-56

Year	*No. of cases*	*Homicide*	*Physical injuries*	*Sexual offenses*	*Damage to another's property*	*Stealing*	*Abuse of confidence*	*Fraud*	*Other*
1946	1698	424	525	107	25	253	11	24	329
1947	1567	374	499	99	31	276	12	12	264
1948	1453	302	502	74	31	219	22	10	293
1949	1546	334	565	90	28	217	8	17	287
1950	1747	333	628	95	28	294	14	24	331
1951	1597	306	475	88	36	337	27	16	312
1952	1479	233	498	69	37	286	11	21	324
1953	1035	275	345	43	16	200	1	11	144
1954	1405	385	442	56	27	234	6	15	240

TABLE 4 (continued)

1955	1462	326	533	59	37	278	14	15	200
1956	1299	255	527	52	40	230	7	12	176
Total	16,288	3,547	5,539	832	336	2,824	133	177	2,900
Percentage	100	21.8	34.0	5.1	2.1	17.3	0.8	1.1	17.8

Secured by Norman Hayner from Pedro Yescas Peralta, attorney of Oaxaca from a manuscript entitled *Delinquency of Minors.*

SYSTEMS OF CONTROL

In the peasant barrio or the transitional village, the integration of all phases of life into a system to meet material, psychological, and social needs is not difficult to comprehend. In the city, this system tends to break down and family and vecindad appear to be highly disorganized; individuals and families break under the strain. Actually, a system has evolved to enable the urban dweller to meet needs in ways impossible or condemned in the village. Some of these needs are basic; others grow out of city life. The low wages scarcely provide for necessities; the middle class sets an impossible standard for the aspiring poor, just as the upper class arouses hopes that are unattainable for the middle class. Illegal ways have become part of the accepted way in which each level seeks to satisfy both needs and aspirations—the petty thievery of the poor, the small *mordida* exacted by lower officials, and the bribes of the higher officials for unfair or illegal favors. Sex becomes the means of upward mobility for the lower-class girl. The system works by an exchange of favors. The *mordida* benefits the official financially and usually saves him some work; it frees the payer of the *mordida* from arrest, delays, or minor irritations. The granting of special privileges for a bribe also promises the official political support, at the same time that it gives the one who pays the bribe an unfair advantage over competitors. Everyone knows of the abuses but no one wants to disturb the system which at some point may be of benefit to him. There are crimes, of course, that cannot be ignored and that call for police action. These range from run-of-the-mill burglaries and attacks to large scale burglary or corruption in government. These are the crimes that appear in official statistics.

REFERENCES

1. BEARD, B. B. "Mexico's Way with Children." *Journal of the American Association of University Women,* 38 (1944), pp. 15-18.
2. HARING, C. H. *The Spanish Empire in America.* Oxford University Press, 1947; Harbinger Books, 1963.
3. HAYNER, N. S. "Criminogenic Zones in Mexico City." *American Sociological Review,* 11 (1946), pp. 428-38.
4. HAYNER, N. S. *New Patterns in Old Mexico.* College and University Press, 1966.
5. LEWIS, OSCAR. *Children of Sanchez, Autobiography of a Mexican Family.* Random House, 1961.
6. LEWIS, OSCAR. *Five Families: Mexican Case Studies in the Culture of Poverty.* Basic Books, 1959.
7. LEWIS, OSCAR. *Life in a Mexican Village: Tepoztlán Restudied.* University of Illinois Press, 1963.
8. LEWIS, OSCAR. *Pedro Martinez.* Random House, 1964.
9. LEWIS, OSCAR. *Tepoztlán, Village in Mexico.* Holt, Rinehart and Winston, 1960.
10. MASLOW, A. H. and R. DIAZ-GUERRERO. "Delinquency as a Value Disturbance," in J. G. Peatman and E. L. Hartley, editors, *Festschrift for Gardner Murphy.* Harper and Row, 1960, pp. 228-40.
11. REDFIELD, ROBERT. *Tepoztlán, a Mexican Village; A Study of Folk Life.* University of Chicago Press, 1930.
12. ROMNEY, K. and R. "Mixtecans of Juxtlahuaca, Mexico," in B. Whiting, editor, *Six Cultures: Studies in Child Rearing.* John Wiley and Sons, 1963, pp. 541-691.
13. SOLIS QUIROGA, HECTOR. "The Criminal Phenomenon in Mexico." *R. Mexic. Sociol.,* 23 (1961), pp. 203-13. Abstract in *Sociological Abstracts,* 11, No. 6, A7032.

4 / India: Tribe, Village, City

The long history of India has been a succession of land invasions from the north and west, and eventually of intrusions of Europeans by sea. The most influential for present conditions was the contact with the British that began with the chartering of the English East India Company in 1600, continued to incorporation of India into the British Empire in 1858, and culminated in the division of Pakistan and India in 1947 and ensuing independence.

India's people fall into numerous cultural groups, some autonomous tribes, some of different religious affiliation, and others intricately related through the caste system. India now contains over 3,000 castes and subcastes as well as numerous noncaste groups and tribes. These groups speak 15 languages and hundreds of dialects, and worship in six major religions, with Hinduism accounting for 85 per cent of the population in 1962. The population is primarily rural; 85 per cent of the people live in some 600,000 agricultural or tribal villages, and 15 per cent in cities.

By the time India gained independence, an English veneer overlaid the many varieties of traditional Indian cultures. Along with English language and educational institutions, England imposed on India its own values, laws, courts, police system, and prisons, many of which were in conflict with the prior Indian political and social organization. When the concept of juvenile delinquency developed in England, embodied in special institutions, these were also transported to India. The present trend is toward a fuller development of western culture, under Indian auspices. Nevertheless, older levels of culture persist, among them some old forms of crime. At the same time westernization has brought its own problems of juvenile delinquency and crime.

In a country of such long and turbulent history and great diversity of cultures, many patterns of crime and delinquency exist, each linked with specific cultural backgrounds. Four situations have been chosen for discussion: autonomous tribes, criminal tribes, villages with a Hindu caste basis of social organization, and large cities.

TRIBAL CRIME

In the classification of groups in India, tribes are distinguished from Hindus, Moslems, and other groups with highly developed literate cultures (11, 12, 13, 30, 31, 33, 34, 35). With the passage of time some tribes have adopted certain Hindu practices. However, it is difficult for them to become incorporated into any caste or to be recognized by Hindus as forming a caste. They are therefore still distinguished as a separate stratum of Indian society, composed of many small independent societies, each with its own language and religious and social system. The tribes number 19 million people, constituting about 5 per cent of the total population of India. They are included in this chapter as another example of small primitive societies in the same general category as the Eskimo and the Mexican Indians, who, adjacent to complex societies, retain many indigenous cultural elements but are disturbed by the impact of the superior society. The tribes in India now are affected by three types of control — the indigenous culture, Hindu influence, and Indian legal systems.

Level of culture and social control

The tribes are widely distributed over India and only incidentally in contact with each other. They are basically agricultural, have a low level of technology, are illiterate, and live at a low subsistence level. The Maria, in eastern India, raise pigs, goats, and fowl. They gather nuts and fruits in the forest, hunt, trap, and fish. Their weapons are bows and arrows, axes, and knives.[1] The Akas, in the sub-Himalayan region, are agricultural and bring their produce to the plains where they are skillful traders.[2] Somewhat in contrast, the

---

[1] Verrier Elwin, *Maria Murder and Homicide,* Oxford University Press, 1950.

[2] Raghuvir Sinha, *The Akas,* Research Dept., Adviser's Secretariat, Shillong, India, 1962.

Dublas, in the extreme western part of India, live in their own hamlets but work for landed Hindus in a pattern resembling serfdom.[3]

The villages in which tribes live are small and often composed of related families. Among the Marias, when a son marries he builds his hut close to that of his father or brother. Relationships are close and, ideally, happy, but tensions and conflicts arise within the villages.

Children are reared in the traditional culture. Since usually there are few social contacts with other tribes or Hindus, and few schools have penetrated into tribal villages, the control of the family over children is strong. One writer states that the strength of tradition in these tribes precludes the existence of juvenile delinquency.[4]

A common pattern of social control outside the family is the village council presided over by a headman. He is a man of prestige and prominence who is chosen on the basis of age, experience, and wisdom. A group of villages of the same tribe may have a larger council composed of the headmen of the village councils. These councils operate with considerable independence of the civil government, and, in fact, have been given jurisdiction in minor criminal as well as civil matters. Serious crimes presumably are referred to the police, who represent the external Indian authority. Often such referrals are not made. People fear the police and distrust the courts. If they are taken to jail or court or sentenced to imprisonment they are removed from contact with their families and village. They may receive severe sentences for legal offenses that the tribe regards as justifiable acts. Also, witnesses object to making the trip to court which may be at some distance from the village. When the local council handles the case, it is in accord with known principles of customary law and the penalties are understood and approved.

Crimes of tribesmen among the Marias

The offenses of tribesmen usually take place within the tribe and grow out of local situations, such as the following:

Thefts are common and usually are of utilitarian objects, with occasional thefts of crops or cattle.

---

[3] P. G. Shah, *The Dublas of Gujarat,* Bharatiya Adimjatisevak Sangh, Kingsway, Delhi, India, 1958.

[4] B. N. Singh, "Delinquent and Juvenile Pattern in Primitive Society," *Eastern Anthropology,* 2 (1948), pp. 107-14.

Tense interpersonal relations explode into quarrels, sometimes between husband and wife or between small groups at fairs or festivals.

Sex crimes often are a violation of tribal laws and customs. Marriage outside the tribe is prohibited and rarely occurs. When it does, the council of each tribe enforces the regulations for marriage in its tribe; the husband pays the bride price as a fine. Women are allowed freedom in sex relations before marriage but not after. Husbands are very jealous and almost certainly kill a lover of the wife or the wife herself.

Murder is a serious crime and is handled by the courts when known. But certain murders are justified in tribal law and may go unreported to the police. Murder usually is unplanned; it develops out of a quarrel or altercation. An incident in 1957 in the Maria tribe may be cited. During a festival, a man asked a member of his tribe to lend him his flute. When the man refused, the first man killed him with a blow of the scythe which he was carrying. In retaliation and anger, the father of the murdered man killed the murderer by cutting off his head with the same scythe. In the eyes of the tribe the second killing was justified.

A special study of murder among the Marias, based on police files, showed that the following were the most common types of cases: murder during drunkenness, and quarrels over sexual offenses, interfamily relationships, and over property and inheritance. The court most often sentenced the convicted murderer to imprisonment, but in 18 out of 100 cases the murderer was executed. In contrast, the village council usually fined a murderer and then concealed the event from the police. However, many cases are reported to the police, or the police learn about them indirectly.

Conflicts with Indian laws

Not all tribal crimes are confined to altercations and thefts within the village. Tribesmen also may violate laws passed by the Indian government for the general welfare. Such laws may not be supported by the tribes and, in fact, may seem an imposition when they run counter to well-established customs that the tribes regard as right.

Violations of forest laws are common. These laws regulate the use of forests, cutting down of trees, and so forth. Many tribes that live near the forests have been accustomed to cutting down trees for fuel, or they clear patches of land for cultivation by burning trees. When the soil becomes exhausted they move to a new site and repeat the process. In the interest of forest conservation, laws forbid or regulate these practices.

Violations of prohibition laws are common. Many tribes use some form of liquor in religious ceremonies and festivals, as well as for immoderate personal drinking. They illegally distill alcohol for their own use as well as to sell. Among the Dublas in 1955 there were only six arrests for murder and seven for sex offenses, but 928 for offenses under the prohibition act, passed in 1949.[5]

Tribes account for only a small proportion of the population of India, and their crimes for a small part of the total crime picture. The discussion of tribal crime brings out several points: the absence of behavior recognized as juvenile delinquency, the centering of crime within the tribe, the conflicts between local control of crime and the Indian system of police and courts, and the rejection of laws that the tribes feel are unjustified and a violation of their rights or tribal values.

CRIMINAL TRIBES AND VIOLENT GANGS

In contrast to the normal tribal crimes that grow out of the tensions and discontents of tribal life are the criminal activities of some tribes, until recently officially designated as Criminal Tribes. These tribes number about four million people, a minute (1.0 per cent) but still troublesome segment of Indian society.

In comparison with normal tribes, Criminal Tribes, in their heyday, had the following characteristics:

Crimes of Normal Tribes	*Crimes of Criminal Tribes*
Incidental to normal social and economic activities	Central means of livelihood, about which the tribe was organized
Internal to the tribe	Directed against outside persons and villages, such as British, Hindus, Moslems
Spontaneous and unplanned	Carefully planned in advance
Murder motivated by anger	Murder for revenge or expe-

[5] Shah, *op. cit.*

	diency, incidental to primary financial motive
Punished by local council	Organized by local council
Individually carried out	Tribal activity
Children not trained in crime	Children carefully trained in crime

Thugs

According to some writers the origin of the criminal tribes was in organized bands of brigands, called thugs, who roamed India in the early nineteenth century and, no doubt, earlier (2, 9). They found wayfarers and travelers to be easy victims in a day of foot travel and lack of police protection. The wayfarer was strangled, his possessions taken, and the body buried.

As the British spread their sphere of influence over India, they made sporadic efforts to control or eliminate the practice of thuggery. Finally, in 1830 the government created a Thugee and Dacoity Department and a determined effort was made to extinguish thuggery. By 1837, 3,266 thugs had been taken into custody; 412 were hanged, and 483 pardoned as approvers—that is, they were accomplices who became state witnesses and were pardoned as a reward. The remainder were either imprisoned or transported. By about 1880 the bands of thugs were considered to be extinct.

Dacoity

As the murderous thugs were suppressed, the Department of Thugee and Dacoity in 1839 turned its attention to dacoity (3, 8, 9), defined as follows by the Penal Code of 1860:

> When five or more persons conjointly commit or attempt to commit a robbery, and where the whole number of persons conjointly committing or attempting to commit robbery, and persons present and aiding such commission or attempt amount to five or more, every person so committing, attempting, or aiding, is said to commit dacoity.

Dacoity is currently defined as armed robbery by gangs which may involve offenses against the person as well as against property. A particularly troublesome form of dacoity was the thefts carried out by gangs of river pirates, some of whom were also expert stranglers. Some of the gangs continued for many years, with sons replacing their fathers as the fathers were imprisoned or died.

On land, dacoity was widespread and continued well into the 1900's. A typical dacoity was the invasion of a small village at night by a gang of about thirty men on horseback, who terrified the residents, ransacked the houses, and carried off anything of value. They then posed as innocent peasants on the road or escaped into forested or mountainous areas not easily accessible.

These gangs, operating by terror and violence, thrived in the villages and along the rivers. As organized police activities, communications, and courts spread over India, their activities were gradually decreased, although not completely eliminated.

Criminal tribes

The fact that the commission of crime was a focus for the social organization of entire tribes was officially recognized in 1871, when the first Criminal Tribes Act was passed by the British government (2, 14, 15, 18, 21, 29). The significance of the term *criminal tribe* is the emphasis it gives to the total tribal organization rather than to the activities of a gang of marauders without regard to their social and cultural background. The criminal activities were recognized as part of the tribal culture.

The social organization of a criminal tribe was the same as that already described for noncriminal tribes—self-contained with its own local council to govern tribal affairs, its own philosophy, rituals, and taboos. In addition to the customary civil and criminal controls of the council, this group also controlled the criminal activities by which the tribe lived. One account states that the council assigned members of the tribe to perform specific criminal acts of theft, disposed of the stolen articles, and distributed the proceeds among the participants in the theft. If members of the tribe were arrested, the council arranged for their defense. The participation of the council in crime was still in operation in the 1950's.

These offenses committed outside the tribe were not considered criminal by the tribe. For example, one tribe justified its stealing as the "exaction of a form of charity which was given willingly in the good old days, but is withheld in these more degenerate times" (1931). Another tribe justified its thefts from money-lenders by pointing out that they falsified their accounts. Theft from the goldsmith was not criminal because he cheated when mixing his alloys.

Pre- or extramarital sex relations within the tribe were condemned, but prostitution outside was justified both as a means to make money and to discover who might have jewels or other valuables.

The crimes of the tribes included a large array of specific acts, many of which continue on a modified scale. Each criminal tribe tended to specialize in one or a few types of crime. In rural India, one tribe stole only cattle, or only goats and sheep, or bullocks and buffaloes. Other specialties were pilfering and petty larceny, counterfeiting of coins, house burglary, theft of edibles, swindling, robbery, daytime picking of pockets.

Children were reared to become criminals and were taught the philosophy of crime of their tribe and the skills needed, just as Hindu children were taught the vocational skills of their caste. One writer reports that a quality highly valued in a husband was skill in crime. Through this transmission of the values and skills of crime to children, the criminal tribes perpetuated their code and skills from generation to generation.

Official attempts to restrain or rehabilitate criminal tribes date from 1871. The first Criminal Tribes Act, passed in that year, had little effect on the tribes since no way was provided for tribesmen to make a living other than by their customary criminal methods. Various revisions followed, providing alternative ways of dealing with the tribes. Some tribes were placed in special settlements, subsidized by the government, where children attended school and an effort was made to teach adults some type of work. The members of other tribes were registered, fingerprinted, and required to report at stated intervals. Repeated offenders could be placed in reformatories.

As criminal activities subsided, the public became critical of designating entire tribes, including the children, as criminal. In 1952 the central government, on recommendation of a special committee, repealed the Criminal Tribes Act, and passed a Habitual Offenders Act which shifted the emphasis from the entire tribe to the criminal individual.

Changing the terminology from Criminal Tribe to Habitual Offender did not immediately solve the problem of tribes whose culture included a variety of criminal acts about which the tribe had no feeling of guilt. Unofficially the stigma of the old title still clings to the members of the former criminal tribes. Many writers refer to them as ex-criminal tribes. Minor offenses are still common among some tribes. Released from settlement and supervision, families may move about the country. In several studies of delinquency in cities, thefts and shoplifting by mothers and children of ex-criminal tribes are noted.

In addition to a continuation of crime, a host of social problems remains which engages the attention of certain welfare agencies. The tribes have become habituated to the settlements where they have lived for years on subsidies. When work is provided, tribesmen are reluctant to take it or to learn a trade. Some members openly state that it is easier to pick pockets than to work in a factory. Parents do not give their children adequate care nor see to it that they regularly attend the schools provided. Boys play truant and gamble outside the settlement.

The social status of the tribes is very low, in a country where status is rigidly defined by the caste system. A survey of the Sansis ex-criminal tribe near Delhi notes that they are untouchables; even the Hindu untouchables may regard the Sansis as beneath them.[6]

Nevertheless, some Sansis (and other ex-criminal tribes) are moving away from the old criminal culture. When they get some education and settle down to steady working, they move toward Hinduism. They give up some of the old customs abhorrent to Hindus, such as raising pigs, burying the dead instead of cremation, and permitting the women to be prostitutes. They adopt some Hindu rituals. These people would like to be accepted as a caste, but are rejected by the established castes.

The study of the Sansis showed that in the sample used, 81 per cent had an inadequate income and were usually criminal; among those with an adequate income, almost as many were criminal. Typical male offenses were theft, excessive drinking, and gambling; typical female offenses were begging and prostitution. Older people were more likely to be criminal than younger, but it is also noted that children are often taken by their parents when begging or stealing.

Both the government and private social agencies are aware of many of the social problems that beset the ex-criminal tribes and

---

[6] P. C. Biswas, *The Ex-Criminal Tribes of Delhi State,* University of Delhi, Delhi, India, 1960.

prevent their complete abandonment of criminal behavior and entrance into employment and social acceptability by the dominant Hindu society. The task is not simple. It is estimated that 2,268,348 members of 128 ex-criminal tribes (out of a total of 3,476,904 members) whose status was changed by the act of 1952, are still in need of rehabilitation to change their orientation toward crime, provide means of livelihood, and bring them into the main stream of Indian social and cultural life.[7]

DELINQUENCY AND CRIME IN VILLAGES

Numerically speaking, village life is the predominate type of living arrangement in India, with 85 per cent of the population living in 585,000 villages, most of which have less than 500 residents. Most of the villages are wholly or primarily Hindu—that is, they follow a common pattern of religious beliefs and ceremonies and are part of the over-all system of castes.

Since India achieved independence, the caste system has been made illegal; all people have equal rights and privileges; old rules of segregation in temples, schools, and public places are inapplicable; and people have the right to move freely as to place of residence, to choose their occupations, to marry into other castes, and so on. But it is not possible to destroy an age-old social system by a few laws. Caste still operates as a social system, with only a few cracks in its rigidity, and these chiefly in cities. Villages are still primarily caste-bound.

The caste system

A word of clarification about castes is needed (18, 23, 29). Originally, there were four main divisions or *varnas,* each with certain duties. The Brahmins stand at the apex of the *varna* hierarchy, with the official function of performing priestly duties, but following other occupations as well. The *Kshatrya varna* stands second, with the traditional function of warriors. The third status goes to the *Vaishya,* or traders. The lowest *varna* is the Sudra, composed of farm laborers and artisans. Outside the *varna* system, and below all, are the untouchables (recently called *Harijans*) who perform necessary menial tasks that are regarded as degrading. At present the original *varnas* are subdivided into many castes and subcastes, each caste with its

---

[7] Biswas, *op. cit.,* pp. vii, 2.

own hierarchical arrangement. One estimate places the total at 3,000. Another says the Brahmins alone have over 2,000 subcastes and the untouchables 563 subdivisions. In any given village only a few castes are represented, often by only a few families. Among them they provide for the basic needs of the village; the castes and subcastes are thus highly interdependent.

Rigid rules define the relationships among castes and establish the roles that caste members may hold. Each child is taught his place in the hierarchy. A system that seems very complex may function with a minimum of conflict when all the roles are accepted and rules followed. When roles and rules are disregarded or defied, as happens now, confusion and even physical combat may result. An example of such combat occurred in one village in the 1930's when a lower caste defied the ruling caste (Rajputs of the warrior caste) and exercised its right to vote. This so enraged the Rajputs that they drove off the cattle of the lower caste, beat the men, and invaded their hamlet where they tore the roofs off the houses. The low caste, aware of the power of the courts, took the case to court. The Rajputs attempted to influence the court by bribes and personal pressure. The case was finally settled out of court.

The village family

Indian villages vary in composition and style of living from one region to another (4, 5, 20, 22, 23). They vary also in terms of the ease of communication with cities, with those in close communication having the highest rate of literacy and the highest percentage in non-agricultural work. Villages in the hinterland have a high rate of illiteracy with four out of five people dependent on agriculture. However, the accounts of a number of writers agree on certain basic characteristics. A small percentage only of Indians are middle-class or wealthy—perhaps not more than 5 per cent. The great mass of the 85 per cent of the population who live in villages are in abject poverty. Within the villages there is little opportunity to improve living standards.

Living quarters are variously described, depending upon the part of India where the village is located. One description speaks of one-story mud huts; another of a long low building for an extended family, with each nuclear unit occupying an alcove. The men may live in a separate building from their wives, daughters, and young sons. In some of the poorer families, stock is housed in one part of the dwelling, while in other families, the stock have a separate building across the courtyard.

Traditionally, the joint family prevailed, in which a father and his sons jointly owned and cultivated land. Now, the joint family is more common in higher castes while among lower castes two-thirds are nuclear. Land has been subdivided until a farm is scarcely large enough to support a nuclear family. The nuclear families usually are part of a local kinship web who feel a strong sense of identity. This feeling prevails among migrants to cities, who send money to their village-bound families when they are able or return to invest savings in land. They do not give up membership in the family and may be reabsorbed in it. The family, especially if there are joint land holdings, forms an anchor of security.

Control of the family rests with the elders, especially the males. This control extends to the choice of marriage partners for the children. It is a sacred duty of parents, especially parents of daughters, to arrange a marriage to someone in another village and outside certain degrees of relationship, but within the same caste. The young couple usually do not know each other. The long drawn out procedure of selection, betrothal, and marriage is controlled by the parents—the prospective bride and groom are merely actors in a play directed and coached by the elders. In spite of its present illegality, marriage and certainly betrothal still often occur for the girl before puberty and for the boy in midteens. The very young girl may remain with her parents until puberty, when she joins her husband's family and comes under the supervision of her mother-in-law. She has no intervening period of adolescence. She is a child in her parental family, then makes an immediate transition to the status of adult in the home of her parents-in-law. She is usually a mother by midteens. The village boy also has no adolescent period. His work in the family group begins in childhood and continues through adulthood. Marriage does not take him out of the family nor bring him independence.

Socialization of children

Gradually, schools are being established in the villages, but attendance is not compulsory and many families fail to see the desirability of sending their children regularly to school (23, 24). Formal education is not well established. Education in the caste values and skills, etiquette, respect for the elders, and future adult tasks are learned within the family. The learning process begins with imitative play in childhood; later it continues by direct participation. The mother-child (and especially the mother-son) relationship is close and warm. The personal father-son relationship is one of restraint on the part of the father, who does not make a companion of his son, and of respect and obedience from the son. Discipline is enforced by scolding, threats, fear, and sometimes physical punishment. If the youthful boy is disrespectful toward his father or rebellious, the father may beat him. However, physical punishment is rare. Usually group pressure and early training are sufficient to insure obedience. As a last resort, a rebellious son may leave the village and make his way to the nearest city.

Behavior that might be thought of as juvenile delinquency—as defiance of caste or village rules and laws—apparently rarely appears. Misconduct is interpreted as a family affair, as disobedience to the parents. This situation may be accounted for by the enclosure of activity within the family and kin, the close association with parents, the early marriage which signifies responsible adulthood but not independence, and the enforcement of authority by the elders. Children learn to fit into the limited social environment and to curb individualism.

Adult crime

Regardless of the conforming rearing of children, adults do not always confine their activities to acceptable behavior (20, 22, 24). A certain amount of stealing of cattle goes on between villages. As harvest nears, it is expedient for a village to post guards in the fields as a protection against thieves. One village study reported the killing of a stranger, without stating the circumstances. These crimes are between villagers and outsiders.

Most village studies that discuss crime indicate that the offenses occur within the village. An occasional study reports the birth of a baby to an unmarried girl, the attempt of the family to maintain a wall of secrecy, and the killing of the newborn baby by an adult male, without a report being made by anyone to the police. Locally the parents are criticized for failing to supervise their daughter, but the killing of the baby is not regarded as a crime. If these deaths come to the attention of the police and courts, conviction brings a heavy penalty. For example, girls who have killed their illegitimate babies have received sentences of imprisonment for life.

Quarrels between men that end in fighting and occasionally in death are reported. Women quarrel within the extended family and the crowded courtyard to which their activities are largely confined. These quarrels may spread and lead to long drawn-out feuds with potential fighting among the men. In one Rajput village the following types of disturbances and crimes were considered in one year by the local *panchayat:* disputes over rights to land, water, and trees; petty theft both of clothing and crops; and use of physical violence against a stranger.

Another village study notes that the greatest crime in some villages is the killing of a cow, a sacred animal among the Hindus. Killing of other animals is also forbidden: dog, cat, jackal, squirrel, horse, or mongoose. Killing of deer and peacocks is also unfavorably regarded by Hindus.

Most of the offenses are handled by the local *panchayat,* an elected assembly of older men in the village. It can impose fines or expel the offender from the village or caste, order a beating (rarely) or disgrace the offender by shaving off half of his hair or beard and leading him around the village to be ridiculed. Expulsion is the penalty for killing certain animals, for incest, or for being beaten by a member of a lower caste. Expulsion, especially in a low-caste village, may be a severe hardship. The person needs the support and security of the village. He is banned from the use of the common well, contacts with his family, and all caste privileges. However, he is accepted back as soon as he repents and submits to the judgment of the *panchayat;* some cases call for purification ceremonies and a fine.

The *panchayat* has little authority to enforce its decisions. The wealthy members of the village may ignore them, and young people may disregard the *panchayat* and hide their violations, especially if they live in a village near a large city where they may spend part of their time.

Beyond and superior to the *panchayat* is the government system of justice, to which more and more villagers turn when they are involved in serious disputes or crimes. However, the general attitude is one of distrust, especially if past encounters with the police have aroused hostility. In one village a detachment of police had been stationed there in the latter part of the nineteenth century in order to stamp out the practice of female infanticide. The villagers, after sixty or seventy years, still regard the police as enemies rather than agents of justice. In general, police are both feared and respected.

The offenses that are either suppressed or punished by the local *panchayat* are usually of a minor and often unplanned nature. Some have been part of the culture for many years and are ways in which unsatisfied personal needs are met. The poor man needs clothing or food for his family. Families or castes try to encroach on the rights of others and a dispute or feud begins. Murder seems to be an unplanned outcome of fighting. Children are aware of all these events and when they enter adulthood they also enter the situations that lead to criminal acts.

CLASH BETWEEN CUSTOM AND CRIMINAL LAW

The traditional Hindu system of marriage and family life included certain practices that horrified the British and led to the passage of laws forbidding them, thus transferring these practices from normal customs to criminal acts. Hindus were slow to accept the change and occasionally still resist, citing the old, often religious, values to support their behavior.

Female infanticide

Sons had high value in the Hindu scale of values, daughters low value (16, 24). A certain amount of female infanticide occurred. As early as 1795, the British declared infanticide to be murder; it was still in practice in 1870, with some indication of its existence as late as 1900. Nevertheless, the evidence does not indicate widespread practice. India did not officially or religiously approve of infanticide, but local groups permitted it as a form of family limitation, especially where girls were concerned. It has been suggested that often formal infanticide may not have been practiced but that girl babies were neglected or their brothers were favored when food was scarce or children were ill, with the result that girls died while boys survived.

Age at marriage

Age at marriage was also a matter of great concern to the British

(2, 4, 16, 28). The tendency was nationwide for parents to arrange betrothal or marriage for girls prior to puberty; they thus assured themselves of having fulfilled their obligation to find a mate for each daughter at a time when she was still a virgin. Part of the British aversion to youthful marriage was to the probability of sexual intercourse by an older husband with a pre-adolescent wife. More recently other considerations have entered in, such as the desirability of education for girls and the granting of free choice of a mate to young people.

Some of the British acts are revealing. In 1860 the Indian penal code defined sexual relations of a man with a wife under ten years old as rape. At this time age eight was thought to be the proper age of marriage for girls and 12 for boys. Various states passed restrictive laws, stipulating specific ages for girls and boys, which were raised as time passed. The Child Marriage Restraint Act of 1929 (Sarda Act) passed by British India fixed ages at 18 for boys and 14 for girls. This act did not cover some 600 states. In 1955 the Hindu Marriage Act forbade the marriage of girls under 15. Laws passed before 1955 tended to represent British sentiment and were more acceptable to upper-caste Hindus than lower-caste and more to urban than to rural people.

The laws run counter to custom and to religiously sanctioned practices and are still often ignored. In 1951 the mean ages for marriage were 15.2 for females and 20.0 for males. At that time there were almost three million married males, six million married females, 66,000 widowers, and 134,000 widows between the ages of five and 14.

Sati

The British early moved against the practice of *sati,* or suicide of the widow upon the funeral pyre of her husband (16). The practice was never widespread and was limited primarily to priestly and noble families among high-ranking castes. It has been estimated that at no time did more than 2 to 10 per cent of widows commit *sati,* even in groups that most highly favored it. The practice was linked to the religious rule against remarriage of widows, who consequently had no vital role to play in the family. Low-ranking castes permitted remarriage and did not expect widows to commit *sati.*

The British passed an act in 1829 for the prevention of *sati;* the act had little effect. In 1856 this act was supplemented by an act permitting remarriage, but again without effect. The decrease of *sati* came slowly, less as a result of laws than of changing attitudes toward the position of women. Nevertheless, *sati* had not completely died out by the 1950's, when an occasional case was recorded. As with infanticide and child marriages, *sati* had social or religious approval or both and could not be eradicated by laws imposed from without.

Polygyny

Another customary practice that the British tried to eradicate by legal action was polygyny (15). The practice of a man having more than one wife simultaneously was never widespread and occurred chiefly when the first wife had not borne a son or had some incapacitating disease. The only exception seems to have been among the Bengali Kulin Brahmins, who did not earn a living from their priestly duties. In the early part of the nineteenth century, some surveys indicate that a Kulin Brahmin might have as many as fifteen or twenty wives, all except the first usually from a stratum of Brahminism slightly lower than that of the husband. From the parents of each wife he received a dowry, and as he went the rounds to visit his various wives, who continued to live with their parents, he was presented with gifts. This practice has died out.

Various laws were passed from 1872 on to control or eliminate polygynous marriages, among all castes and tribal groups. None of the laws was very effective. In 1955 the Hindu Marriage Act forbade marriage of either man or woman who already had a living spouse. Violation constitutes bigamy and is punishable under the Indian penal code.

JUVENILE DELINQUENCY AS A PUBLIC PROBLEM

Juvenile delinquency, unrecognized and perhaps nonexistent in the villages, is prevalent in certain areas of Indian cities, especially those undergoing rapid industrial development.

Background of juvenile delinquency

In common with many other Asian and Far Eastern countries, Indian laws do not define juvenile delinquency in terms of specific behavior (7). Juvenile delinquency refers to offenses carried out by children between the ages of 7 and 15 or 16. Between ages 7 and 12 a child is not regarded as responsible for his conduct unless he has become sufficiently mature to judge the nature and consequences of his conduct. The upper age of 15 or 16 varies from state to state. Above these ages, the offender is handled in adult courts.

The concept of juvenile delinquency and methods of dealing with delinquents in India were based on usage in England when the British controlled India. In general, this pattern continues to the present. India has provisions for juvenile courts, referral clinics, and several types of institutions for confinement and treatment. As is true in most countries, these services are unevenly distributed, with cities being most fully provided with such facilities.

Migrants and slums

The contrast between rural misbehavior, a family problem, and urban delinquency, a public problem, is marked (1, 6, 10, 17, 21, 25, 27). The mere number of delinquents in itself creates a problem in some urban neighborhoods. More pertinent is the inability in certain areas of the city of family, caste, and neighborhood to indoctrinate and control children and youth.

The areas of high delinquency rates are the slums, peopled not only by permanent residents but by large numbers of unsettled and restless migrants from rural villages. The problems of these migrants, which extend far beyond delinquency and crime, have become accentuated as cities have moved, in education and technology, further and further away from the static villages. The gap between the levels of living in cities and rural areas constantly widens. Although advances have been made in providing schools and social services for villages, only a little inroad has been made on illiteracy and poverty —on bringing villagers into the modern current of Indian culture and technology. Many rural families are unable to make a livelihood from the small plots of worn-out land, and new land is not available for cultivation. At the same time the demand for village handicrafts has declined. Meanwhile the population has steadily increased. Added to these economic factors that decrease the attractiveness of village life—that "push" people out of the villages—are the attractions that pull people to the city: possibility of education, factory jobs, exercise of new political rights, and the possibility of shaking off the handicaps of low caste.

Migrants draw heavily from the lower castes and untouchables. They come into the city as families or as individuals, including teen-aged boys. They come without reserves of cash to tide them over and poorly equipped in personal habits, education, or skills to cope with city life.

Many migrants, unable to fit themselves into city jobs and ways of living, become floaters, moving from city to city or between city and village. A study of Marathi-speaking migrants in Bombay showed that a fifth required longer than two years to secure work, half up to two years, and only a third no longer than a month.[8] Some personality differences may separate the steadily employed from the floaters. The steadily employed are described as well-behaved, temperate, hardworking; they keep a connection with their relatives in the village, sending money to them. In contrast, floaters exhibit undesirable behavior, for example, rowdyism, excessive drinking, and abandonment of old people and children. The family is frequently beset by quarrels. Separation and divorce are commonplace and may be followed by a period of promiscuity for both men and women with eventual remarriage. Begging, stealing, and picking pockets also are evident.

It is impossible for most cities to absorb the number of migrants who come in. Housing is so limited that many cannot find space in the crowded tenements and resort to living in the alleys and on the pavements. Some families with small children are in this predicament, and large numbers of uprooted men and boys, without property or extra clothing, live in this way.

The unity of the village family tends to disappear in the city. Usually only a nuclear family or a detached individual migrates and both the help and the controls of the larger family are lost. The father cannot provide work for his children nor control their leisure activities. Families often disintegrate under the pressures and the customary male model is absent in a situation where no adult male relative is at hand to step in as a substitute. In the village the caste throws another circle of control around individuals. Caste lines often become blurred in the city; many low-caste members or untouchables

[8] P. N. Prabhu, *The Social Implications of Industrialization and Urbanization* (section on Bombay), UNESCO publication from Research Centre on the Social Implications of Industrialization in Southern Asia, Calcutta, India, 1956. See also section in same publication on Delhi, by M. B. Deshmukh.

are willing to have it be so in order to escape the disabilities of their caste membership.

Types of juvenile delinquency

Juvenile delinquency in the cities is primarily part of the general "culture of poverty," and not part of a subculture of delinquency with self-contained values and standards supported by organized gangs of boys and cliques of girls, such as exist in many American and some European cities (3, 32, 37). A study of Bombay showed that gangs of delinquents were uncommon and not well developed; they were in a formative, rudimentary stage.[9] Loyalty and solidarity were shortlived; an arrested delinquent was ready to tell the names of his companions. Such gangs as existed were usually headed by an adult, who taught the delinquents the techniques of his particular type of crime and guided their exploits. The adult was respected and regarded as a benefactor, probably because 72 per cent of the gang boys studied were homeless boys living without regular employment on the footpaths and pavements. These adult-led gangs often specialized in some one type of crime and had regular customers for the stolen goods. A few cases were found of more highly organized and socially dangerous gangs, whose members carried knives and stole goods worth large sums of money.

The most common offense is against property, that is, thefts or possible destruction of property, according to a study of court cases in Greater Bombay, Ahmedabad, and Poona made in 1954. Table 5 gives the distribution of all cases, and Table 6 the types of theft. Most of the things stolen are easy to sell for cash and are not for the immediate use of the delinquent. Few would bring any large sum of money. Some of the money makes possible the hand-to-mouth existence of many delinquents; but the author notes that some is used to buy luxuries that the boy's family cannot afford or that a well-to-do family regards as unnecessary.

Much juvenile stealing is an offshoot of adult crime. The exploitation of small gangs of boys by adult thieves has already been described. Boys may be paid by adult criminals to transport stolen goods, which the child may or may not know has been stolen. Some-

[9] H. Sheth, *Juvenile Delinquency in an Urban Setting,* Popular Book Depot, Bombay, India, 1961: see also S. S. Srivastava, "Sociology of Juvenile Ganging," *Journal of Correctional Work,* Lucknow, India (Sept. 1955), pp. 72-81.

times the boy's family exploits him. For example, a father who had a small brass and copper shop had his son steal brass plates. Street peddlers may encourage a child to steal while they show their wares, or a child may steal in a store while his parents make a purchase. Adults from ex-criminal tribes may teach their children to steal. Some employed boys steal.

TABLE 5

Juvenile Offenses in Greater Bombay, Ahmedabad, and Poona, from Juvenile Court Records, 1954*

(Percentage Distribution)

Offense	*Greater Bombay*	*Ahmedabad*	*Poona*
Against property	56.1	47.3	52.2
Against rationing and prohibition rules	29.5	23.6	8.7
Ticketless travel	0.4	2.7	26.1
Hawking and trespassing without license	4.1	20.9	2.2
Other	9.9	5.5	0.8
Total	100.00	100.00	100.0

*Hansa Sheth, *Juvenile Delinquency in an Urban Setting*. Popular Book Depot, Bombay, 1961, p. 105.

TABLE 6

Types of Theft in Greater Bombay, from Juvenile Court Records, 1954*

(Percentage distribution)

Types of Theft	*Percentage of Total Thefts*
Metals (scrap iron, small brass pieces, metal pipes, etc.)	34.5
Cash and costly articles (fountain pens, watches, jewelry, cameras, bicycles)	20.6
Clothes	11.0
Railway material (leather hide, bulbs, iron rods, battery cells, electric fans)	6.7

TABLE 6 (continued)

Edibles (grains, vegetables, coconuts, tea-packets, chocolate tins)	5.9
Miscellaneous articles	13.3
Not known	8.0
Total	100.0

*Hansa Sheth, *Juvenile Delinquency in an Urban Setting.* Popular Book Depot, Bombay, 1961, p. 107.

Boys are often used by adults in evading such laws as the rationing and prohibition laws. Offenses against rationing and prohibition are violations of specific laws. Rationing of essential food grains was begun in the city of Bombay and the suburban area in 1943 and was gradually extended to other parts of Bombay State. The law covers the acquisition, possession, distribution, and transportation of food grains. City adults want grain in excess of their ration to use or sell; villagers wish to sell grain. Children are often hired to carry the grain; if they are arrested the adult is relieved of responsibility.

Bombay State has total prohibition of alcoholic beverages and has arrangements with nearby states not to sell alcohol in Bombay State. This situation opens the way for the illicit manufacture and sale of liquor. Again, boys are employed to transport liquor, or smuggle it into the city, using such containers as milk cans, cycle or motor tubes, rubber balloons, bottles, bags, and so forth. The child may be instructed to travel on the train without a ticket for which he may be put off the train or arrested. Parents may be the ones who make such use of their children. In other cases, juveniles may be employed in distilleries to protect from arrest the adults who operate the plant. Many boys are legitimately employed but carry liquor as a side line.

Gambling is common among juveniles. Fifty per cent of the gambling offenses in Bombay State were by juveniles. The gamblers are less likely than the thieves to be poor boys. They were often well employed as it was necessary to have money in hand. The author surmises that the motive was recreation, excitement, or curiosity.

Other offenses that may lead to arrest are traveling on the railroad without a ticket, hawking wares without a license, trespassing, assaults, and disorderly conduct. These offenses are not regarded as criminal by the offenders and sometimes are overlooked by the police.

Another offense, not included in the Bombay study of juvenile court cases but that is widespread throughout India, is the combination of vagrancy and begging. Legal authorities may proceed against vagrants and beggars as constituting a public nuisance. In most states, begging in railway premises and public places is forbidden. These provisions have not prevented vagrancy and begging among both adults and children.

A study of vagrancy of boys in Lucknow and Kanpur is revealing. In the sample of vagrants used, few were below nine years of age and the average age was 13.7 years.[10] Vagrancy tapered off above age 14; the author surmises that in the later teens boys either settled down to normal life or passed from vagrancy into full-fledged criminal careers. The boys, studied while loitering on the streets, varied from full-time vagrants who lived and slept on the streets to boys still living at home but spending their days wandering and begging.

The family backgrounds of the vagrants were marked by a high proportion of broken homes with desertion by the father, the presence of a step-father, or lack of either parent, and drinking, gambling, and irregular sex habits on the part of the parents. Comparable data for the general population are not given, but the percentages of these factors for the vagrant boys seem higher than one would expect in general.

The boys do not attend school or have other institutional affiliations. They associate with each other but usually without strong bonds. Only a fifth had an active gang life; 41 per cent had no fixed peer-group affiliations; 34 per cent were in loosely defined groups.

The boys' behavior is deviant from that expected of the teen-age Indian boy and indicates hedonistic living in the present, without orientation to future plans. They are described as stubborn, impertinent, and rude. Lying is a protective activity. Obscenities and vulgarities are common as are homosexuality and masturbation. The boys may exhibit themselves sexually, thought to be a carry-over from early childhood when nakedness was disregarded. They have a minimum of heterosexual relations. Other activities include gambling of a simple type and use of a variety of intoxicants.

The activities of the boys easily move into delinquency and crime as the boys try to maintain themselves without work. Petty thefts by

---

[10] S. S. Srivastava, *Juvenile Vagrancy.* Asia Publishing House, Bombay, India, 1963.

individual boys or small groups are common, usually taking the form of shoplifting or theft of edibles. Higher rewards come from pocket-picking or snatching money or articles from women and children. Boys still at home steal from their parents.

Begging is an easy way to obtain money with little risk of arrest. Among the vagrant boys in Lucknow and Kanpur, 75 per cent were regular beggars and additional boys begged occasionally.

Sex offenses

Sex offenses pertain primarily to girls, who may be handled as nonoffenders by the juvenile courts which treat them as in need of supervision (32). One type that may be listed in the record as the victim of kidnapping or rape refers to girls who elope with men without marriage but after having had sex relations. The customary supervision of girls is difficult in the city slums and especially so if the home is broken or both parents are employed. Another type of sex offense in which the girl is the victim follows exploitation by parents or other adults which results in the girl becoming a member of a house of prostitution. Other girls drift to the city, cannot find work, and solicit on the streets.

The exploitation of women and girls is recognized in the Indian penal code which provides imprisonment up to ten years and fines for procurement, buying, and selling of girls under 18 for prostitution. Another act of 1958 applying to all of India provides punishment for keeping a brothel, living on the earnings of prostitutes, procuring, inducing, or taking a woman or girl for the purpose of prostitution, detaining a woman or girl in premises where prostitution is carried on, for prostituting in or in the vicinity of public places, or seducing or soliciting for the purpose of prostitution.

The criminal milieu, the family, and the future

In view of the varieties of exploitation of both boys and girls by adult criminals the statement made by the sociologist Hauser seems justified: delinquency in India is not a question of drifting into criminality as an attempt to solve problems of social adjustment, but is the result of recruitment of the young by criminals already in existence in the city.[11] The extent of this recruitment is held in

[11] P. Hauser, editor, *Urbanization in Asia and the Far East,* UNESCO Research Centre on the Social Implications of Industrialization in Southern Asia, Calcutta, India, 1957.

check by other factors.

Clinard, who is familiar with the problems of India's cities from first hand contacts, states that, as in all cities, the slums are noted for juvenile delinquency, crime, prostitution, professional begging, and use of drugs. He adds: "These problems appear, however, even allowing for differences in the extent of reporting and arrests, to be not so serious as in the slums of the West. In fact, India presents evidence that poverty alone does not explain deviant behavior in slum communities." He attributes the low incidence of delinquency in India, as compared to the West, to the degree that the family and caste act as agencies of social control. He anticipates a rise in rates of deviant behavior as India becomes more highly industrialized and urbanized.[12]

Middle-class children and youth

The emphasis on juvenile delinquency in the slums should not obscure consideration of the middle class, where young people are still primarily members of organized families and castes that follow customary patterns. Parents and older members receive the respect and obedience of children and youth, shelter their daughters, either select or influence the selection of marriage mates, provide education, and to a large extent guide occupational choice. Young people may deviate from strict family compliance but usually not in the form of delinquency or crime. They pull against family controls and create tensions especially between grandparents and youth, but in general the family still is the milieu for daily living from infancy into adulthood. Beyond the family, the caste system still exerts control, regardless of recent laws seeking to obliterate caste lines. The castes of middle and upper rank seek to hold the line against intrusions of lower castes and have little motivation to move out of their own privileged caste placement.[13]

Contrary to the general orderliness of middle-class youth is the disorderly conduct of groups of male college students, which apparently is a carry-over from the early 1940's when they participated in

---

[12] Marshall Clinard, *Slums and Community Development, Experiments in Self-Help,* Free Press, 1966, p. 88.

[13] An excellent discussion of the urban family is given by Aileen D. Ross, *Hindu Family in its Urban Setting,* University of Toronto Press, Toronto, Canada, 1961.

the struggle for independence.[14] The current reasons for protests and strikes are usually related to college problems, sometimes of a trivial nature. Typical precipitating incidents include objections to examinations, an increase in college fees, to secure the return of a popular teacher, and other college situations. In a study made in 1961-62, Ross suggests that the real basis of protests and unrest may be changes in economic and social problems. For example, even well educated youth may find it impossible to secure employment in a country where the rate of unemployment is high and the rate of industrialization low. Another area in which there is lack of adjustment is in changes in sex roles and the partial emergence of girls and young women from the seclusion of the home to the college campus and employment. Three or four male students will set out to find a girl or several girls whom they will tease, ridicule, and subject to rude remarks. They have earned for themselves the derisive title of Roadside Romeos. So annoying are their attentions that the largest women's college in Bangalore found it necessary to secure police services to warn or arrest the men students when they congregate before the college.

Other types of undesirable public behavior include stopping or stoning trams, buses, or trains, raiding a motion picture theater, and destruction of a women's college residence. The activities may be as limited in time as one morning, or may last for five months or go on indefinitely.

ADULT CRIME

The discussion of juvenile delinquency has already suggested the close relationship between delinquency and adult crime. (19) The girl or boy, detached from family controls, not attending school, and unemployed finds an open avenue to adult crime, first as a kind of apprentice under the tutelage of mature criminals, and later as an adult criminal himself. The types of exploitation of the young indicate some types of adult crime: picking pockets, thieving, begging, and evasion of rationing and prohibition laws. Table 7 expands the list and shows the frequency distribution for Bombay State in 1955. The highest proportion of crimes falls into the classification of minor property crimes, followed by serious offenses against the person and

[14] Aileen D. Ross, "Student Indiscipline in a Developing Country," paper presented at the Annual Meeting of the American Sociological Society, 1962.

property or property alone, and serious offenses against the person. The most frequent offenses are of a minor nature, being ordinary theft, lurking and house trespassing, and "hurt" or minor personal injury. Some of the troublesome crimes of the past occur only in small numbers: exposure of infants or concealment of birth, dacoity, and belonging to gangs of thugs. On the other hand, new crimes originating in recent laws are numerous, as shown by 106,798 crimes under the heading "Offenses under special and local laws declared to be cognizable." Most of these crimes are violations of prohibition laws.

As is true for any official record of crime, Table 7 does not include crimes that are tolerated, undetected, or that do not end in conviction at the time of trial. For example, it is difficult in the table to isolate white collar crimes, that is, crimes inherent in the way a business is operated. Nevertheless, such crimes exist in India as in all urbanized nations. A newspaper clipping of 1967 headed Calcutta concerns "black money," or money not reported by business men in their official records, a technique whereby they evade payment of taxes. Black money may account for as much as a third of income. The concealed income may be used personally or to bribe minor officials to grant the "innumerable permits" required in the operation of a business.[15]

TABLE 7*

Cognizable Crime in Bombay State, 1955**

Offense		*Number of offenses*
Class I.	Offenses against the State, Public Tranquility, Safety, and Justice	
	1. Rioting or unlawful assembly	973
	2. Personating public servant or soldier	35
Class II.	Serious Offenses against the Person	
	3. Murder	1,347
	4. Attempts at murder	145
	5. Culpable homicide	83
	6. Rape by person other than husband	163

[15] *Chicago Daily News,* January 17, 1967.

TABLE 7 (continued)

Class	Offense	Number
	7. Unnatural offense	22
	8. Exposure of infants or concealment of birth	269
	9. Attempts at, and abetment of, suicide	345
	10. Grievous hurt	1,854
	11. Administering stupefying drugs to cause hurt	57
	12. Hurt	3,232
	13. Kidnapping or abduction, selling, etc. for prostitution, dealing in slaves	447
	14. Hurt and assault to deter a public servant from duty	599
	15. Rash or negligent act causing death or grievous hurt	456
Class III.	Serious offenses against person and property or property alone	
	16. Dacoity and preparation and assembly for dacoity	453
	17. Robbery	1,638
	18. Serious mischief and cognate offenses	1,194
	19. Mischief, by killing, poisoning or maiming any animal	328
	20. Lurking, house-trespass, etc.	10,517
	21. Belonging to gangs of thugs, dacoits, robbers and thieves	2
Class IV.	Minor offenses against the person	
	22. Wrongful restraint and confinement	692
	23. Rash act causing hurt or endangering life	647
Class V.	Minor offenses against property	
	24. Theft of cattle	1,462
	25. Ordinary theft	19,012
	26. Criminal breach of trust	1,772
	27. Receiving stolen property	171
	28. Cheating	858
	29. Criminal house-trespass or house breaking	74

Class VI.***

Other offenses

31. Offenses under special and local laws declared to be cognizable	106,798
Total of true cognizable cases	158,676

*Perin C. Kerawalla, *A Study in Indian Crime.* Popular Book Depot, Bombay, 1959, citing official reports, pp. 82-83.

**A cognizable crime is one for which police may make an arrest without a warrant.

***Class VI crimes are non-cognizable. Examples given in another connection are offenses relating to marriage; intimidation, insult and annoyance; and keeping a lottery office.

Political corruption is another form of white collar crime that is mentioned in various accounts.

White collar crimes have little to offer the typical juvenile delinquent from the slums, but open the way for educated middle-class youth to move into criminal activities.

The young adult offender

Bridging the gap between juvenile delinquents and adult criminals is the young adult offender (19, 38). In India, in 1955, according to the Jail Administration Report, among males convicted of crime and imprisoned, 22 per cent were below the age of 22. They were almost double the proportion of the total population in this age group (12 per cent). But this did not compare with the disproportion for the group 22 to 30 years old; 53 per cent of the jail population as compared with only 16 per cent of the total population fell into this mature adult group. For ages 31-40 the proportion of male criminals only slightly exceeded the proportion of the population, and above age 40 the proportion of criminals was less than the proportion of the population.

Among women the distribution was somewhat different. Below age 22 the proportion of female criminals was less than the corresponding proportion in the total population.[16] Between ages 22 and 60, the proportion of criminals was approximately two or three times the corresponding proportion in the population. Male criminals bulk large in the young and mature age groups, women in the middle-age range.

Property crimes are the most frequent offenses of young adult

[16] Kerawalla, *op. cit.*, pp. 52-53.

offenders in India, and prominent among such crimes are burglary and dacoity.[17] Minor offenses for which young adults are arrested include vagrancy, begging, travelling on the railroad without a ticket, gambling, excise offenses, and an assortment of other minor offenses. The statistics of five Indian states show that such offenses account for 55 per cent of total arrests (excluding arrests for excise offenses) for persons aged 17 to 21. Since many of these offenders cannot pay fines, they serve prison terms.

The above offenses are not greatly different from those of juveniles or of the common run of adult offenders. They point to a continuity of offenses from childhood into adulthood, with the addition in adulthood of more serious crimes and of white collar crimes. Young adults have little opportunity for white collar or political offenses.

THE TREND OF DELINQUENCY

In India various types of juvenile delinquency and crime coexist, linked with various phases of political-economic-social changes. Some types are left over from the past, such as the intra-tribal crimes of still isolated primitive tribes, and the now minor offenses of the remnants of criminal tribes. Belonging essentially to the past are the intra-village crimes that will change as communication and transportation increase. The delinquency and crime of cities, struggling from village-ways to industrial-urban ways, are of the present and point to the future. The trend of change is from tribal to Hindu organization, and from village to city. It seems very probable that delinquency and crime will increase and change in character in the cities and perhaps in the villages as a result of the displacements of old personal patterns of family life and village control by as yet incompletely developed new and formal patterns and controls. The very attempt to solve certain problems may create new ones. For example, the move to eliminate caste distinctions weakens caste control. The migration to the cities relieves pressure on the farms and villages but creates many new economic problems, some of which are eased by the widespread juvenile delinquency and petty crime. The emphasis on higher education with the slow development of comparable positions creates unrest and public disorders

At present, city delinquency, like much of city life itself, is in a

[17] *Young Adult Offender,* Department of Economic and Social Affairs, United Nations, New York, 1965.

rudimentary stage of development. It grows out of poverty, dire need, and lack of social organization in the slums. Adult criminals prey on rootless children and youth. Financial welfare measures, typical of Europe and the United States, are in a beginning stage. Compulsory school attendance and varied youth organizations, typical of more mature cities, have not yet appeared. However, these provisions may not eliminate delinquency. In western cities, with their bulwarks against poverty and provided with schools and youth agencies, delinquency, far from disappearing, has seemed to feed on these provisions. Thefts are not for necessities but for luxury items. Schools are often a source of frustration, calling forth retaliatory vandalism and violence. Youth agencies provide a new form of activity and sometimes of delinquency. Gangs, now in a rudimentary phase in India, are a recognizable form of delinquent groups in Europe and reach a high point of organization and ruthlessness in some of the most highly urbanized parts of the United States.

India is sometimes referred to as an economically underdeveloped country. If it is, a part of its underdevelopment is in the area of juvenile delinquency. A crucial question is whether India can incorporate its young into constructive and conforming ways of life and thus bypass the more highly organized, destructive, and violent forms of delinquency that have accompanied the processes of industrialization and urbanization in the West.

REFERENCES

1. BHATIA, V. B. "Juvenile Delinquency in the City of Lucknow." *Journal of Correctional Work,* (India), 12 (1965), pp. 108-25.
2. BISWAS, P. C. *The Ex-Criminal Tribes of Delhi State.* University of Delhi, Delhi, India, 1960.
3. BOSE, G. "Delinquency in India." In K. R. Eissler, editor, *Searchlights on Delinquency.* International Universities Press, 1956.
4. CHANDRASEKHAR, S. "The Family in India." *Marriage and Family Living,* 16 (1954), pp. 336-42.
5. CHANDRASEKHAR, S. "The Hindu Joint Family." *Social Forces,* 21 (1943), pp. 327-33.
6. CLINARD, MARSHALL. *Slums and Community Development, Experiments in Self-Help.* Free Press, 1966.
7. *Comparative Survey on Juvenile Delinquency,* Part IV, *Asia and the Far East.* United Nations, Department of Social Affairs, Division of Social Welfare, 1953.
8. COX, SIR EDMUND C. *Police and Crime in India.* Stanley Paul and Co., London, no date.

9. CURRY, J. C. *The Indian Police.* Faber and Faber, Ltd., London, 1932.
10. DESHMUKH, M. B. *The Social Implications of Industrialization and Urbanization* (section on Delhi). UNESCO, Research Centre on the Implications of Industrialization in Southern Asia, Calcutta, India, 1956.
11. ELWIN, VERRIER. *Maria Murder and Suicide.* Oxford University Press, London, 1950.
12. FUCHS, STEPHEN. *Children of Hari, A Study of the Nimar Balahis in the Central Provinces of India.* Verlag Herold, Vienna, Austria, 1950.
13. FUCHS, STEPHEN. *The Gond and Bhumia of Eastern Mandla.* Asia Publishing House, Bombay, India, 1960.
14. GHURYE, G. S. *The Scheduled Tribes.* Popular Book Depot, Bombay, India, 1959.
15. GILLIN, JOHN L. *Taming the Criminal: Adventures in Penology.* Macmillan, 1931.
16. GOODE, W. J. *World Revolution and Family Patterns.* Free Press, 1963.
17. HAUSER, PHILIP, editor. *Urbanization in Asia and the Far East.* Proceedings of the Joint UN/UNESCO Seminar (in cooperation with the International Labour Office) on urbanization in the ECAFE Region, Bangkok 8-18 August, 1956. UNESCO, Research Centre on the Social Implications of Industrialization in Southern Asia, Calcutta, India, 1957.
18. HUTTON, J. H. *Caste in India, Its Nature, Function, and Origins.* Oxford University Press, 1961.
19. KERAWALLA, P. C. *A Study in Indian Crime.* Popular Book Depot, Bombay, India, 1959.
20. LEWIS, OSCAR. *Village Life in Northern India.* University of Illinois Press, 1958.
21. MAMORIA, C. B. *Social Problems and Social Disorganization in India.* Kitabmahal, Allahabad, India, 1960.
22. MARRIOTT, MCKIM, editor. *Village India: Studies in the Little Community.* University of Chicago Press, 1955.
23. MAYER, A. C. *Caste and Kinship in Central India, A Village and its Region.* University of California Press, 1960.
24. MINTURN, L. and J. T. HITCHCOCK. "The Ràjpùts of Khalapur, India." In B. B. Whiting, editor, *Six Cultures: Studies in Child Rearing,* John Wiley and Sons, 1963.
25. PANAKAL, J. J. *Prevention of Types of Criminality Resulting from Social Changes Accompanying Economic Development in Less Developed Countries.* Part I. United Nations: Department of Economic and Social Affairs, 1960.
26. PATEL, T. "Some Reflections on the Beggar Problem in Ahmedabad." *Sociological Bulletin* (India), (March, 1959), pp. 5-15.

27. PRABHU, P. N. *Social Implications of Industrialization and Urbanization* (section on Bombay). UNESCO, Research Centre on the Social Implications of Industrialization in Southern Asia, Calcutta, India, 1956.
28. ROSS, AILEEN D. *Hindu Family in its Urban Setting*. University of Toronto Press, Toronto, Canada, 1961.
29. SETHNA, M. J. *Society and the Criminal*. Leaders' Press, Bombay, India, 1952.
30. SHAH, P. G. *The Dublas of Gujarat*. Bharatiya Adimjatisevak Sangh, Kingsway, Delhi, India, 1958.
31. SHAH, P. G. *Tribal Life in Gujarat*. Bharatiya Vidja Bhavan, Chaupatty, Bombay, India, 1964.
32. SHETH, HANSA. *Juvenile Delinquency in an Urban Setting*. Popular Book Depot, Bombay, India, 1961.
33. SHUKLA, B. K. *Daflas of the Subansiri Region*. North-East Frontier Agency, Shillong, India, 1959.
34. SINGH, B. N. "Delinquent and Juvenile Pattern in Primitive Society." *Eastern Anthropology*, 2 (1948), pp. 107-14.
35. SINHA, R. *The Akas*. Research Dept., Adviser's Secretariat, Shillong, India, 1962.
36. SRIVASTAVA, S. S. *Juvenile Vagrancy*. Asia Publishing House, Bombay, India, 1963.
37. SRIVASTAVA, S. S. "Sociology of Juvenile Ganging." *Journal of Correctional Work*, (India), 2 (September, 1955) pp. 72-81.
38. *Young Adult Offender*. Department of Economic and Social Affairs, United Nations, New York, 1965.
39. ZINKIN, TAYA. *Caste Today*. Oxford University Press, London, 1962.

5 / The Soviet Union: Change of Ideology

The Soviet Union well illustrates the close relation of criminal concepts and behavior to the basic political and economic ideology. The Revolution of 1917 was not simply a rebellion against the Czarist government, but a destruction of a complete social system for the purpose of instituting a communist regime designed to affect all phases of life. Communist ideology not only controls government and the production and distribution of goods, but sets moral standards to which all are urged or compelled to conform. Crime is defined in relation to the central ideology and includes offenses not found in western nations but which constitute a threat to the principles of communism. More specifically, crime is regarded as having its origin in capitalism; it is said to be a vestige of capitalism or the result of contaminating contacts with capitalist countries. Juvenile delinquency is of great concern since it indicates a failure of family, school, and various communist organizations for youth to instill the principles of communism in children.

As is generally true in any society, crime and delinquency are a threat to the basic values and principles of the society, in this case, communism. The relationship is more evident than in societies of longer standing, since the origin of a communist society in Russia and the affiliated republics is of recent origin and its progress toward an ideal goal has been a slow and torturous one, with many changes in interpretation of basic principles and consequently in the formulation of criminal concepts and methods of dealing with both delinquency and crime.

COMMUNIST CONCEPTS RELEVANT TO CRIME AND DELINQUENCY

Communists believe that, in an ideal communist society, crime and delinquency could not exist (18, 26, 27, 30). All needs would be satisfied; all people would live together in peace and harmony. Crime and delinquency are regarded as linked to the capitalist system, in which, according to communist principles, the powerful, rich elite and the successful middle class oppress the working class or proletariat. In the ideal communist society there would be no need for a formal government—the state would "wither away." Since there would be no crime, the need for criminal laws, police, criminal courts, jails, and prisons would also disappear. A few years of experience after the Revolution of 1917 taught the communist leaders that the proletariat did not eagerly accept the ideal state. Force and compulsion were required to wrest private property from them and place it under the ownership of the government. All the trappings of crime detection, arrests, and punishment typical of modern states continued, with various modifications to fit them into communist ideology. In the 50 years since the Revolution criminal laws and methods of dealing with offenders—youthful and adult—have changed with the social situation of a developing industrial country and with changes in leadership.

Government also has responded to changing needs and crises. Far from withering away, government has become a rigidly controlled hierarchy of authority and power, with ultimate and unquestioned power resting in a small central authoritarian group, the Presidium, and a Central Committee.[1] The authoritarian government is justified by the phrase, the dictatorship of the proletariat, and its elimination of opposition as the necessity of removing the last vestiges of the capitalist system. At successive lower levels of authority are the Party Committees of National Republics and Ethnic Territories, Party Committees on Local Levels, and the Party's rank and file. Each level is answerable to the level above it for fulfilling its responsibilities and is charged with surveillance of the level below. With this system and a strong police force, the small proportion of the people who are in the Communist Party (5 per cent) exerts supervision and control of some 230 million people in the Soviet Union. Decisions are made at the top and are expected to be accepted without question, debate, or an opportunity to protest or to vote on an issue by the millions of

[1] T. A. Thomasic, "Social and Political Structure of the Soviet Union and the United States," paper delivered at the Annual Meeting of the American Sociological Association, 1966.

people lower in the scale. Protests, objections, or refusal to follow directives constitute crimes of varying degrees of seriousness and lead to disciplinary action.

Although communism ideally introduces a classless society, the Soviet Union is far from classless. One student of the Soviet Union lists 12 occupational classes, corresponding to different levels in the political hierarchy.[2] The highest category includes the military, governmental, managerial, and various intellectual classes, followed by lower levels of intelligensia, technicians, and clerks—in short, all who do some form of mental work. Corresponding to the party's rank and file are labor supervisors and foremen, skilled and unskilled laborers, and agricultural laborers on state farms. The collective peasantry, a large agglomeration with little place in party membership, follows. At the bottom of the hierarchy are convict laborers, at times an important element in the industrial development of the Republics.

Another classification notes essentially the same hierarchy of authority but adds three additional categories.[3] One is termed by the author the "activists," who may or may not be party members but who as volunteers become very active in furthering the ends of the Party. A second category is termed "outsiders," people who quietly ignore the party commands but do not openly resist or oppose. The first of these two categories, the "activists," is very likely to become upwardly mobile; the second, the "outsiders," is relegated to lower occupational levels. The third category contains the "enemies of the people," that is, of communism. They oppose the state directly or commit the ordinary run of crimes. They fall outside the legal categories, are disciplined in the community, or make up the prisoners in ordinary prisons or forced labor camps.

Placement of the various categories is in part related to the almost total control that the Party exerts over both private and public affairs of all people, whether or not they are members of the Party. This control is possible through the dispersion of the various levels of the Party hierarchy into all levels of society. Those who adhere to the Party directives and principles are favorably considered for

---

[2] Thomasic, *op. cit.*

[3] John Kosa, *Two Generations of Soviet Man,* College and University Press, 1962, pp. 67-76.

favors, education, and promotion. Higher education is another factor in placement—but the opportunity for higher education is in part in the hands of the Party, and in part related to the position of the student's father. The ability of the young student also helps to determine his future education. Thus the young person and his parents are not free to make choices of education and occupation. The growing class divisions and the difficulty of moving from class to class occasion dissatisfaction and some criminal behavior among those who feel frustrated or unfairly treated.

A fundamental principle involves the transfer of means of production and distribution of goods from private ownership to joint ownership by the working classes (the state). The state controls the establishment of factories and the placement of citizens in jobs, places a quota of production on each enterprise, pays workers a wage, and fulfills many of their needs as a social service. Hospital care, education, and recreation are strictly controlled as well as paid for by the state. Private property is limited to a small vegetable plot and a few farm animals for farmers, and household and personal possessions for urban dwellers. A large proportion of crime consists of thefts of utilitarian or luxury items from other individuals or from state-operated enterprises as people seek to satisfy individual interests, to augment their scanty goods, or to improve their standard of living. These goals are difficult to accomplish under mass concepts and limited wages. State provisions are for the masses and do not take account of individual interests.

A basic communist principle is that work is a sacred duty of every able person, male or female. Consequently everyone, except children and old people, is obligated to work, from the highest classes down to the convict laborer. Work may differ from level to level, but no one is officially exempted. Quotas of production and income are determined by higher authorities. Work assignments come from above. The slogan encompassing this principle has changed slightly from time to time. At first the expression was "from each according to his ability, to each according to his needs." A later expression that allows for differential payment to persons in different levels of the occupational hierarchy is "from each according to his ability, to each according to his work." Refusal to work, absenteeism, failure to reach assigned levels of production, and habits such as alcoholism that interfere with work are all censured and the offender in some way disciplined. Special laws passed in 1960-61, called anti-parasite laws, placed severe penalties on such offenders.

Communism has created its own standards of morality. The highest moral principle is furtherance of communist society; the most severe punishments are for crimes against communism, euphemized as crimes against the people. Whatever supports communism is good; opposition is not tolerated. According to Kosa, the individual is expected to "merge his wishes and interests with those of the party" and accept the norms and values of the Party as his highest goal.[4]

JUVENILE DELINQUENCY

As with adult crime, juvenile delinquency is related to the political-economic framework and is expected to disappear with the last vestiges of capitalism. Its solution lies in thorough training of children in the principles of communism and close supervision of youth.

Delinquency in the 1920's and 1930's

The communists inherited a horde of detached youth from the years of World War I, prior to the Revolution (1, 6, 7, 34, 35, 42). In October, 1916, a Moscow newspaper referred to the "endless number of child volunteers," 11 to 16 years old, who returned to Moscow with adult war prisoners. They were supposed to be separated from adult prisoners but conditions were such that they were housed with the adults. The number of detached children was swelled by war orphans and refugee children, who roamed the streets and gathered on street corners. The chief delinquencies of these floating children were vagrancy, theft, and prostitution.[5]

After the Revolution, juvenile delinquency continued. Not only the upheaval of the Revolution followed by civil war, but famine and pestilence, and disturbances of traditional forms of family life released children and youth from group controls.[6] Not all such children were delinquent. Many might be considered potential delinquents because of the confusion of ideals and means of social control.

---

[4] Kosa, *op. cit.*, pp. 24-25.

[5] W. A. Lunden, *War and Delinquency,* Ames, Iowa, The Art Press, 1963, pp. 22-23. For comparison with World War II, see Chapters 7 and 8.

[6] I. S. Wile, "Present Problems of Mental Health in Russia," *Mental Hygiene,* 22 (1938), pp. 42-43; B. Madison, "Contributions and Problems of Soviet Welfare Institutions," *Social Problems,* (Spring, 1960), p. 299.

In 1921 it was estimated that there were eight million homeless "wild" children, among whom were 75 thousand delinquents. The solution was thought to lie in gathering these children into institutions and in educating them in correct communist philosophy. The task was beyond complete accomplishment. In 1922 only 540,000 of the homeless children were housed. Many children were released after only a short period, in order to make room for other children.

After some decrease in delinquency in the decade of the 1920's came an increase. One author states that if the year 1931 is taken as the base in Moscow, in 1932 the number of delinquents had increased 28 per cent, by 1933, 65 per cent over 1931, and by 1934, 85 per cent.[7] Communist leaders were disturbed not only over the increase itself but because in theory delinquency should have decreased markedly as communism established itself. The earlier attitude of tolerance and the protection of homeless children no longer seemed applicable. Most of the delinquents of the 1930's were living at home and attending school. They could no longer be looked upon as the innocent victims of an earlier capitalist period and of the exigencies of social crises. The shift in attitude placed the responsibility for delinquency on the parents, who were charged with neglecting their moral responsibility for rearing good communist children. Also, as children were held responsible for their offenses a new punitive attitude replaced the earlier attitude that delinquents were the victims of social conditions. Regardless of change in attitude and treatment, delinquency has continued and is still a matter of deep concern to communist leaders.

Soviet youth

Juvenile delinquency since World War II is best viewed in relation to the general trends among Soviet youth, rather than a thing apart (8, 13, 16, 28, 40). The present generation of youth did not experience the Revolution with its emphasis on the sacred duty of all to fight capitalism and to strive for the achievement of socialism and eventually communism. They have had little experience with the extreme repressions and harsh punishments of Stalin's regime. They have been reared primarily in the freer and more tolerant period that began with Khrushchev's assumption of the position of highest authority. They are not motivated by a fanatical fervor for

[7] *Ibid.*, p. 43.

communism nor by the great terror that accompanied the purges of the 1930's. The attitude is general among youth that socialism (even communism) has been accomplished. They seek a relaxation of the drive toward submergence of the individual in the state and an opportunity for individual motivation, a time for pleasure, and an acquaintance with western culture, both intellectual and material. Surreptitiously, if not openly, they violate many laws restricting the written expression of non-communist attitudes, listen to forbidden music, and debate freely among themselves the common values of communist and capitalist ideas. More openly, and especially in the cities, a small proportion of youth engage in stealing and speculation (selling for profit), and others form the drifters classified as hooligans.

The development of social classes in Russia with different levels of income and education has created a stratified youth, all of whom, however, are subject to laws passed when it was assumed that there would immediately be a classless society. Dissatisfactions abound among both favored and unfavored youth. Partial familiarity with western culture also creates dissatisfactions with restrictions imposed by the government. Delinquency is found in the different social strata in Russia at the present time.

Hooligans

An account published in 1962 but based on the author's observations in large Russian industrial cities during 1955-59 states that the group that has attracted most public attention is the *stilyagi* or style-chasers who copied gaudy and extreme types of American clothing, adopted American nicknames, and played American jazz and rock-and-roll music, illicitly recorded (16, 40). At first the *stilyagi* were not delinquent but clung to the margin between conformity and deviancy. Later, the connotation of the term was extended to include antisocial behavior. Another and more serious type of behavior, definitely delinquent in character, is called hooliganism, a term applied to adults as well as youth. A central ingredient of hooliganism is public drunkenness combined with brawls and fighting. The sale of alcohol to minors is forbidden, but they are able to secure it in ample supply. General disorderliness, rudeness to passers-by, and obscene language are other expressions of the rebellion of hooligans against conforming behavior. A further step in delinquency comes when youth either avoid work or supplement wages by stealing and selling goods belonging to the state or engage in illicit trade or barter with tourists.

Other items that round out the picture include the fact that youth are unable to secure firearms, although they have knives with which attacks can be made. They cannot secure cars and hence are not very mobile. They cannot become full-time delinquents, since they are expected to be either in school or working and their absence from either is soon noted and investigated.

The statements on hooliganism do not link the behavior with age range, but the references to drinking, work, and buying and selling imply that the hooligans are older adolescents or youth. The background of most hooligans is residence in lower-class slums. Family life is meager; typically both parents work. The home is a few crowded rooms in an old apartment building, with the kitchen shared by several families. The drabness of home and family life is in sharp contrast to the activities and freedom of the streets.

In comparing the delinquency in Russia with that in the United States, one writer points out the absence of organized delinquent gangs, the relative lack of violence, or of spectacular crimes. Without gang affiliations, a delinquent subculture has not developed to provide support and status for the delinquent through the performance of daring acts. Drunkenness is a major problem; drug addiction, found among some delinquents in the United States, is not mentioned.[8]

Upwardly mobile youth

A second category consists of upwardly mobile youth, whose parents are in the working class. Most members of this category conform to communist expectations. A few, unable to move into the elite group through parental influence or higher education, have developed means of illicit trade to bring them fast wealth. They are often able to trade goods characteristic of Russia for articles that tourists have with them, which are of better quality than similar Russian goods. These are then sold at a high mark-up to Russians. Sometimes the aspiring Russian youth travels and returns with

[8] Paul Hollander, "Youthful 'Survivals' and Destructive 'Innovators'; The Problem of Delinquency in the USSR and the USA." Paper delivered at the Annual Meeting of the American Sociological Association, 1966.

illicit goods which he sells, varying from books to clothes. The trader makes money and lives well but is socially unacceptable among those with whom he trades.

Gilded youth

A third category of deviant youth has been termed gilded youth; they are the children of the elite, who receive high salaries, fine living quarters, cars, and many privileges. Although these young people are often pampered by their parents and have the generous use of the family car, some of them supplement their income in much the same way as the delinquent youth of working-class origin. Excessive drinking and carousing in some city drinking spot may be followed by wild parties at home in the parents' absence or at the family's country home. When their behavior outstrips law and public tolerance, they depend upon the position of their parents to save them from public disgrace or legal punishment. These youth do not form delinquent gangs, but published accounts suggest that the excesses are carried out by peer groups much as any recreation might be. Presumably most of these young people are eventually drawn back into conforming adult life.

Causative factors

Special reasons are cited for each category of delinquents: the lower class—lack of family life, dullness of life, the lure of the streets and alcohol; upwardly mobile—low pay and envy of the elite; and the gilded youth—pampering by the family, restlessness, boredom, and objection to compulsory common labor during college years. Several more general factors may be suggested. Whatever the class of youth, all are subjected to the strict and rigid regime from which many wish to escape into more freedom, more individual choice, and more excitement. Many wish to know more about the rest of the world, to travel more widely, to own and make use of western products, and to work out their own ideology. Various deviant ways have developed to evade the regulations without being detected, arrested, and punished.

This account is not intended to imply that most Soviet youth are deviants in any serious sense, delinquents, or young criminals. Most of them conform, accept the ideology of communism, fit themselves into the prescribed pattern of work and cultural pursuits, trim their aspirations to realistic proportions, and fulfill their needs within the communist program. It should not be overlooked that many needs are automatically if not lavishly fulfilled: education, health care, and guarantee of work and a place to live. Many of the hard self-sacrificing demands of the 1920's and 1930's are apparently part of history.

TRAINING OF CHILDREN

The Soviet government has imposed certain responsibilities upon families and schools to instill communist ideals in children. Furthermore, it has established a series of special organizations to shore up any deficiencies in families and schools and to carry the training on into the young adult period.

The family

The attitude of the state and the laws regulating family life have swung from one extreme to the other (11, 17, 19, 26, 36). These changes and various abrupt and violent social changes initiated by the state have tended to disrupt the family.

Just after the Revolution, a part of the ideology of communism was that the family was a hindrance to the development of a communist society. Disbanding the family would destroy it as an economic unit in competition with the state. It would also release the wife from domination by the husband and set her free for industrial work. In the 1920's and early 1930's the attack of communism on the family was direct. Marriages could be loosely formed and as readily broken apart. Abortions could be obtained at the request of the woman. Most already established families did not disintegrate, but many new unregistered families and truncated families came into being.

At this early period of communism the family was regarded as an unreliable agency for rearing children in communism. The traditional authoritarian Russian family was not amenable to the transfer of authority to the state. One writer states, "The communist movement fought the family as an enemy of the new social order, a bulwark against change, a seedbed for antistate tendencies."[9]

During this same period, families were losing their property to

[9] L. A. Coser, "The Case of the Soviet Family," in R. L. Coser, editor, *The Family: Its Structure and Functions,* St. Martin's Press, 1964, p. 59.

the state. Resistant families were broken up and members were sent to forced labor camps or resettled in other areas than the one where they and their parents had lived, perhaps for generations. Many resistant adults were killed. Other families suffered disorganization through the pressuring of women to take factory jobs or to do "men's work" on the farms. As a result of these many disturbances of family life, children ran wild as they had immediately after the Revolution.

As part of the state plan to dispose of the family, the state began a program of completely communistic living with institutional provisions for kitchens and child care. These plans did not work out; they were expensive to implement and were strongly resisted. However, state nurseries were opened in connection with factories that employed women. Schools and youth organizations took over much of the training of children in communist ideals and behavior.

In child care the family thus became a competitor of the state. Even when children lived with their parents, they often became alienated from loyalty to them. At one period children were urged to report to state authorities any anticommunist utterances or behavior of their parents.

During this period of loose family ties and despite the efforts of the state to train children in communism, delinquency increased. Whether for this or other reasons, by the mid-1930's the state began to reverse its attitude about the dissolution of the family. The family now came to be regarded as a valuable unit in communism and a partner of the state. Its authority over and responsibility for rearing children were increased. It was also held responsible for the delinquency of children. The local party units were admonished to encourage lasting marriage, discourage frequent changes of partners, and condemn neglect of the family by the husband. Divorces were limited to three, with an increasingly higher fee charged for each one. Abuse of alimony was to be discouraged and, where granted, to be strictly enforced by the courts. Abortion was reinterpreted as indicating an egotistical and light-minded attitude toward the family; it was banned except for strict medical reasons. Since 1944, when new marriage laws were passed, great emphasis is placed on permanence of marriage. The laws do not recognize marriages that are not registered, and increase the difficulty and expense of securing a divorce. The great freedom of sex relations of the early days of communism now is decried and pressure is exerted to restrict sex relations to a responsible personal relationship. In fact, so strict have the laws and pressure become that some writers on Russia believe they do not leave enough freedom and will lead to nonconformity as people seek to meet individual needs and to escape from relationships that have become oppressive.[10] It is important to remember that the parents to whom the 1944 laws apply were themselves reared in communism. If any family member now represents the pre-Revolutionary family, it is likely to be an old grandmother, who may be incorporated into a family to care for young children while both parents work. But she has learned the value of silence.

The schools in communist character-building

Education in the Soviet Union is closely tied in with communist policies (1, 6, 41). A major goal is to provide education not only for children but for illiterate older youths and adults.

Another objective is the training of children and youth in the skills needed for the continued economic development of the Soviet Union. As time goes on education in science is emphasized. Although all children are entitled in theory to have equal educational opportunities, with any favors going to the children of the working class, actually in higher education the educated and elite class has a higher representation than the working class. Urban children have more opportunities than rural. In this situation lies part of the basis for different categories of youth and the accompanying differences in delinquency.

A third objective is the indoctrination of all children in communist ideals and goals. Children are taught that their primary loyalty is to the state, not to their families. Textbooks emphasize the greatness of the Russian people, reaching back into the past for heroes and the rightness of the communist regime. Pride and patriotism are major points of emphasis.

Fourth, schools also give moral training. Morality is not established by religious precepts nor is religion thought to contain absolute values. Morality consists of obedience to the basic moral rules and truths as these are formulated by the Communist Party. Thus morality may change as the central organization of the Party decrees. Each educational level has a formal program for the teaching of Soviet morality, consisting of specific rules to be followed. The pro-

[10] Coser, *op. cit.*, p. 39.

gram bears heavily on obedience, a sense of duty, patriotism, and the value of work.

State sponsored youth organizations

The *Komsomol* or Young Communist League is the most important of the youth organizations, planned to embrace all youth either through membership or supervision in all phases of life (15, 18, 27, 33). The organization dates back to 1918, and in 1945 had reached a membership of 15 million or approximately half of the eligible youth. Since then membership has declined.

The *Komsomol* is the upper level of three youth organizations. Training of children into the ideals of communism begins with membership in the Little Octobrists, for children under nine, at which age the child passes into the Young Pioneers, a transition marked by a colorful and impressive ceremony. Young Pioneers are eligible for membership in the *Komsomol* at age 14 if they meet certain requirements and secure the necessary recommendations. Usually they are eager to join, even though later they may drop out. *Komsomol* is closely tied in with the Communist Party, which dominates it. Members are indoctrinated in political ideology, taught to them by Party members. *Komsomol* is the avenue by which youth move upward in the Party hierarchy.

Komsomol is an important segment of the communist system. The members provide a ready supply of workers for the great projects undertaken by the state; they oversee, supervise, and reprimand members as well as nonmembers to curb deviant behavior; they also help train members of the younger children's organizations. Both *Komsomol* members and others are held in line by threats and fears of arrest for nonconformity or open opposition. Control of behavior is exerted positively through identification with the Party and rewards of status, and negatively through fears and threats.

The three youth organizations work closely with the schools and extend their activities into leisure hours, thus in theory controlling almost all the hours of the day for children and youth. If the system worked perfectly, it would make delinquency impossible. Its failure to work as planned is most obvious among the older teenagers.

LEGAL PROVISIONS FOR DELINQUENTS

In the period immediately after the Revolution, state leaders made special provisions for delinquent and neglected children (5, 7, 10, 21, 22). The basic nature of children was regarded as good and conforming; misbehavior called for care and reeducation.

Commissions and courts

The first agencies to assume the care of delinquent children were Commissions for Cases of Juveniles, established by the state in 1918. Children up to age 17 (after 1920, age 18) were referred to these Commissions. The Commission could refer children over age 16 to the People's Courts (lower level courts), and after 1930 all over age 16 went to the courts.

In 1936 the Commissions were abolished and a much more severe attitude was taken toward delinquents. Children of 14 and over were tried in the criminal court and for serious crimes, children of 12 and over. The serious crimes were larceny, violence, bodily injury, maiming, murder, or attempted murder. If found guilty, the delinquent was subject to any kind of punishment applicable to adults—which included the death penalty. It is not clear whether the death penalty actually was applied to young children. In 1940, the list of crimes was extended to include acts endangering railroad traffic such as loosening rails, placing objects on the tracks, and so forth. In 1941 all other offenses of minors aged 14 and over were made subject to criminal prosecution.

In 1960-61 came another reversal, when the various Republics of the Soviet Union again established Commissions with extensive powers for the care of both delinquent and neglected or wayward children. The Commissions have charge of all delinquents under the age of 14, except for the serious crimes listed above, which still are handled by the criminal courts unless specifically referred to the Commission. A variety of disciplinary measures may be used, including a public or private apology by the delinquent, warnings, probation for one year, making restitution, arranging for medical services, or commitment to a residential educational institution if the delinquent poses a serious threat to the public. The completely punitive system initiated in 1935 has shifted toward a policy of retraining.

Correctional institutions

The concern about delinquency in the 1930's led to the establishment of a series of institutions for emotionally disturbed, wayward, and delinquent children, under appropriate ministries of the central government (1, 20, 44). Among the institutions were reception units and reformatories for the more confirmed and hardened juvenile delinquents, operated by the Ministry of Internal Affairs. These are of two types, Educational Colonies and Work Colonies.

Although visits to the correctional institutions by foreigners seem to be discouraged, several descriptions from visitors are available. The Educational Colony, Zenigorod, that serves Moscow and its area is about 40 miles from Moscow.[11] Equipped for 225 boys, at the time of the description (1958) it had approximately 200 boys. The staff totalled 41 members plus 10 guards and maintenance personnel. Most numerous of the staff are the *Educateurs,* who might be described as counselors and who live in the institution, teachers, and work foremen. Medical care, physical education and sports, supervision of leisure, a radio-television, a game room, library, and auditorium for concerts are part of the setup. The boys have academic classes and training in a choice of trades. Units of Young Pioneers and *Komsomol* have been formed within the institution. Parents may visit once a week and actually come about once a month. The boys may have occasional visits home and are sometimes taken to Moscow for special events. The establishment, built in 1941, consists of a number of buildings, adequately, even attractively, furnished.

Misconduct within the institution is handled in a number of ways; discipline seems to depend chiefly upon the pressure of disapproval from other boys. Specifically, the methods are: discussion with the boy; discussion of the case before the boy's group and public censure; discussion and public censure before larger groups of boys; posting of a public notice of the offense; and isolation in a room for not over three days, a rare punishment. The most effective method is the public censure before a large group of boys. If these measures fail and a boy seems unable to adjust to the Colony, his case may be referred to the court, which may reassign him to a Work Colony.

Boys are released in small groups of four or five. A celebration is arranged, which the parents attend. The Commission which sent the boy to the Colony assumes some responsibility for supervision of the

---

[11] H. Grand, *Enfance Déficiente Mentale et Délinquance Juvénile en U.R.S.S.,* Imprimeries Réunies, Valence-sur-Rhone, France, 1961, pp. 73-86. A similar description for a different colony is given in Harriett Wilson, "A Visit to the U.S.S.R.," *British Journal of Criminology,* 1 (July, 1960), pp. 69.73.

boy, which may include supervision by the labor union or *Komsomol.*

The Work Colonies are for boys who have committed serious offenses; they also receive transfers from the Educational Colonies. The one that serves Moscow and the surrounding area is the Colony of Ikeha. Built to accommodate 400 boys, in 1960 it had 57 residents. It resembles the Educational Colony except that more time is spent at work, an average of five hours daily as compared with three or four hours in the Educational Colony. More contacts with the outside are arranged, including some work in nearby establishments. With exemplary conduct and a good record of study and work, the boys may be released after serving a third of their sentences. The usual commitment is for three years, the usual number served is two.

In describing the Work Colony that she visited, Wilson comments: "No club activities seem to exist in the labour colony. The general impression here was that of a punitive institution. The colony is a closed one guarded by armed soldiers in little turrets around the outer wall. The boys are not given leave, but parents may visit."[12] She also noted that in the Educational Colony almost all the staff, including the governors (wardens), wore military uniforms.

Girl delinquents

In a diligent search for information on delinquency and crime in the Soviet Union, totalling over 40 references, no specific information was found about girl delinquents, their delinquencies, or special provisions or institutions for them.

ADULT CRIME

The communist philosophy underlying juvenile delinquency and the handling of many juvenile cases in the criminal courts bring delinquency into close relationship with adult crime. Lack of available statistical reports prevents any statement as to how many juveniles are actually processed through the adult courts or subjected to penalties designed for adults.

From the Revolution to Stalin's death

Immediately after the Revolution individuals and groups actively opposing the new regime were dealt with speedily by execution (18, 21, 29, 30, 31, 39). All vestiges of capitalism were to be smashed by

[12] Wilson, *op. cit.*, pp. 71-72.

whatever means were necessary. Many peasants and working class people (the proletariat), who theoretically should have grasped communism eagerly, resisted a change of status. Peasants *(kulaks)* who had acquired a little land and livestock and small businessmen *(bourgeoisie)* were especially unwilling to give up their property and enter a collective manner of living. These resisters were also disposed of by death or sent *en masse* into forced labor camps.

With various ups and downs the movement of suppression extended into the 1930's reaching its climax in the great purges during the latter part of this decade, whose announced purpose was to purify the Party. Many people were executed either individually or in groups. Death was often preceded by extreme physical torture to force confession. Lesser offenders were sent to forced labor camps, expelled from the Communist Party, or reassigned to different positions. In 1933, 800,000 members were expelled from the Party and in 1934 over 340,000.[13] The inner circles were not exempt from the purge. In 1934, of 139 members elected to the Central Committee, 98 were subsequently executed. Over half of the delegates who attended Congress in 1934 were later arrested on the charge of committing anti-Revolutionary crimes. Lawyers trained in pre-Revolutionary law were arrested, tried administratively (without a court trial) and never again heard from: 200 in 1931, 400 in 1935, and 165 in 1938.

Terror mounted; informers could be found in factories, housing units, and all sorts of local groups. People feared to speak freely for fear of accusations that would lead to their arrest. As a dramatic exhibition, occasional public trials were held, beginning in 1928-29 and continuing at intervals through the 1930's.

After the end of World War II, no further great purges were carried out, although from time to time individuals or small groups were executed for political crimes. After Stalin's death, the terrorism and mass punishments declined. It was revealed that many people had been falsely accused and executed or sent to the labor camps. Many prisoners were released. Since the middle of the 1950's a policy of liberalization has been instituted with many new laws passed in the early 1960's.

[13] M. T. Florinsky, editor, *McGraw-Hill Encyclopedia of Russia and the Soviet Union,* McGraw-Hill Book Co., 1961, pp. 464-65, 514-15; E. Kamenka, "The Soviet View of Law," *Problems of Communism,* 14 (March-April, 1965), pp. 8-16.

The secret police

The resisters and rebellious persons were covered by law, but few of their cases were heard in court (12, 18, 30). Political expediency rather than justice ruled the day. The political police—the secret police—were granted total power of control over these cases; they received complaints, made investigations, reached conclusions about guilt, passed sentence, and carried out the sentences without the assistance of a court and without the right of the accused to be represented by an attorney or even to hear the accusation against him. The prisons and forced labor camps into which many persons were sent were under the control of the secret police. One interpretation is that the need for political communist orthodoxy was so great that a trial that observed due process of law could not be risked; guilt had to be asserted even though not proved.[14]

The power of the secret police was extended by the obligation placed upon the ordinary citizen to report to the police any "errors" or violations of communist principles or laws known to him. Heavy penalties were imposed on anyone known not to make such reports. This voluntary surveillance was augmented by the use of paid informers. Suspicion and fear were prevalent. Nevertheless many citizens were reluctant to inform on others. The laws of the 1960's have reduced the power of the secret police and thrown certain safeguards around citizens.

Speculation

The Soviet Union has crimes of the familiar traditional type, such as thefts, damage to property, murder, manslaughter, mayhem, rape, illegal abortion, forgery, counterfeiting, giving or taking bribes, and a long list of other offenses. These are all regarded as vestiges of capitalism, as distinct from crimes against communism. Some of the ordinary crimes have a special significance in a communist framework and are regarded as only a little less serious than opposition to the communist system itself.

Speculation is the term applied to thefts from the state, which carry more severe punishment than thefts from individuals (13, 23, 43). To steal from the state is an attack on the basic economic sys-

[14] D. R. Cressey and W. Krassowski, "Inmate Organization and Anomie in American and Soviet Labor Camps," *Social Problems,* 5 (Winter, 1957-58), pp. 217-30.

tem and is interpreted as stealing from all the people who in theory have joint ownership of state property. Speculation covers a wide variety of offenses. The farmer may sell part of his produce privately rather than turn it over to the state. State-owned equipment may be diverted to private use. Patients have been known to carry away beds when they leave a hospital. Building materials disappear from a construction site. The manager of a fruit and vegetable market may divert money to his private use—a crime that may bring a long prison term. Theft from the state often involves bribing or transporting goods from one part of the country to another and secretly reselling it. In major cases of speculation a complex pattern of crime with many participants may evolve.

The public is apathetic toward speculation against the state; in contrast they resent thefts from individuals. People who know of speculation are loath to report it to the proper officials. Local authorities may quietly transfer a speculator to another position or use other disciplinary measures rather than report the offense. Sometimes the crimes begin as ways to speed up production, for example, illegally supply material to a project that otherwise could not meet its time limitation. This side-stepping of regulations may lead to distribution of goods for private profit.

Parasitism

Parasitism, or refusal to enter fully into the work program, is a matter of major concern (4, 9, 32, 33). In the Soviet system it is mandatory that everyone work; the adolescent passes directly from school into employment. The college student is not exempt. Work is required along with academic studies as well as during the summer. Upon completion of education, at whatever level, the person is assigned to appropriate employment, which he may or may not like.

Anti-parasite laws were passed in the various Soviet Republics in the 1950's and made uniform in 1961. The laws are directed against "able-bodied citizens leading an anti-social, parasitic way of life, deliberately avoiding socially useful labor and likewise those living on unearned income."[15] Cases are tried either by a People's Court

[15] Quoted by L. Lipson, "Hosts and Pests: The Fight against Parasites," *Problems of Communism,* 14 (March-April, 1965), pp. 72-82.

or by a public meeting of workers. The offender is given a warning before a hearing is held and allowed sufficient time to find a job. The offender does not acquire a criminal record but may be sentenced to exile or to compulsory labor for two to five years, or property illegally acquired may be confiscated. A study of the early 1960's in Russia showed that among 600 anti-parasite cases, 20 per cent were sentenced to two years in exile; 25.5 per cent to three years; 11.5 per cent to four years; and 43 per cent to five years.[16]

In effect, exile is an attempt to force people to work and thus increase production. It also removes them from adverse influences in their place of residence. The law has been used by communities to free themselves at least temporarily from undesirables, such as drunkards, prostitutes, troublemakers, people engaged in illicit financial pursuits, and young people living off their parents. Their behavior is not quite criminal but is opposed to communist ideology.

Many complaints have been made against the anti-parasite laws. They are loosely phrased and open the way for prejudiced action. They also place the assignment of heavy penalties in nonlegal hands, such as the workers' groups. They are a part of a general movement in Russia to place social controls in the hands of citizens as a further step toward complete communism.

The residents of places to which offenders are exiled have many complaints. Offenders are reluctant to work and encourage each other to resist reformation. Troublemakers in their home communities, they continue to be troublemakers in exile, creating disturbances and corrupting residents. It seems clear that many of the offenses for which "parasites" are sent into exile are not crimes but deviancies that indicate general lack of adjustment.

Hooliganism has already been discussed in connection with juvenile delinquency and youth offenses. The same type of behavior is found also among adults. Although the behavior is not criminal, it is regarded as undesirable in itself, and contrary to the ideal image of a communist, who is expected to be devoted to work, self-improvement through educational and cultural pursuits, and service to the state. Hooliganism is incompatible with steady work and soon leads to absenteeism; eventually the anti-parasite law may send the hooligan into exile.

---

[16] L. Lipson, "Commentary on 'The Future Belongs to . . . Parasites?'" *Problems of Communism,* 12 (May-June, 1963), pp. 1-6.

Alcoholism

Excessive use of alcohol and drunkenness are a continuing problem, which seems to cross class lines to affect all categories of people (2, 14, 16, 35, 39). Russians themselves trace the use of alcohol back for centuries as an age-old custom, a necessary feature of festivals, celebrations, and recreation. Alcoholic sales were a source of revenue to the czars through the imposition of taxes and, after 1900, through a government monopoly. From group controlled celebrations, the use of alcohol passed into another area of activity and became associated with gambling, prostitution, and crime.

Under communism, production of alcohol is a state monopoly. Private production of alcohol is a criminal offense. On the one hand, the state profits from the sale of alcohol; on the other, rails against its excessive use. The concern of the government is not with abolition of drinking but with its control.

Constant propaganda against the evil effects of alcoholic use is carried on in newspapers, lectures, and instruction of the young. Concern is not only with physical and mental deterioration, but also with decrease in production as a result of deterioration and absenteeism from work. The relation of drunkenness to delinquency and crime is emphasized. It was asserted in 1964 that 90 per cent of all crimes are committed in a state of drunkenness, ranging from hooliganism to murder. Another report in 1965 said that half of all violations of law were accounted for by alcoholism, ranging from one-fourth of automobile accidents to 90 per cent of cases of hooliganism.[17] A sobering-up station and psychiatric clinics are provided for treatment, whether on a voluntary or compulsory basis is not clear. Punitive measures may be taken through the public display of name, address, and position of the drunkard.

The solitary drinker—the true alcoholic—is rare. Most drinking goes on as a social activity. Drinking is a deeply ingrained custom of men. Women rarely drink in public. Men gather in restaurants where hours may be spent by a congenial group around a table which becomes theirs for the evening through the purchase of drinks. This predilection is linked with the crowded conditions of apartments and almost total lack of privacy. The street and above all the restau-

[17] M. D. Shargorodskii, "Causes and Prevention of Crime," *Soviet Sociology,* 3 (Summer, 1964) pp. 24-39; *Current Digest of the Soviet Press,* 17 (July 28, 1965), pp. 10-19.

rant become the substitutes for the home. Efforts to reduce the use of alcohol and limit sales has the effect of driving people back to the dissatisfactions of the home and thereby increasing tension and frustration.[18] As a substitute for comradely drinking, the state has instituted alternative activities of duty to the state and courses of study. It is difficult, however, to substitute organized activities for the free recreation sought by young people.

Labor camps and prisons

Convicted criminals fall into two categories: political and economic offenders who are grouped together because both are a threat to communism; and "ordinary offenders" whose crimes are violations of the rights of other individuals, such as murder, assault, or theft of private goods (3, 12, 18, 30). Penalties are much heavier for the offenders in the first category, as they are regarded as having willfully moved against communism. Ordinary criminals are regarded as the victims of capitalist influences, who are sadly in need of reeducation in communist doctrines and retraining to accept the philosophy of the value of labor.

From 1919 on, forced labor camps have been in existence, called by various writers at different periods concentration camps, forced labor camps, corrective labor camps, and since 1956 corrective labor colonies. The number of people sentenced to these camps varied, reaching a peak apparently during the 1930's. After Stalin's death and the end of the purges, the number of sentences declined and many prisoners were released under amnesty. Some of the camps (or colonies) were closed; others are still in use.

During the heyday of the labor camps, conditions were described as "appalling." Inadequate protection against the weather, unlimited hours of work, inadequate food, and lack of medical care were typical. Beatings, solitary confinement, and shootings were commonplace. Prisoners had no legal protection, and, in fact, political prisoners were sentenced by the secret police without legal trials. Political prisoners were treated more harshly than ordinary prisoners although both were in the same camps. After World War II, the two categories of prisoners were separated.

Prisons, as distinct from labor camps, are also in use and are

[18] J. R. Azrael, "Notes on Soviet Urban Attitudes toward Leisure," *Social Problems,* 9 (Summer, 1961), pp. 69-78.

reported to be the most harsh of all the penal institutions. They house political prisoners, persons who have committed serious crimes, and dangerous recidivists.[19] "Corrective labor" is compulsory.

A news report of 1964 states that unwalled prisons were opened in 1963 as supplements to the labor colonies.[20] The report is based on an article published in the August, 1964 issue of *State and Law,* a Soviet publication, concerning the Perm Oblast prison, approximately 500 miles northeast of Moscow. In this Russian innovation in their prison system, the prisons are organized as state farms, on which the prisoners work for the same number of hours as is required on the outside, although they are paid less. The prisoner's family may live with him on the prison grounds; therefore schools and other community facilities have been opened. The prisoners are restricted in their movements and are under supervision of a small staff; there are no guards. The offenses represented vary widely, with 56.7 per cent being various forms of theft, 26.6 per cent murder, 5.9 per cent rape, and 10.8 per cent "other." Prisoners are transferred from corrective labor colonies after they have served at least half of their sentences and demonstrated their fitness for the open institution by exemplary behavior.

A major part of the regime in all prisons is labor; this is in accord with the communist doctrine that labor is an obligatory duty of all citizens. Compulsory labor is thought of as reeducation for a return to civilian life. It also makes a measurable contribution to industrial development. In the 1930's the labor camps were assigned a certain percentage of the total production for the country. Prisoners by the thousands were put to work to develop the basic industrial foundations for converting the Soviet Union from an agrarian to an industrial economy. They were put to work in mines, to secure raw materials; they built railroads, canals, and highways.

Comrades' Courts and voluntary police

The basic system of courts consists of a USSR Supreme Court which hears few cases but is occupied with appeals and protests; Republic Supreme Courts, which are primarily courts of appeal

[19] P. Barton, "An End to Concentration Camps?" *Problems of Communism,* 11 (March-April, 1962), pp. 38-46.

[20] *Chicago Daily News,* October 1, 1964.

occupied with review of cases from the lower courts; and the People's Courts, which hear most of the cases (9, 18, 33, 37). At the lowest level are the Comrades' Courts, a grassroots type of court which has been experimented with off and on since the early years of communism. Several times the Comrades' Courts were abolished and revived. In the 1950's interest revived and was crystallized in a new law in 1961. The Comrades' Courts handle a variety of types of offenses, usually minor in nature; they are expected to operate through measures of social influence which include public reprimands, censure, demands for a public apology, and warnings. The Courts may also exact small fines. They may make recommendations to state agencies, which may lead to punitive measures.

Comrades' Courts may be set up wherever a collective exceeds 50 people—in apartment blocks, educational institutions, or agricultural or industrial collectives. The personnel is nonprofessional, that is, comrades of the same background as the offenders. These courts have been interpreted in several ways. They are a move away from official courts, at least so far as minor offenses are concerned, and toward supervision by fellow-workers. This is regarded as a step toward the communist ideal. However, they bring ever more types of behavior under the scrutiny and within the control of officially established agencies. The penalties are light but the spread of supervision is wide.

The move toward supervision of people by those they are closely associated with at work, in organizations, or residentially is not confined to the Comrades' Courts. A system of voluntary police has appeared from time to time and in 1959 was revived and given formal recognition. The *Komsomol* has taken an active part in the organization and staffing of this movement. By 1960 there were two and a half million members in 80,000 units, often organized within industrial and agricultural enterprises. Their purpose is to warn offenders and report recidivists to the police or Comrades' Courts. However they have tended to expand their activities to all types of supervision and interference with the activities of individuals, sometimes beating young people of whose conduct they disapprove.

The Comrades' Courts and the voluntary police are revised manifestations of early vacillating attempts to remove control from regularly established police and courts and place it in the hands of peers through informal supervision. The movement attempts to use moral suasion and public opinion to hold everyone to the line of approved communist conduct. Discussion pro and con and many shifts toward and away from more formal control continue in the Soviet Union.

THE SLOW PROCESS OF CHANGE

The Soviet Union is a country still in the process of moving from one ideology to another. The form of government that has evolved in the process—a strictly enforced control from the top that works down to the lowest mass level of society—is the opposite of the communist ideal of cooperative people deeply devoted to and identified with a system that operates fairly for the equality of all. The seeming instability and vacillation of definitions of delinquency and crime, of police, courts, and correctional institutions are in the nature of experiments attempted by the top authority to bring the Soviet Union quickly into communism and as quickly into modern industrialism. Many of the experiments have failed and been abandoned; some measures that failed earlier have been revived, modified, and tried again.

Both offenses and treatment of offenders are closely related to the basic doctrines of communism. The virtual abolishment of private property and the principle of universal work for the state and only indirectly for the workers are at the basis of many criminal offenses. The attempt to restrict leisure activities to educational and cultural pursuits is at the base of other offenses. The submergence of the individual in the state and the denial of individual choices and decisions in many areas of life lead others into criminal offenses.

The treatment accorded delinquents and criminals is phrased in terms of reeducation. For delinquents especially, schools and the work of the *Komsomol* within correctional institutions try directly to instill communist principles. Compulsory work in both juvenile and adult institutions is supported by the principle of obligatory work for all.

More than in any other of the societies included in this book the Soviet Union exemplifies the definition of delinquency and crime as a threat to the values of society. Other nations have changed bits and parts of social values or have made more basic changes slowly, in each case incorporating threatening behavior in the criminal code. Russia, at one stroke, sought to revolutionize the entire system, in effect, to turn the value system upside down. Acts that had been meritorious under the previous system became crimes.

Russia's experience demonstrates that it is difficult suddenly to reverse values and a social organization by force. Nor has its parallel attempt to educate the young and reeducate delinquents and criminals been fully successful in a situation of incomplete isolation from the outside world and the conflict of values within.

REFERENCES

1. ALT, HERSCHEL and EDITH. *Russia's Children.* Bookman's Associates, 1959.
2. AZRAEL, J. R. "Notes on Soviet Urban Attitudes toward Leisure." *Social Problems,* 9 (1961), pp. 69-78.
3. BARTON, PAUL. "An End to Concentration Camps?" *Problems of Communism,* 11 (March-April, 1962), pp. 38-46.
4. BEERMAN, R. "Parasite Law in the Soviet Union." *British Journal of Criminology,* 3 (1962), pp. 71-80.
5. BEERMAN, R. "The Soviet Law on Commissions for Cases of Juveniles." *British Journal of Criminology,* 2 (1962), pp. 386-91.
6. BEREDAY, G. Z. F., W. W. BRICKMAN, and G. R. REED. *Changing Soviet School.* Houghton Mifflin, 1960.
7. BERMAN, N. "Juvenile Delinquency under the Soviets." *Journal of the American Institute of Criminal Law and Criminology,* 30 (1939), pp. 68-76.
8. BILLINGHAM, J. H. "Soviet Youth is Getting out of (Party) Line." *University, a Princeton Quarterly,* No. 27 (Winter, 1965-66), pp. 9-13.
9. BOITER, A. "Comradely Justice: How Durable Is It?" *Problems of Communism,* 14 (March-April, 1965), pp. 83-92.
10. "Children's Courts in Russia." *Survey,* 47 (November 19, 1921), pp. 278-79.
11. COSER, L. A. "The Case of the Soviet Family." In R. L. Coser, editor, *The Family: Its Structure and Functions.* St. Martin's Press, 1964.
12. CRESSEY, D. R. and W. KRASSOWSKI. "Inmate Organization and Anomie in American and Soviet Labor Camps." *Social Problems,* 5 (1957-58), pp. 217-30.
13. *Current Digest of the Soviet Press* (almost every issue has pertinent material).
14. EFRON, VERA. "Soviet Approach to Alcoholism." *Social Problems,* 7 (1960), pp. 307-15.
15. FAINSOD, M. "The Komsomol: A Study of Youth under Dictatorship." *American Political Science Review,* 45 (1951), pp. 18-40.
16. FIELD, M. G. "Alcoholism, Crime, and Delinquency in Soviet Society." *Social Problems,* 3 (1955), pp. 100-09.

17. FIELD, M. G. "Social Services for the Family in the Soviet Union." *Marriage and Family Living,* 17 (1955), pp. 244-49.
18. FLORINSKY, M. T., editor. *McGraw-Hill Encyclopedia of Russia and the Soviet Union.* McGraw-Hill Book Co., 1961.
19. GEIGER, K. and A. INKELES. "The Family in the USSR." *Marriage and Family Living,* 16 (1954), pp. 397-404.
20. GRAND, H. *Enfance Déficiente Mentale et Délinquance Juvénile en URSS.* Imprimeries Réunies, Valence-sur-Rhone, France, 1961.
21. GRZYBOWSKI, K. "Soviet Criminal Law." *Problems of Communism,* 14 (March-April, 1965), pp. 53-62.
22. GSOVSKI, V. *Government, Law, and Courts in the Soviet Union and Eastern Europe.* F. A. Praeger, 1959, II.
23. GSOVSKI, V. "Reform of Criminal Law in the Soviet Union." *Social Problems,* 7 (Spring, 1960), pp. 315-28.
24. HAZARD, JOHN N. *Settling Disputes in Soviet Society.* Columbia University Press, 1960.
25. HAZARD, JOHN N. "Unity and Diversity in Socialist Law." *Law and Contemporary Problems,* 30 (1965), pp. 270-90.
26. INKELES, A. and R. A. BAUER. *Soviet Citizen, Daily Life in a Totalitarian Society.* Harvard University Press, 1959.
27. INKELES, A. and K. GEIGER, editors. *Soviet Society, A Book of Readings.* Houghton Mifflin Co., 1961.
28. JUVILER, P. H. "Communist Morality and Soviet Youth." *Problems of Communism,* 10 (May-June, 1961), pp. 16-24.
29. KAMENKA, EUGENE. "The Soviet View of Law." *Problems of Communism,* 14 (March-April, 1965), pp. 8-16.
30. KOSA, J. *Two Generations of Soviet Man.* College and University Press, 1962.
31. "Law and Legality in the USSR." *Problems of Communism,* 14 (March-April, 1965), p. 1.
32. LIPSON, L. "Commentary on 'The Future Belongs to . . . Parasites?' " *Problems of Communism,* 12 (May-June, 1963), pp. 1-6.
33. LIPSON, L. "Hosts and Pests: The Fight against Parasites." *Problems of Communism,* 14 (March-April, 1965), pp. 72-82.
34. LUNDEN, W. A. *War and Delinquency.* The Art Press, Ames, Iowa, 1963.
35. MADISON, B. "Contributions and Problems of Soviet Welfare Institutions." *Social Problems,* 7 (1960), pp. 298-307.
36. MOSELY, P. E. "The Russian Family, Old Style and New." In R. N. Anshen, editor, *The Family, Its Function and Destiny.* Harper and Bros., 1959.
37. RITVO, H. "Totalitarianism without Coercion." *Problems of Communism,* 9 (November-December, 1960), pp. 19-29.
38. SCHAPIRO, L. "Prospects for the Rule of Law." *Problems of Communism,* 14 (March-April, 1965), pp. 2-7.
39. SHARGORODSKII, M. D. "The Causes and Prevention of Crime." *Soviet Sociology,* 3 (Summer, 1964), pp. 24-39.

40. SHERMAN, G. "Soviet Youth, Myth and Reality." *Daedalus,* 91 (1962), pp. 216-37.
41. WIDMAYER, R. "The Evolution of Soviet Education." *Harvard Educational Review,* 24 (1954), pp. 159-75.
42. WILE, I. S. "Present Problems of Mental Health in Russia." *Mental Hygiene,* 22 (1938), pp. 25-56.
43. WILLETS, HARRY. "The Wages of Economic Sin." *Problems of Communism,* 11 (September-October, 1962), pp. 26-32.
44. WILSON, H. "A Visit to the USSR — Some Observations on a Visit to an Educational Colony, a Labour Colony, and a Remand Home for Young Delinquents." *British Journal of Criminology,* 1 (1960), pp. 69-73.

6 / Sicily: Ineffective Government and the Criminal Society – the Mafia

Mafia refers to a criminal organization prevalent in western Sicily, whose roots are deeply entwined with the development of Sicily from a simply organized society through feudalism into present day industrial growth.

A criminal society is a recognizable group that exists within a larger society organized on conventional lines (2, 7, 13). The larger society typically has a government, economic system, and religious and educational institutions, which function, whether poorly or efficiently, to serve the needs of the whole population. Under certain conditions, some segments of the population control the government for their own benefit, while other segments are neglected, oppressed, or exploited. Sometimes the government nominally serves all people but is weak and poorly run. Under such conditions powerful, ruthless criminal groups may terrorize other groups or individuals, forcing them to pay large sums of money to avoid injury, death, or destruction of property. At the same time they protect and help other groups. Such terrorizing groups may fall into the category of a criminal society. They tend to develop where government is weak. They do not actually replace government but, unimpeded by police or military forces, they take over many functions of government in addition to their direct criminal activities. The Sicilian Mafia is a criminal society. It is included here because children of Mafia families are indoctrinated with the philosophy of the society and readily step into criminal roles as they grow up.

Mafia is discussed under five headings: the social background, the traditional operation of Mafia, the transitional period, the contemporary period, and organized crime in the United States which is sometimes said to be an offshoot of Mafia.

SOCIAL BACKGROUND OF THE SICILIAN MAFIA

Sicily, an island of approximately 10,000 square miles, is separated from the mainland of Italy by the Strait of Messina, which is two miles wide at the narrowest point. In some areas, high cliffs running down to the sea further increase the isolation of the island. Even today, with improved transportation and communication, the island is to some extent cut off from the mainland. Within the island, meager contacts and communication have created regional isolation.

2,600 years of invasion

Sicily has an old population running back to the paleolithic period (20). Its easy access from the sea invited a succession of Mediterranean invaders, each group leaving behind some of its people and culture when it was succeeded by later intruders. There are indications that the Phoenicians were in Sicily prior to the eighth century B.C. At irregular intervals the island was taken over successively by the Greeks, Rome, the Vandals, the Byzantine Empire, the Saracens, the Normans, the Germans, the French, the Spanish, Great Britain. In 1860, Garibaldi conquered Sicily and the island became part of united Italy.

Even after Sicily became part of the united Italian kingdom, it was a country cousin and has not yet fully entered into the process of industrialization that has brought northern Italy into line with European urban-industrial development. It is closer to the traditional way of life, more inclined to follow entrenched semi-feudal patterns of living, and still addicted to its opposition to law enforcement. The western part of Sicily is especially characterized by these traits. It was in western Sicily that Mafia developed as a pervasive type of social organization—a criminal society operating within the larger society.

Mafia as philosophy and as criminal organization

The word *mafia,* origin unknown, seems to be local to Sicily (15). Traina's Sicilian-Italian dictionary (1869) defines the word *mafia* as a neologism denoting any sign of bravado. Another dictionary, Mortillaro's, in 1876 stated that *mafia* was a word of Piedmontese origin, meaning gang.

Although Mafia (gang) seems to be of recent usage, *mafia* (bravado) refers to a traditional philosophy of Sicily. According to *mafia,* individuals were expected to settle their own disputes and personal conflicts without referring the matter to local authorities. A theft was interpreted as a personal insult, since it indicated that the thief did not fear vengeance from his victim. Adultery was a deep personal insult to the husband that called for reprisals. Only personal retaliation could remove the mark of dishonor. Referral to local authorities was a further mark of dishonor.

The philosophy or attitude of *mafia* was supported by a code of honor called *Omertà*. According to this code, "a conspiracy of silence" was maintained toward all law enforcement officers and strangers regarding the activities of one's companions. Another part of the code was absolute obedience of younger persons to elders. Violation of *Omertà* was judged by the elders, and execution of a penalty (often death) was in their hands.

The organization now called Mafia (gang) is based on the philosophy of *mafia* (bravery, honor) and the code of *Omertà* (total loyalty to the organization).

Development of Mafia

Mafia, as a recognized social institution, appeared in the latter part of the nineteenth century, approximately in the 1860's, the period when the word Mafia was first applied to the organization (6, 7, 14). However, Mafia-like groups and activities preceded this stage, probably extending back as far as the eleventh century when the Normans introduced feudalism to Sicily. Hobsbawn, an Englishman who has made a scholarly study of Mafia, speculates that such an organization served as an intermediary force between the wealthy, local, feudal lords who owned the estates and the powerless peasants.[1] The civil government was so remote and so spasmodic in its action that it seemed to be a foreign oppressor, whose tax collectors and police were thought of as predators, similar to the local bandits. The three groups that were most defenseless were the peasants in the fruit-growing area near Palermo and on the inland feudal estates, and the sulphur miners of the south central area. It was in these areas that Mafia was most strong. Earlier Mafia-like activities tended to disappear in the eastern, more highly developed part of the island.

Feudalism in Sicily was officially abolished in 1812-38. The way

[1] E. J. Hobsbawn, *Primitive Rebels,* Manchester University Press, Manchester, England, 1959, Chapter 3.

was opened for further organization of local intermediary groups and the development of Mafia. Hobsbawn refers to Mafia as "a parallel machine of law and organized power" and says that such a parallel system was "inevitable in a society such as Sicily, in which the official government could not or would not exercise effective sway." For the rank and file in Mafia territory, Mafia provided the only recognized means of control.

TRADITIONAL OPERATION OF MAFIA

Organization of Mafia

Although Mafia is usually referred to in the singular, there was never a tightly organized association spread over a wide region (2, 12, 15). There was rather a loosely integrated network of local groups or Mafias. The territory of a specific Mafia tended to be the area within which personal contacts might be maintained before telephones and automobiles enlarged the areas of personal communication. Thus, in basic organization there were many Mafias, each operating independently in its local territory. Internally, a given Mafia was loosely organized and can scarcely be spoken of as a structure. There was no written or even formulated constitution or by-laws. The code of *Omertà* was honored by all members and rigidly enforced.

In one rural village several Mafias could function independently provided their activities differed. One Mafia might control the usage of a local spring that supplied water for an area, and another the marketing of some specific product. It was then expedient for several Mafias to come to a working agreement. This alliance developed gradually, with one group being recognized as the most powerful and its leader being accepted as their superior by the leaders of several Mafias. Such alliances still function.[2]

The loose leadership system did not include a rigid hierarchy or formal methods of advancing from one status to another. The leader was a man with natural qualities of leadership who attained his position primarily by demonstration of these qualities. Only occasionally did a leader rise to more than local prominence. No statement has been found of the qualities of leadership, but a careful scrutiny of descriptions of outstanding leaders reveals these qualities:[3] the leader

[2] L. Barzini, *The Italians,* Atheneum Publishers, 1964, pp. 270-73.

[3] Barzini, *op. cit.,* pp. 273-81.

commanded respect and his authority was accepted even when he was a young man; people turned to him for advice and he was always ready to listen to even the most humble of them; his manner was humble and courteous; he was a man of his word and could be relied upon; he was flexible and could adapt to changing social conditions. At the same time that he had these qualities that suggest amenability he had a hard inner core. He was a good organizer and a firm disciplinarian; crimes, down to the smallest, were fitted into a pattern, and a "cut" was received from even the most insignificant thief. He exerted discipline not by violence and disruptive actions but by respect and fear instilled by the knowledge that deviations would bring stern reprisals. These leaders were widely respected and always referred to as Don, a Spanish title for a lord or gentleman. The above were the qualities discernible in Don Vito Cascio Ferro, who was the outstanding Mafia leader from about 1900 until the late 1920's, and Don Calò Vizzini, whose rule over Mafia ended in 1954 when he was 77 years old. It should be noted that both of these outstanding leaders held their high position for many years. Locally there were of course many leaders of lesser caliber.

Once a member of a Mafia it was difficult to withdraw and impossible to become a member of an opposing group, especially the police. Primary loyalty was to Mafia and a disregard for this loyalty quickly led to death. An often-cited illustration can be given from the nineteenth century. The young cousin of a powerful Mafioso joined the *carabiniere* (police force). When he was discharged and returned home, the family leaders removed the stain on their honor by arranging for his death.

The functions of Mafia

The overall function accomplished by Mafia and the similar organizations that preceded it was to act as a balance between the oppressed peasants and sulphur miners and the owners of land and mines, who were often absent and disinterested nobles (5, 7, 12, 14, 15). The leading Mafiosi held in control the bandits or outlaws, forced the landlords into submission to their financial demands, and protected the peasants from unendurable oppression. They often held the position of manager of a feudal estate and later when feudalism was abolished often rented large areas from the landlords and sublet sections to peasants, or acquired land in their own right. In time they became a rural middle class with propensities for profitable activities.

Mafia operated by threats of force, the actual use of force, and in time by the fear generated by their misdeeds. The most successful Mafiosi were those who aroused so much fear that actual violence was not necessary. Some of their methods of operation follow:

1. Cattle might be driven off, presumably by bandits, but actually by an accomplice of the Mafia estate manager. The theft was reported to the owner. An ally of the manager then told the owner that he had seen in another district some cattle that resembled the stolen ones. If the owner cared to pay his expenses he might be able to bring back the cattle. The payment often equalled a third or half the value of the cattle.
2. In agricultural areas, a "tax" might simply be levied on the landowner for the protection of his property. If he failed to pay, his crops, trees, and vines would be mysteriously destroyed.
3. Sometimes the wife or child of a wealthy man would be kidnapped and held for ransom. Public opinion, lenient toward some other Mafia operations, opposed kidnapping and the killing of the victim that might follow. Kidnapping declined about 1900-15, with the last killing of a kidnapped person occurring in 1900 and the last actual kidnapping of a child or woman in 1920 (according to an account written in 1930).
4. Some Mafias acted as middlemen between the peasants or landowners and the merchants in cities, negotiating the sale and purchase of perishable fruits. Prices paid to the producer and those paid by the city merchant were arranged with a high profit for Mafia.
5. Sometimes frankly extortionist letters, very politely phrased, were sent to wealthy men.

The general procedure was for the victims to accede to the demands of Mafia, without referral to the police. Refusal to comply led to further victimization; and the police were and admitted themselves to be helpless.

In addition to these financial operations by which money was siphoned off from the rich to themselves or the peasants, each Mafia exerted a general regulatory control over its territory. It was opposed to miscellaneous or individual crimes. Rape was contrary to the Mafia code of honor. Disorderliness was to be avoided. Mafia supervised community activities and punished criminals. Mafia members did not define their own depredations as criminal but as necessary manipulations to rectify injustices.

In better organized communities many of the functions of Mafia would have been performed by the police; others would have been suppressed by the police. Mafia was linked to disrespect for the law, which seemed foreign and remote, without roots in the needs of the community. It existed because of weak and often corrupt law enforcement. Rule by Mafia thus served as a substitute for law enforcement, setting up its own system for distribution of goods, its own code of desirable behavior, and its own ways of enforcing its demands. In more recent times, as will be explained later, it has shifted from this homegrown type of social regulation toward a more thoroughly criminal organization. As law enforcement has grown stronger, Mafia has retreated from its more general regulatory functions to its more specific and Mafia-centered criminal functions.

Socialization of children for Mafia

The organization of a local Mafia was closely related to the close family and kinship organization on which Sicilian society rested, and which is still strong in all Italy (1, 5, 23). The basic social unit was the nuclear family, augmented, aided, and controlled by the extended kinship web, which included other closely organized nuclear families. In the relatively isolated communities of the nineteenth century, there was much in-marriage so that the ties of kinship brought many families into a system of mutual responsibility. It was therefore quite natural that the basic unit in Mafia was the family and that its membership tended to follow these kinship lines. Family members and relatives could be trusted, and only them, fully. The stranger, the outsider, was never to be trusted. The trusted group was further expanded by the system of godparenthood. This system was used to reinforce personal ties within a Mafia by the practice whereby the head of Mafia, or a leading member, became the godfather of the son of a Mafia member. Thus a boy, in a sense became dedicated to Mafia at birth.

In a family where father, uncles, and other adult male relatives were Mafia members, children grew up to accept Mafia as a normal part of the social order. Just as in the United States a child accepts without question the occupation and social-class level of its parents, in Sicily children similarly accepted a future in Mafia.

Boys were taught the philosophy of *mafia* and the code of *Omertà*. As they matured they accompanied their fathers into Mafia activities and by observation and informal teaching moved gradually into Mafia membership. Women were not members of Mafia, but they supported it by complete silence about it. Girls were taught to observe the philosophy of *mafia* and the code of *Omertà*.

Except for their devotion to Mafia, Mafiosi followed the general pattern of family life in Sicily. Families lived in small villages and worked the land as a unit. Each village had its patron saint, to whom the villagers were devoted, honoring him annually with a procession and gifts on his special day. The bond of a common patron saint gave the village unity. Families, not officials, controlled the behavior of individuals. The father was the chief authoritarian member, with the mother in a subordinate but supporting role; boys took precedence over girls. When a conflict arose between two families, its resolution was a family affair. A system developed to avoid blood vengeance. An intermediary would bring together the heads of the quarrelling families and if possible induce them to come to some agreement. The agreement was sealed by drinking together, with each man agreeing to act as godfather to the next child born to the other man. The reciprocal godparenthood was regarded as a type of kinship, indeed as creating a stronger tie than blood relationship. If agreement could not be reached, the two families might feud until all members of one were killed.

Marriages also were family affairs, and every effort was made by the groom's mother—the official matchmaker among the peasants—to find a desirable wife for her son from the village, that is, from among those who honored the same patron saint. The progression of the engagement, the wedding ceremony, and the succeeding festivities followed a ritualistic pattern. The prospective groom had a limited amount of initiative after the engagement was arranged by the two families; the girl had none. The couple could visit each other only in the presence of relatives.

Although young children of both sexes played together, from puberty on girls were closely supervised and in general remained within their parents' household. It was essential that the girl should be a virgin at the time of marriage.

The Mafia family was a typical Sicilian village family. Mafia leaders were as devout as other men and participated in religious ceremonies. Their daughters were protected and it was a violation of the code for a Mafia man to rape a woman. Marriages of sons and daughters were arranged by the elders, with emphasis on marriages that would strengthen the local Mafia organization.

Mafia itself followed a family pattern of organization, with an authoritarian leader and deference and submission of youth to elders. Women held the same low status as in the family. Thus when youth passed from primary loyalty to their families to primary loyalty to Mafia they were not changing the pattern of their lives but were substituting a large primary group for a small one, without abandoning the small one.

Banditry not part of Mafia

Some writers on Mafia make the error of confusing Mafia with banditry which has also flourished from time to time in Sicily, as well as in southern Italy (7, 12, 14, 19). Bandits were of two types.

One type of bandit was the result of failure of a revolt. Those who had been defeated escaped to the mountains, where they formed bands and carried on a kind of guerilla warfare. The conquerors usually moved strongly against them as they were a constant threat.

In the second type, an individual committed a legal offense or crime. The offense might have been small, but in resistance to arrest or as a result of a sentence thought to be unjust or excessive, the offender might kill an official. Such a murder might readily be regarded as a "just homicide" by the man's own community. To avoid arrest and trial for the homicide, the offender "took to the hills." His whereabouts remained a secret with his friends, who often provided him with food and clothing. Some bandits even continued to live with their families, always ready to leave hurriedly if word came that the police were looking for them. These bandits supplemented what they were given by the peasants with thefts from the rich. They also at times avenged themselves on the rich or the police for assumed wrongs. They often were heroes in the eyes of the peasants. Usually bandits were tolerated or aided by Mafia and prevented from making unreasonable encroachments on the community or the landowners with whom Mafia cooperated. Mafia did not hesitate to dispose of a troublesome bandit. Bandits survived in this role for only a few years. They might be killed or arrested for continued crimes or they might quietly fit themselves back into their home community, unbetrayed by the residents, who sympathized with them.

The differences between bandits and Mafia are clear. Bandits were renegades, fugitives from the police, who performed no useful function aside from sporadic help to the poor. Mafia was part of the normal social organization of a community, keeping order, punishing violators of their own "criminal" code, and maintaining some kind of equilibrium between the rich landowners and the peasants. Their methods were often criminal according to the law but justified in their own system of standards.

THE TRANSITIONAL PERIOD: 1860 to WORLD WAR II

After Sicily became part of the United Kingdom of Italy (1860), it felt the impact of the national government and was subject to many stresses as it slowly progressed from a village society in which, in western Sicily, Mafia played a major role to a semi-urban society in which Mafia was challenged by the national government. Many changes came concurrently, sometimes independently, often interlocked.

Reduction of physical and social isolation

The transitional period brought Sicily out of relative physical and social isolation (5). Transportation between Sicily and Italy improved, and the building of highways on the island linked western Sicily with other regions.

Education improved and the aspirations of young Sicilians, including the children of Mafiosi, reached upward toward business and professional levels. Some new industries were established in Sicily, although not to the extent that was true for northern Italy. At the same time, western Sicily remained essentially agricultural.

Contacts with foreign countries increased through travel, some of which was the result of police campaigns against Mafia which led to temporary refuge in nearby countries. Other contacts resulted from immigration to the United States, the return of immigrants, and to a small extent the deportation of criminals of Italian birth from the United States to the country of their birth. Knowledge of the world came also through motion pictures, and later radio and television.

Perhaps more important in drawing Sicily and Italy together than the economic and cultural contacts was the influence of the right of Sicilians to vote in national elections.

The vote

The first important granting of the franchise to Sicily was in 1882, with universal franchise coming in 1912, giving everyone the right to vote (7, 12, 14, 15). Mafia was able to enter into national politics. In return for various bribes and concessions, Mafia could guarantee election for candidates of the political party able to bestow the greatest benefits on it. The peasants were not much concerned with politics but could be intimidated or persuaded into voting as the local Mafia dictated. Members of Mafia were sent to Rome as deputies, where they obtained concessions and entered into fraudulent activities beyond the opportunities open to local Mafia in Sicily. The way was eased for obtaining weapons and manipulating the police.

Mafia, although used by Mussolini in the elections of 1924, supported the Liberal Party and hence did not support him—a factor in the movement of Mussolini against Mafia. Under fascism, also, local representatives to the national government were no longer elected and Mafia thus lost much of its value to political parties. With the death of Mussolini, Mafia reemerged into national political life. Through the right to vote and to participate in the national government, Mafia lifted itself from a local and provincial association into a political influence. Its roots and area of most intense influence remained in Sicily.

Decline of feudalism

Mafia developed out of the social and economic inequalities of feudalism and the helplessness of the peasants (2, 7, 14). The slow decline of feudalism changed the role of Mafia but did not destroy the organization. Feudalism was legally abolished in Sicily in 1812, but the actual movement from large landed estates to small individual holdings and the liberation of peasants from feudal status extended over many decades, broken from time to time by limited peasant revolts. By the 1890's, socialist movements provided the peasants with an alternative to dependence on Mafia for protection. The way was opening for a modern, business-type relationship of peasants with landlords and for political influence.

The effects on Mafia seem to have been two. The leading Mafiosi fitted themselves into the changing social situation. They became the medium for negotiations between estate owners and landless workers who wished to acquire land, and in the process they acquired land for themselves. The second effect on Mafia was their movement into various business relationships where they could exploit legitimate businessmen. Some of the exploitation was related to agriculture and the control, through fear, of prices on products. But Mafia also moved into urban economic activities through extortion of money from businessmen to prevent various misfortunes, such as the collapse of scaffolding and the injury or death of workers. If the money was paid to one strong Mafia, it maintained order, not only holding its own members under control but preventing rival Mafias or individual criminals from stealing or vandalism.

The abolition of feudalism changed Mafia from a loosely organized village association into closely organized urban groups, each specializing in some form of extortion. It also raised the leading Mafia members into the middle class.

Attempts of government to control or eliminate Mafia up to World War II

The Sicilian government has never been able to control the activities of Mafia—in fact, it was due to its ineffectiveness that Mafia became so deeply rooted in Sicilian life (4, 6, 9, 15). The local government and police became tools of Mafia; later, Mafia infiltrated various local governmental units. The relation of government representatives and Mafia has changed from time to time but has never been such that Mafia was controlled or stamped out. The attitude of the national government toward Mafia has been ambivalent, alternating between using Mafia influence to swing votes to certain candidates and moving in force against Mafia in an effort to stamp it out.

Soon after Sicily became part of Italy, an attempt was made to crush Mafia. In 1860, General Medici appointed Nicotera to this task. He did not make much headway, his arrests being primarily of ordinary criminals and political enemies.

In 1878 Prefect of Police Malirsardi was given authority over Sicily by the Italian Prime Minister of the Interior. He exiled several hundred criminals to the coastal islands. In time Mafia in Sicily reorganized. Members opened shops and practiced a trade as a respectable front behind which to carry on their criminal activities.

In 1894 another attempt was made when Premier Crispi sent General Morro di Lauriano and Commissioner Count Codronchi to Sicily, with a large army. Other accounts say that Crispi was moving against the cooperative movement in Sicily which was active between 1890 and 1900 and which tended to take over the betterment of the peasants' position with which Mafia had been concerned, leaving to Mafia more thoroughly criminal activities. Whatever the main objective, after this move, Mafia was declared dead but actually it had simply become temporarily quiescent.

Mussolini made a serious effort to stamp out Mafia. In 1926 he issued a decree that anyone suspected by public opinion of breaking the law could be arrested and sent without a trial to detention islands off the coast. Since only the opinion of fascists carried any weight, the way was open for fascist leaders to get rid of political enemies as well as criminals. Faced with the possibility of arrest, important Mafiosi joined the fascists or migrated to Tunisia or the United States. The result of two years' effort netted 147 members of Mafia who were brought to trial in Termini Imeresse, Sicily. For the most part, these people, arrested for all types of crime, were rank and file members of Mafia or other criminal elements. It was difficult to prove that outstanding Mafiosi were connected with vicious crimes, as younger members actually carried out the crimes under orders from the leaders. However, one outstanding Mafioso, Don Vito Cascio Ferro, at the time an old man, was imprisoned and died before the completion of his sentence. In his lifetime he had been acquitted of 70 crimes, including 20 homicides. It is obvious that in terms of numbers, 147 was an insignificant proportion of Mafia members. It was extremely difficult to persuade people who had been victimized by or had witnessed Mafia crimes to testify in the trial. Even those who had talked to the investigators privately could recall nothing when placed on the witness stand, so great was their fear of almost certain reprisal. The trial lasted three months. The public prosecutor asked for penalties ranging from hard labor for life to prison terms of five years. The jury required only three days to reach their decision, which was for conviction.

Mafia was suppressed until World War II and the death of Mussolini, after which it revived with many men of a younger generation and a different orientation.

MAFIA SINCE WORLD WAR II

The end of World War II saw Sicily in a state of great confusion. Mafia again came to the fore; it was active in freeing Sicily of the many bandits who infested it, many of them criminals who had escaped from jails damaged by Allied bombs. Only with the aid of a powerful and ruthless bandit, Giuliano, were the bandits finally subdued. Giuliano and his band served as a kind of emergency force for Mafia; the leader was eventually killed, presumably through the connivance of police and Mafia, after he had overstepped the limits of public tolerance.

Mafia in internal conflict

As order returned to Sicily, Mafia found itself torn by internal conflict (8, 12, 18). Power did not pass easily from older to younger Mafiosi as in the old days. In the post-war period two factions became active: one was composed of the old members who predated the war and advocated the old methods of operation, control, and dispensation of justice; the other was made up of young men, including some returned from the United States, who did not acknowledge the authority of the elders nor follow the old known methods of control whereby those who offended Mafia knew what action to expect from them.

The new members had no interest in the peasants nor in maintaining a balance between the rich and the poor. They were criminals per se. Some reportedly could be hired as killers for 325 dollars. New methods were used to kill opponents. Bombs replaced the daggers of an earlier period. In one incident, seven police and soldiers were killed by a bomb that had been concealed in an abandoned car. A shop was broken into and rifles (the old weapon) were left, while 114 revolvers were stolen.

But the old Mafia still exists and uses many of its customary methods. Non-Mafiosi still cooperate with them. A notorious case is that of several friars of Mazzarino who were arrested for typing extortion notes for the Mafiosi (who had no typewriter) and carrying them to intended victims. If they did not pay, the monks told the victims, they would probably be killed. The friars were arrested and brought to trial in Italy proper in 1962. They defended themselves by pointing out that they were simply giving the victims good advice—in similar circumstances in the past, men had been killed for not yielding to the demands of Mafia. The friars were at first acquitted but later convicted. The old type of inter-Mafia feuds still occur with outbursts of murder and refusal of witnesses or victims to testify on the witness stand.

Modernization of Mafia

The setting for the new conflict and activities is partly economic and partly political (2, 8, 17, 21). Economically, Sicily is the scene of a large scale drive to modernize and industrialize the island, involving an extensive program of public works. Mafia is using its power to obtain contracts and licenses. When the effort fails, Mafiosi force the successful contractor to make payments in return for which they agree to prevent property damage or personal injury. The set-up is a lucrative one for Mafia but occasions conflicts and killings between rival Mafia organizations.

Politically, Sicily seems powerless to control these and other Mafia activities. The ineptness and collusion of local officials is encouraged by the reluctance of the central government to intrude on local autonomy. Police action between the four western (Mafia) provinces of Sicily is not coordinated; there are not enough police and they are not well equipped for their task; no fingerprints are taken nor physical records kept.

A further development is the involvement of Sicilian Mafias in illicit international narcotic drug trade, especially since World War II. Opium, originating in Turkey, is smuggled to the Near East ports where morphine is extracted, then to France where Corsican racketeers process the morphine base into heroin, much of which is then smuggled to the Mafia in Italy or Sicily, and from there to overseas ports, including the United States.

Efforts at government control

The continued Mafia activity and the seeming inability of police and courts in Sicily to function have had several results (2, 8, 12). Some trials are now held in Italy; and the central government in 1963 appointed a commission to study Mafia as a preliminary step in a movement against the organization. The commission had 30 members, representing the eight political parties in the same proportion as their numbers in the Chamber of Deputies. However, half are Sicilian. This dispersion of political affiliations made it difficult to get a working majority within the commission.

In a book published in 1964, Luigi Barzini, after a close examination of Mafia, stated: "There is no denying that the Mafia in western Sicily is fundamentally a criminal organization, which causes great suffering among the people, condemns a majority of them to a primitive life of shame, squalor, poverty, hunger and fear." But it is not, he continues, simply a criminal organization: "It is believed to be also a spontaneous way, developed by the people themselves through many centuries of misrule, to administer a rough and archaic form of justice, a way to keep one kind of peace and ensure the safety of the inhabitants, an *ersatz* of legal government." He concludes: "The situation is worse now than it ever was." He calls Mafia "an exaggerated cancerous form of the milder disease prevailing in all Italy," whereby individuals attempt to supplement the defects of government by their own efforts and thereby prevent corrections of the government.[4]

ORGANIZED CRIME IN THE UNITED STATES

The possible relation of Mafia in Sicily to organized crime in the United States has been of long-standing interest to crime investigators and journalists (1, 3, 10, 11, 16, 17, 22). The United States has long had criminal gangs of one sort or another. The advancing line of frontier settlement, poorly policed, provided a year-round open season for mobile criminal gangs, one of the most notorious of which was headed by Jesse James. There has never been any implication that these early open-country gangs had any connection with Mafia; they were strictly home-grown. Cities also had their gangs long before the major immigration from Italy and Sicily, their members tending to be drawn from whichever immigrant group was the newcomer at the time. The cry of Mafia came after the heavy immigration from Italy and Sicily began in the 1890's and centered around the use of a black hand drawing as a symbol of criminal groups. At present, membership lists of organized criminal groups are heavily interlarded with Italian and Sicilian names, but not limited to them. They represent of course only a minute percentage of the total Italian and Sicilian population in the United States.

The sociologist Daniel Bell places the development of organized crime in the general framework by which all immigrant groups in the United States have climbed the social class ladder from obscure manual labor to a position of desirable status in business and the professions and of power in politics.[5] The Irish made their climb through the construction business, the Catholic Church, and politics. The Jews made theirs through banking, merchandising, and the professions. Some Italians, finding these avenues closed, found a way to wealth through criminal activities that more and more have taken

[4] Barzini, *op. cit.*, pp. 285-86.
[5] Daniel Bell, *The End of Ideology*, Free Press, 1962, Chapter 7.

the form of providing illicit services that are much desired by Americans. At an earlier period, the chief service was through organized houses of prostitution; briefly, during the prohibition period, it was distribution of alcoholic beverages; at present, it is gambling and for a limited clientele narcotic drugs. With the acquisition of wealth from these activities, and the passing of a generation or two, the leaders have attempted to move up the social class scale, to adopt the manners of the upper middle class, to move into well-to-do suburbs, and to send their children to college.

Various surveys have revealed the interconnection of gambling rings in different cities. It is sometimes asserted that a certain ring or certain leader dominates or actually controls the gambling rings in many cities. This is the network that is usually referred to as the Mafia in the United States. Whether such a system exists is a moot question. That leaders meet and confer seems certain, especially since the discovery of the meeting of leaders of organized crime at Apalachin in 1957. This meeting has been variously interpreted as proving the existence of a nationwide system of organized crime with central control, or as simply a meeting of men in the same line of business to discuss mutual problems and establish policies to prevent cutthroat competition, similar to meetings on a national basis of men in legitimate lines of business. The present network has replaced the violent competitive struggles between different organized criminal groups in the 1920's and 1930's, when disputes over territory or control of specific types of crime inevitably were settled by so-called gang wars during which leaders were systematically killed until one gang had established its superiority and dominance. The penalty of death is still inflicted when someone tries to break into the present established system or reveals criminal acts to the police or an investigating commission. Whether control is centralized or decentralized among cooperating rather than conflicting groups, it seems certain that some type of affiliation exists—that organized crime is a special stratum of American business life, less condemned by the public than serious individual crimes, more condemned than the white collar crime of legitimate business.

Organized crime in the United States has many resemblances to the Sicilian Mafia. They may have originated in the attitudes and customs that Sicilian immigrants (some of whom undoubtedly were Mafia members in Sicily) brought with them; however, some may be protective devices that any criminal group would develop to protect its interests from competitors, reformers, and the police. These methods may have originated in Sicily and have been passed on to younger men and presumably to men of non-Sicilian origin. The statement is sometimes made that only men of Sicilian ancestry can become members of Mafia. Be that as it may, organized criminal groups in the United States include men of other ethnic backgrounds who presumably follow the same protective devices as Sicilian ethnics.

When Sicilians immigrated to the United States (with or without Mafia backgrounds), it was inevitable that they should bring with them the attitudes and customs subsumed under the general heading of *mafia.* They kept their affairs to themselves, settled their own disputes—by death if personal honor was involved—did not appeal to the police, and were close-lipped if arrested. The code of *Omertà,* general to the culture of Sicily and to some extent of Italy, was a part of the culture and personality of the immigrants and continued to function in the United States. Other cultural groups brought with them other cultural characteristics: Jews, a love of learning and business sagacity developed in European urban life; the Irish, a tendency to turn to physical labor, to settle personal disputes with their fists, and to maintain a devotion to their religion. Each immigrant and ethnic group used its initial characteristics to gain a foothold in the United States. Each group has fitted itself into some facet of American life, usually in a legitimate manner. A residue has failed to enter a normal channel and makes its way through crime (corrupt politics, white collar crime, organized crime). To what extent the form of crime is a direct inheritance from a European background is difficult to say.

The most revealing information about organized crime in the United States has come from the criminal Joseph Valachi who, fearing that he was marked for murder even through in prison, revealed his knowledge of organized crime gained through 30 years as a low-status member (a "soldier") in an organized criminal group. His statements, made to the Permanent Subcommittee on Investigations of the Senate Committee on Government Operations, were confirmed in large part by information from various city police departments, especially New York City, and from other witnesses versed on the operations of organized crime.[6]

[6] *Organized Crime and Illicit Traffic in Narcotics.* Report of the Committee on Government Operations . . . Report 72, Senate, 89th Congress, 1st Session. Government Printing Office, 1965, pp. 30ff, 283-284.

According to Valachi, the term *Cosa Nostra* has replaced the term Mafia for the American version of Sicilian Mafia. It is interpreted in America as meaning "our thing" or "our family," and by the Italian writer Barzini as "our own affair, something which must be guarded from intruders." In the principal cities where organized crime prevails, a number of "families" may operate; New York City is said to have five, whose leaders run *Cosa Nostra* in that city. Other cities have their own units of *Cosa Nostra.* Within each unit or "family" a hierarchy of leadership exists with different roles and functions at each level. Men in the lower ranks have no contact with the top men, but have the function of carrying out criminal operations dictated from above. This hierarchy with specialization of functions approaches a bureaucratic organization similar to the organization of legitimate urban business.[7] The old familial and kinship ties typical of Mafia in Sicily still exist; some sons follow their fathers into *Cosa Nostra,* and there is also a network of marriages between the sons and daughters of members of *Cosa Nostra* in different cities. But the movement is toward bureaucratization, apparently to a greater degree than is true of Mafia in Sicily. Leaders of different units of *Cosa Nostra* within a given city cooperate and, between cities, leaders meet for consultation and planning. Evidence has not been found of one overall boss.

The general conclusion of investigators is that *Cosa Nostra* is a lineal descendant of the Sicilian Mafia but is not an integral part of an international organization. In certain types of crime, such as the illicit drug trade, *Cosa Nostra* may cooperate with Mafia but it is an independent organization, several generations removed from its original Sicilian members. It is shaping itself to the American urban pattern of economic operations while at the same time retaining a criminal orientation and some of the old codes and on occasion violent methods of the original Mafia.

REFERENCES

1. ANDERSON, ROBERT T. "From Mafia to Cosa Nostra." *American Journal of Sociology,* 71 (1965), pp. 302-10.
2. BARZINI, LUIGI. *The Italians.* Atheneum Publishers, 1964; also Bantam Books.
3. BELL, DANIEL. *The End of Ideology.* Free Press, 1962.

[7] R. T. Anderson, "From Mafia to Cosa Nostra," *American Journal of Sociology,* 71 (1965), pp. 308-10.

4. DI GREGORIO, JOHN. "Mussolini and the Mafia." *Nation,* 126 (1928), pp. 263-65.
5. GUERICO, FRANCIS M. *Sicily, The Garden of the Mediterranean, The Country and Its People.* London: Faber and Faber, 1938.
6. "Has Mussolini Demolished the Mafia?" *Literary Digest,* 96 (January 28, 1928), pp. 40-44.
7. HOBSBAWN, E. J. *Primitive Rebels.* Manchester, England: Manchester University Press, 1959.
8. "Hunting the Mafia." *Economist,* 209 (1963), pp. 369-70.
9. "Italian Mafia." *Outlook,* 72 (1902), pp. 5-6.
10. JOHNSON, EARL, JR. "Organized Crime: Challenge to the American Legal System." *Journal of Criminal Law, Criminology, and Police Science,* 53 (1962), pp. 399-425.
11. KEFAUVER, ESTES. *Crime in America.* Doubleday, 1951.
12. LEWIS, NORMAN. "The Honored Society." *New Yorker,* 39 (February 8, 1964), pp. 42-105; (February 15, 1964), pp. 39-111; (February 22, 1964), pp. 35-91.
13. MACNAMARA, DONAL E. J. "Criminal Societies," *Encyclopedia Americana,* 1962, vol. 8, pp. 200f.
14. MERLINO, S. "Camorra, Maffia (sic) and Brigandage." *Political Science Quarterly,* 9 (1894), pp. 466-85.
15. MOSCA, GAETANO. "Mafia." *Encyclopedia of the Social Sciences,* 1933, vol. 10, pp. 36-38.
16. *New York Times,* February 14, 1965.
17. *Organized Crime and Illicit Traffic in Narcotics.* Report of the Committee on Government Operations, United States Senate, made by its Permanent Subcommittee on Investigations, together with Additional Combined Views and Individual Views. Report 72, Senate, 89th Congress, 1st Session. Washington, D.C.: Government Printing Office, 1965. (Includes testimony of Joseph Valachi.)
18. RENTON, BRUCE. "The Angry Young Men of Palermo." *New Statesmen,* 63 (1962), 294.
19. SEDGWICK, H. D., JR. "Musolino, the Bandit." *Outlook,* 71 (1902), pp. 1057-60.
20. "Sicily." *Encyclopedia Britannica,* 1963, vol. 20, pp. 602ff.
21. STERLING, CLAIRE. "Shots in Sicily, Echoes in Rome." *Reporter,* 23 (August 4, 1960), pp. 35-36.
22. TYLER, GUS. *Organized Crime in America.* University of Michigan Press, 1962.
23. WHYTE, WILLIAM FOOTE. "Sicilian Peasant Society." *American Anthropologist,* 46 (1944), pp. 65-74.

7 / England: The Mature Industrial Nation

England was the first nation to develop the industrialized city that is now, the world over, the central breeding ground of juvenile delinquency. In earlier years it passed through stages of change just now being experienced by many nations in earlier phases of urban industrialization. England also set the pace for Europe and the United States. Historical and current aspects of delinquency and crime in England provide a background for some preceding chapters and form an introduction to the chapter that follows on delinquency in certain European countries.

Britain was in an extreme corner of the ancient world. After the discovery and settlement of the Americas, along with the agricultural, commercial, and industrial revolutions, England became the center of the modern world. Industrial, financial, political, and naval leadership was British. England's methods of solving problems illuminate similar situations in other nations; for example, often her solutions for crime were exported directly to her colonies (as in India), or her criminals were physically transported (as to the American colonies or Australia). At a later period, an exchange of ideas and methods of dealing with criminals went on among the countries of the western world, with England sometimes being the recipient, sometimes the originator, of innovations. Some of Britain's attempted solutions for crime succeeded; some failed. England's experience often gives a foreview of how current proposals just now being considered elsewhere actually worked in practice; it can add a kind of hindsight to the immediate attempt at foresight.

ENGLISH HISTORICAL DEVELOPMENT

England provides a picture of the transition from the feudal to the contemporary, from farm village to great metropolitan London, from the medieval artisan to the huge factory and industrial corporation, from the town shop or annual fair to the worldwide network of trade, finance, and Empire. In the realm of crime and its treatment, England moved from the state and its courts, giving cruel, brutal punishment and repression, to the present-day juvenile court, acting as beneficent foster parent, admonishing, redirecting, providing for many needs, with a whole series of supplementary institutions—industrial and reformatory schools, Borstals, Approved Schools, remand homes, classification centers, parole and probation services, and the like. In the much too brief space here, we can try to see, against the general historical background, items and episodes in the long, slow shift from the feudal to the modern ways in handling the young offender.

The situation in England reflects a midway point between that in the civilized western world and that in primitive cultures such as the Eskimo, the village community (which is little changed although in a modern nation, as in the Sicilian mountains, Mexico, or India), or the masses of transplanted villagers found in cities like Mexico City or Bombay.

The history of English development including its criminal aspects is sketched in four periods.

Sixteenth to mid-eighteenth centuries

For some two centuries, beginning with Henry VIII, several trends stand out. Great increases occurred in population, towns, wealth, trade, and foreign contacts, and the pattern of medieval England moved toward modern forms. Control by an uneasy cooperation of the crown and the great magnates of the nobility with the Church was fading. The Church, in its medieval form, was a major political power, huge landowner, source of many of the king's dominating ministers, and setter of a unified pattern of thinking. All this was being liquidated. Differences of opinion, perhaps most visible in the area of religion, became gradually more evident and acceptable. The urban population, merchants, and traders acquired numbers, wealth, power, and much land. The forerunners of the Industrial Revolution—still to come—can now be seen in the growth of towns and cities, the commercial and agricultural revolution, the rise to major importance of the wool trade and of the export of cloth, but especially in the increase of the middle class in numbers and wealth, in the accumulation of capital, and in public influence.

In regard to offenses and younger offenders, when a youth committed an offense, he received the same harsh treatment as an adult. Law and the system of justice was by and for the powerful, bearing down on threats to property and the *status quo,* showing no compassion to women or the young. Hundreds of offenses carried the death penalty. Executions were frequent and glaringly public, justice harshly executed, jails incredibly inhumane. The concept of "adolescence" had not emerged, nor had that of the juvenile and younger adult as requiring special ways of handling in the system of dispensing justice or as needing special institutions. The system involved the repression of "sturdy beggars," the workhouse, the laws of settlement, and poor law activity, administered by those most hurt by any increase of local taxes that would have been required for less punitive treatment. Humanitarianism was expressed through the Church. By the end of the period, a multiplicity of churches and sects had come into being, but without the tolerances and adjustments needed to make a plural system work smoothly. Almost the only practical measure for prevention of crime among the young was apprenticeship; schools were only for the few.

From the Industrial Revolution to Waterloo, 1750-1815

From the introduction of the general use of new inventions and machines through that turbulent generation stretching from the fall of the Bastile to Waterloo, a new world took shape, a world of currents and forms much like the present (8, 15, 18). Urbanization and large scale production replaced the earlier pattern of cottage and village manufacture. Great wealth and bitter poverty grew side by side, and the disparity grew. Slum living increased in the cities.

War changed from feudal forays to mobilization against Napoleon of the entire manpower and economic power of the nation, with rises in wages and prices. With the defeat of Napoleon came demobilization, surpluses, and the collapse of prices and wages. Adjustment was made to a new world, with added continents but the loss of the American colonies. This loss symbolized change toward a new system of international and economic organization: the American republic became the "first new nation," undeveloped, unindustrialized, but independent and pioneering in the new way.[1]

The Church faded as the place for the shaping of ideas, for charity, refuge, and education. From the varying churches and sects, there came a flood of individual philanthropists and reformers, local and national groups and societies, overlapping in their efforts at benevolence, piety, education, and reform. In competition, secular public opinion, rational and middle-class, increasingly became influential. Action by the state was becoming the method of accomplishing goals, the long trail toward the welfare state was being blazed. Social progress and reform seemed to come in the wake of the individual who could somehow strike fire in general interest and draw followers, such as John Howard and Elizabeth Fry in the field of jail reform. For all the discussion, however, actual conditions were little changed.

Children as little adults

At the time that the Industrial Revolution was gaining force, children past infancy were regarded as little adults. Before the Revolution, when weaving was a cottage industry, children of four or five were set to work by their parents. Children of seven were apprenticed to the ironmakers at Birmingham. When factories began to replace cottage industries in spinning and weaving, parents at first rebelled against placing their children in factories. The children of paupers or abandoned children, however, were apprenticed to mill owners at an early age and separated from their parents. Soon, under the threat of poverty, parents working in the mills permitted their young children to work there also. This employment of children was not deplored but was regarded as an admirable arrangement, whereby children as young as four or five were supporting themselves, like adults, and adding to the wealth of the nation. In 1785, a clergyman recommended the general adoption of a rule applied in Rutland that relief should be denied to any family that had a child above six years of age who could not knit or a child above nine who could not spin or weave.

Conditions in the factories were deplorable from the point of view of health. Children were required to work in some factories up to

[1] S. M. Lipset, *The First New Nation, The United States in Historical and Comparative Perspective.* Basic Books, 1963.

16 hours a day, six days a week, and a ten hour day was regarded as benevolent. Apprentices lived in buildings constructed near the factories and usually had no time nor place for recreation. They were forced by severe punishments to work diligently and carefully.

The conception of children as adults carried over into marriage, permissible under English common law at 12 for girls and 14 for boys. Among wealthy families, children were often betrothed by their parents well before puberty, and married soon after.

None of the present elements of child rearing—a loving association with adults, opportunity for friends of their own age, attention to health, and provision for education—were even thought of in connection with the children of paupers and only minimally so for children still with their parents. Childhood did not exist in the modern sense.

The forcing of children into adult modes did not necessarily mean that the children had independence. They were little adults in some respects but under the strict surveillance of older adults—parents, employers, local officials—in others.

In view of the situation just described, it is not unusual that in the area of crime and criminal justice children tended to be treated in the same manner as adults. In English common law, children under seven were pardoned for all acts; between ages eight and 14, children were held responsible for their misdeeds if they were sufficiently intelligent to understand the nature of their behavior and could distinguish between right and wrong. Over age 14, they were considered to be adults. Children over seven who were adjudged guilty of criminal acts were subject to the penalties applied to adult criminals.

Death, usually by public hanging, was the punishment for as many as 200 crimes during the eighteenth century. As many as 12 to 20, or occasionally as many as 40, condemned persons might be hanged in one day. Hanging day in some places came once a month. It was a day of revelry, ribaldry, and rioting. In London, the cart that carried the condemned from jail to the gallows forced its way through thousands of people. For the most notorious criminals, their execution was watched from grandstands which had been erected for part of the huge crowds of spectators. Most of the executed criminals were men, often youthful, but some were women and young children. It is not known how many children received the extreme penalty. Blackstone, writing in 1795, refers to earlier cases in which children were executed: a girl of 13 burned to death for killing her mistress; a boy of 10 hanged for killing a companion; a boy of eight hanged for burning two barns; and a boy of 10 executed for killing his bedfellow.[2] In 1785, two boys, aged 12 and 14, were convicted of highway robbery and hanged. As late as 1833, a child of nine was convicted of housebreaking when he broke the window in a shop and took two pennies' worth of paint. The witness was another child of nine. He was sentenced to death but never executed.[3]

Crime in the cities

A distinction should be made between London and other cities of England (15). The Industrial Revolution struck the smaller cities directly; they experienced the transition from cottage industries to factories, the influx of workers, and the difficulties of integration between essentially village ways of life and the more impersonal ways of the city. London was less directly affected but experienced many problems of growth and social control in the eighteenth century. Factories tended to be established outside the city; the trend in London was toward a commercial, trading, and financial center. The population spread far beyond the central city; the metropolitan area became an uncoordinated patchwork of local laws and administrative units. The evils of the century, especially in the first half, are pointed up by such phrases as these: exposure and desertion of abandoned infants or their "wholesale slaughter in the workhouse or by parish nurses," alleviated to some extent in London by the Foundling Hospital; poor who begged or starved on minute parish doles; lack of sanitation and high death rate; crudeness and brutality; drunkenness and gambling; robbery and violence in the streets that made people fear to leave their homes at night. Police protection was totally inadequate—it was not until 1829 that the Metropolitan Police of London was established, and then only after a struggle against those who opposed it as a semi-military force that would lead to centralized despotism.

[2] Cited by Frederick B. Sussman, *Juvenile Delinquency,* Oceana Publications, 1959, p. 12.

[3] The Hon. Edward Cadogan, *The Roots of Evil, Being a Treatise on the Methods of Dealing with Crime and the Criminal during the 18th and 19th Centuries in Relation to Those of a More Enlightened Age,* John Murray, London, 1937, pp. 82-83.

Exposure of children and youth to crime

As industrial and commercial cities developed, so did the problem of crime among youth, and of public concern for that crime (6, 15). The *Report of the Committee of the Society for the Improvement of Prison Discipline, and for the Reformation of Juvenile Offenders,* published in 1818, states that the information of their study, "unites in demonstrating the lamentable fact, that juvenile delinquency has of late years increased to an unprecedented extent, and is still rapidly and progressively increasing; that the crimes committed by the youthful offenders are often of the worse description; and that an organized system for instruction in vice, and the encouragement of depravity is regularly maintained."[4]

Young children were exposed to many conditions that inured them to crime and set the stage for vagrancy, begging, and eventually crime. Writing of the eighteenth century, Cadogan speaks of the "herds of very young children" who were driven into the streets each morning by indigent or profligate parents who could not find employment nor apprenticeships for them. They were warned that a flogging awaited them if they returned empty-handed. Other children shifting for themselves were orphans, whose means of livelihood was begging and stealing.

Somewhat older children of both sexes gathered in disreputable public houses, known as "flash houses," where thieves and prostitutes habitually gathered. The mature and skilled thieves tutored the young in the methods of successful pickpocketing. Girls were soon reduced to prostitution. In some instances, boys and girls divided into small groups of two or three, scattering out over the city, and returned later to divide their plunder which might equal as much as £400 in one night. Some of the "flash houses" catered almost exculsively to boys and girls, one having accommodations for as many as 400. Money stolen in the daytime was spent at night in gambling and in brothels. Young teenagers were frequently among the youth engaged in these activities.

Children were brought into contact with ne'er-do-wells and depraved, as well as poor and improvident, persons through the custom in debtors' prisons of permitting parents to have their children

[4] *The Report* was from the Society for the Diffusion of Knowledge upon the Punishment of Death and the Improvement of Prison Discipline, Bensley and Sons, London, 1818, p. 11.

with them where no attempt at classification by age was made. One account in the early 1800's says that it was not uncommon for 300 women with children up to the age of 16 to be crowded into four rooms, where they were in charge of an old man and his son. A netting in front of the women's portion of the prison failed to screen them from the view of the men prisoners.

Men were allowed to visit their wives in prisons, where they could associate with them only in the cells crowded with other women and children. Wives and prostitutes visited the male prisoners; boys could receive their sweethearts who passed themselves off as sisters. Accounts of Newgate jail in London emphasize the drunkenness, the revelry, the cruelty of prisoner to prisoner, and the imprisonment with depraved or hardened criminals of a small number of young boys.

Apprenticeship

The system of apprenticeship, designed to train boys in useful trades and girls in domestic work, was regarded as providing an open door to delinquency.[5] Many apprentices had spent their earlier years in workhouses as orphans or abandoned children. At the age of 14 or 15, they were apprenticed to masters, who often were little concerned about how the boys spent their nonworking hours. In London, and no doubt elsewhere, the system was criticized, especially when the apprentice did not work or live in the house of his master, but traveled daily to another location. Instead of returning promptly to his master's house at the end of the work day, he and his companions remained on the streets. In other cases, masters permitted their apprentices to spend their free time as they wished. In their public relations, apprentices were variously described as demoralized, disorderly, drunken, insolent, and as frequenting taverns, associating with prostitutes, and engaging in fights with other apprentices. Undoubtedly many apprentices learned a trade and became steady workingmen, but many others are cited in the literature of the times as ending up as serious criminals or on the gallows. They had ample opportunity to mingle with adult ne'er-do-wells and criminals in alehouses and other public places. Second-hand dealers encouraged them to steal by buying the stolen goods from them. In London, masters

[5] M. Dorothy George, *London Life in the Eighteenth Century,* Harper and Row, 1964, Chapter 6.

could complain to the Chamberlain, the guardian of the apprentices, about the shortcomings of their apprentices. The boys (and girls also) might then be sent to the House of Correction where, until the last quarter of the eighteenth century, they were not separated from the prostitutes and vagrants who were the chief inmates.

In the jails for criminals, young boys were often found awaiting trial for some minor offense but crowded in with convicted adults. One report speaks of seven or eight children between the ages of nine and 13 in the infamous jail at Newgate, London. Somewhat later, when some segregation was instituted, boys aged eight to 16 or 18 were housed together, without regard to the opportunities for tutelage in crime of the young first offender by the older boy skilled in criminal ways.

Not all, and certainly not the most serious offenses, were committed by boys. Accounts of life in London in the eighteenth century are filled with instances of robbery on the dark, poorly policed streets, often at the point of gun or knife. Much of it was attributed to the Irish and Jews (the then current immigrants) who were unable to find adequate work for support. But not all crime originated with the poor. It was a time of corruption in many aspects of life. Public offices were bought, the cost of this being covered by fees exacted for the services of the office.

Before the end of the eighteenth century, awareness of great problems of ignorance, poverty, and crime was forming, with many legal and voluntary movements to prevent crime and reform criminals. The term "juvenile delinquency" appeared in various published materials. The writings of John Howard, the great advocate of prison reform, appeared between 1777 and his death in 1790. The slow process of change had begun that was to come to fruition in the nineteenth century.

The ferocity of the law

In handling offenders, judges and public alike were beginning to be sickened by the brutal punishments—the flogging, physical mutilations and brandings, and the executions (2, 6, 13, 34). Children and youth were still handled as adults, except when a compassionate judge or jury softened the sentence. In 1816, near the close of the period under discussion, there were in London prisons more than 3,000 inmates under 20 years old, of whom half were under

17; some were as young as nine or ten. A thousand of these young people had been convicted of felonies, and many were destined to be hanged or transported.

Transportation to the American colonies was ended by the American Revolution. An emergency measure that tended to become permanent was the incarceration of prisoners in the hulks of old ships anchored in English rivers and harbors and fitted for close security. They had all, if not more than, the defects of prisons—overcrowding of all ages of men and boys, lack of sanitation or medical attention with a high death rate, and lack of any means of reform. After 1787, prisoners were transported under appalling conditions on shipboard to Australia and nearby islands, where their treatment was perhaps a little less brutal than in the prisons and on the gallows in England, but much more prolonged. Boys and girls in small numbers were included among the transported criminals.

FROM WATERLOO TO SARAJEVO, 1816-1914

Relative to the past centuries and the decades to follow, the century between Napoleon's defeat at Waterloo and the opening of World War I was unique: a century of peace, with growth by almost every index, and political stability under middle-class control and leadership.

Economically, it was a wonder century. The railroad, steamship, automobile, and airplane, in turn, appeared and were assimilated. They made possible the great factory, port, and metropolis. Wealth and productive power increased miraculously; English dominance in industry, commerce, and finance was clear. Political and military power was high. It was the time of Empire.

It was also the century of optimism; men came to believe in the "progress of mankind, onward and upward forever." Thought changed; the old controlling views might seem unchanged on the surface, but they had lost the power to control events. New "prophet-thinkers" (Marx, Darwin, Freud) destroyed the very foundations of old patterns of belief. Perhaps John Dewey should be included, with his pragmatism, moral relativism, and progressive education imported from America. Tax-supported free education at the elementary school level was made available, then compulsory. Higher education grew in volume and quality. Voluntary groups for reform mushroomed, and the state gradually approached thc welfare state.

Representation in Parliament and the structure of local government were reformed and rationalized.

The marvel was that this was done without much force or bloodshed, rather gradually and by consent. Unlike the experience of the Continent, there were not, in England, bloody struggles at the barricades, communes, overturns of dynasties, or bitter, visible struggles between hostile classes.

Changed attitudes toward crime

With regard to criminal behavior, significant trends of the period seemed to be the appearance of a concept of juvenile delinquency, as opposed to a general concept of crime to be dealt with irrespective of age; emphasis on youth, the youthful offender, and younger convict; classification by depth of criminal attitude as well as by sex and age; differential treatment of women and children; and concern to reform and rehabilitate rather than to deter and punish by harshness or to eliminate from British life by execution or transportation. The modern pattern thus replaced the medieval. By the end of the nineteenth century, the offender was treated less as a soul to be converted or indoctrinated and more as a person to be helped and remotivated.

Voluntary efforts to prevent or correct delinquency

The start toward prevention and rehabilitation of child and youthful offenders came in the latter part of the eighteenth century from volunteer groups and only later was incorporated into the laws (13, 16, 41). An early group was the Marine Society which opened a school as early as 1756 "for waifs and strays and the children of convicts," who were fed, clothed, and, at an appropriate age, sent to sea. At first, both men and boys were sought by the Society to supply men for the navy and to save boys from a life of vagrancy and crime. After three years, the Society gave all its attention to boys. In 1769, the Society was reorganized and a drive was made for funds to outfit boys and apprentice them to masters of ships; approximately 300 boys were outfitted and apprenticed. In 1786, a ship was secured to be used as a training ship for these would-be apprentices. Under the control of a capable naval officer, a staff was provided consisting of a boatswain, boatswain's mate, carpenter, cook, and schoolmaster.

Another society to aid the children of convicts was the Philanthropic Society, established in London in 1788 to provide for abandoned and vagrant children who had criminal associations. They were described in the First Report of the Society as belonging to no rank of the civil community, as "links which have fallen off the chain of society, and which going to decay, injure, and obstruct the movements of the whole machine."[6] This Society established three cottages, each housing 12 children, where they received some vocational training.

The work of voluntary groups extended into the nineteenth century. The first Ragged Schools were established in 1818. To these judges could send destitute, abandoned, or orphaned children for day education. During the first half of the nineteenth century, many private schools or reformatories were opened, at the expense and sometimes near the homes of wealthy men who were moved both by compassion and awareness of the almost certain future criminal career of the waifs they gathered in. Children were not sentenced to these private institutions by the courts. Certain parts of cities swarmed with abandoned, begging children, whose chief contact with adults was often in a disreputable public house or with an adult criminal who taught children to pick pockets and directed the youngsters' thefts for his own benefit.

Public responsibility for special institutions

When interest extended from prevention to reformation, the first reformatories were in private hands (13, 41). They were recognized by the courts, and certain categories of young convicted offenders, aged 16 to 20, were sent to them. Formal recognition by Parliament came in 1854 when the first Reformatory Schools Act was passed. This act made it possible for the courts to commit offenders under 16 to the reformatories, still in private hands. The offender had first to spend at least 14 days in prison, after which he might be transferred to a reformatory for from two to five years. From then on, various acts were passed for financial assistance and inspection, until eventually the government took over the establishment and control of reformatories.

Industrial schools, also in private hands, were legally recognized in 1857 by an Act of Parliament which was amended in 1860,

[6] George, *op. cit.*, p. 223.

1861, and 1866. These acts assigned to the Schools the function of training schools for children under 14 years of age. Many of the children were incorrigibles or dependent and neglected. Children under 12 who had committed offenses might also be sent to the Industrial Schools.

A further step for the separation of the young from adult criminals came in 1838 in the Parkhurst Act, which set aside a former military prison on the Isle of Wight to be used as a prison for young offenders. Those under 18 and including some under 10 who had been sentenced to transportation might be sent here, where the emphasis was on reformation rather than on punishment. The inmates might later be transported to the colonies or pardoned and transferred to a reformatory. After the passing of the Reformatory Act, this pioneer prison passed out of existence.

Looking back, one might say that the first half of the nineteenth century witnessed the swelling of interest and efforts on the part of the public to care for neglected and potentially delinquent or criminal children, the latter half, the assumption of this responsibility by the government. Despite these efforts, children under age 16, and especially between 16 and 20, were still sent to adult prisons, but in decreasing numbers. The Prison Act of 1865 required that those under 16 should be separated in the prison from those above that age. Finally, in 1948, the Criminal Justice Act formally prohibited the imprisonment of persons under age 15 and placed restrictions on imprisonment of young offenders up to age 21. Special institutions, separate in administration from prisons, were used for children under 15.

The whole movement concerning institutionalizing children and youths in special institutions had several motives. One was to gather vagrant and homeless children who were associating with criminals and rapidly becoming demoralized and criminal into homes or schools for training that would prevent their further immersion in crime. The other was to bypass imprisonment along with adults for convicted young offenders and place them in special institutions or reformatories.

Foundation of present system

Three acts passed in 1907 and 1908 "laid the foundation stones of the contemporary penal system in England: they were three—

the Probation of Offenders Act, 1907, the Children Act, 1908, and the Prevention of Crime Act, 1908. . . ." according to Lionel W. Fox[7] when he was Chairman of the Prison Commission for England and Wales (5, 13, 39). These acts crystallized the movement to prevent delinquency and avoid imprisonment of children in prisons. The Children Act was known at the time as the Children's Charter. Children under age 14, often more neglected than delinquent, were to be sent to Industrial Schools, which first had been recognized legally in 1857. Offenders from the age of 12 up to, but not including, 16 were destined for reformatories.

For the next age group, 16 to 20, guilty of serious crimes, a special institution was devised, based in part on the new reformatory system instituted in Elmira, New York, in 1876. This American reformatory singled out an age group above that long recognized as juvenile and set it apart from the mature adult criminal category, a group now often referred to as the young adult offender. The special English institution is known as a Borstal, from the name of the village in Kent, England, where an experimental program was successfully carried out. Borstals, by that name, have spread into many countries in Europe and, beyond, to former English colonies.

The Children Act of 1908 also provided for juvenile courts for offenders under 16.[8]

The change in attitude and treatment of juvenile delinquents was only part of a general change in values and services that characterized England in the century between 1816 and 1914, as was outlined just above, in the first paragraphs of this section. As is true now of developing nations, England was not without problems, but it had established the trends that still continue as to methods

[7] Lionel W. Fox, *The English Prison and Borstal Systems,* Routledge & Kegan Paul, London, 1952, p. 334.

[8] England was not the first country to establish juvenile courts or similar agencies to keep children out of criminal courts. The Scandinavians bypassed juvenile courts for delinquent children; in 1896, Norway established child welfare boards to deal with delinquent and dependent children, and Sweden and Denmark soon followed their lead. The first juvenile court per se was established in Illinois in 1899, and gradually other states passed the necessary legislation, the last being Wyoming in 1945. However, the justification for the juvenile court system in Illinois was found in earlier English common law practices. By combining laws for the care of dependent children by courts of chancery with age definitions of delinquency, delinquent children were kept out of the criminal courts. England thus furnished the base for juvenile courts in the United States.

of solving these problems through organized governmental services and legal procedures.

Many changes have been made in the acts of 1907 and 1908, but the basic principles remain: recognition of special periods of childhood and youth when the emphasis should be on prevention and reformation; complete separation by different age groups and by sex; assumption of responsibility by local and national government. To avoid confusion in terminology, one change should be noted: the old terms, reformatory and industrial school, were given up, and the term, Approved Schools, was applied in 1933 to the institutions for boys or girls under age 17. From time to time wide-sweeping new acts are passed or recommendations made. An example is the White Paper on "The Child, The Family, and the Young Offender" issued by the English government in August, 1965, which concerns methods of accomplishing the basic values rather than a change in the values themselves.

WORLD WAR I TO WORLD WAR II

After World War I the tide ebbed. The Empire was gradually liquidated; world dominance disappeared. Political parties seemed to represent the division of social classes now in sharp conflict, and optimism faded (7, 24). It was the era of the gigantic in everything —in industries, commerce, cities, labor organization, and governmental structure. Social problems became of major importance, too; the ideal was the welfare state. Problems were so intricate and the costs of every solution suggested so huge that the ordinary man or group seemed impotent; everything was to be left to government at the center, believed to have unlimited wisdom and infinite resources to conquer every problem. Leadership was no longer by the patricians, of noble birth and large land ownership, as in the time of the Tudors, or by those thought to represent enlightened public opinion and "the best minds of the better people." Leadership was by the majority in Commons of those elected to represent the wishes and demands of the masses. Welfare legislation produced great national systems, inevitably bureaucratic and costly. The decades after World War I saw the great loss of wealth and lives of that war, the depression of the 1930's, World War II, the cold war, and the fading of Empire. It was a time of much confusion.

Building on the foundation laid prior to World War I, England improved its courts and created an amazingly effective (and unarmed) policing force. It developed its psychiatric and counseling service; created special types of Borstal Institutions and Approved Schools for each type of youthful guest, with diagnostic and classifying units; created a system of youth clubs and services; and experimented with detached workers and attempts to reach the unattached youth. Research of many types was carried out and the reports appeared in print.

Trends in delinquency rates

Both World War I and World War II witnessed an acceleration in the number of children in courts for indictable (serious or criminal) offenses (23, 36). Prior to World War I, the number of delinquents under age 16 increased by 21 per cent between 1910 and 1914; the percentage is based on the number of children rather than rates, and does not take account of any increase in the estimated child population that may have occurred. Between 1914, the year the war began, and 1917, the year of peak delinquency, the number of delinquents increased 64 per cent. The number remained high through 1918, the year the war ended, and then dropped abruptly to the pre-war level where it remained during the 1920's, with irregular minor fluctuations during the 1930's.

The figures on delinquency for the World War II period are for children (ages 8-13) and young persons (14-17). The rate per 100,000 male children guilty of indictable offenses almost doubled between the first and last years of the war, and the corresponding increase for female children was 77 per cent. The increase in rates for young persons was 58 per cent for males. The rate for female young persons more than doubled, with the peak coming in the middle of the war period. After the end of the war, rates declined briefly and then rose, reaching a new high in 1951 for boys that exceeded the war rates; for female young persons the rate fluctuated, coming back several times to the war high, while for female children, the rate between 1948 and 1952 exceeded any previous rate before or during the war. It was not until well into the 1950's that the rates were noticeably below the war rates, but substantially above the pre-war rates.

The above figures, even for the younger age groups, are all for serious (criminal) offenses. Minor misdeeds and the peccadillos of children are not included.

The social disruptions and offenses of World War II

Many of the institutions in which the activities of children and youth normally are contained were seriously disrupted for at least part of the war years (3, 4). These disruptions did not all reach their peak simultaneously, and, even while the war continued, steps were taken to offset the damaging effect on children and youth.

For the security of children, a widespread system of evacuation from London to designated reception centers, located at a distance from the city, was put into effect. By February, 1941, in the second year of the war, five out of six children in the County of London had been evacuated. But children were not content, and parents longed to have them at home. During lulls in the war, many children returned home, only to be evacuated again when the war quickened. Some children moved four times in the course of the first year of the war. Not only did the London children find it hard to adjust to new ways of living and separation from their parents, but the families with whom they were placed found it hard to adapt to their city charges. Schools and other community facilities in the reception areas could not crowd in the additional children. In time, new agencies were opened in reception areas to ease the pressure: 240 hostels for difficult children, 443 social centers with occupational clubs, and 157 social clubs.

Children who returned to, or remained in, cities found their homes damaged or threatened by bombing. By November, 1942, one dwelling in five in England and Wales had been damaged, and in some areas two or three out of five. The rate of damage in London was double that for the rest of the country.

The partially bombed buildings opened tremendous opportunities for adventurous play. Children climbed through the ruins with abandon. They dug through the rubble and kept whatever toys, candies, or other attractive objects that they found. Many were brought before the courts where they found that their treasures were regarded as stolen material. They fell under the strict regulations against looting —an activity by adults that netted much larger returns than did the minor depredations by children. The restoration of homes was carried out even while bombing continued. Out of 2,750,000 homes damaged, 2,500,000 had been repaired and restored to occupancy by September, 1942.

The extensive bombing had its corollary in the use of air raid shelters in which families took refuge night after night. More than a million people "lived" in the shelters during the height of the bombing. Many children spent 15 out of 24 hours in the shelters and young workers often circulated between shelters and jobs, going home only on the weekends. There was no privacy in the shelters and also nothing to do. Adolescents drifted from shelter to shelter, often losing contact with their parents. Runaways found it easy to "lose themselves" in the shelters.

School age children who remained in London—about a fifth of the normal number—often found themselves left to their own devices. With their fathers in service and many of their mothers employed, they completely lacked normal supervision and care. Mothers of children under age 14 were not conscripted for war work but often voluntarily took full-time jobs. School buildings were badly damaged or transferred to other uses. Truancy skyrocketed both in London and in the overcrowded schools of reception areas. Few attendance officers remained and often did not insist on attendance. Some children never attended. An effort was made to restore school services and by January, 1941, 81 per cent of school children still remaining in London were in school; by July, 1941, 99 per cent of the child population of the country were in school.

Children above school age (that is, 14 and over) were employed, and often worked overtime. Their wages rose above anything they had known before. They were freed from family control through the conditions cited; and their money was quickly spent in undesirable types of recreation. Girls found soldiers attractive. The increase of delinquency, high for all ages and both sexes, had its peak among girls under 14.

Tensions increased among adults because of fatigue, anxiety about relatives, air attacks, rationing, transportation problems, financial problems, and the future. Children either reacted to the states of mind of their elders or directly shared in the tensions, in addition to which they suffered special tensions of their own, such as an urge for sexual experience in the face of an uncertain future and a desire to share in the excitement of the war or find a substitute for direct participation.

The accounts of the war years do not indicate any radical change in types of delinquency but a distortion of earlier patterns. Thefts and truancy increased radically. Money was spent indiscriminately and sometimes harmfully. Sexual misbehavior of girls increased. Delinquency of both boys and girls increased, but in greater proportion for girls. Special concern was felt for the increase among girls under 14.

While the war was yet in progress, services for children were expanded and plans were laid for improvements as soon as possible. Youth services, recreation, and physical training were increased. Recommendations were made to local authorities for improved methods of handling delinquents. Large country houses were secured and opened for additional Approved Schools. In these and similar ways, an attempt was made to reduce delinquency and to expand facilities.

It is important to note that although services for delinquent children were strained and officials overworked, although short cuts had to be made to care for delinquents (such as sending some youth to prison when Remand—detention—Homes and Borstals could no longer crowd them in), the system for controlling and handling the delinquents did not collapse. Although the normal institutions of family and school were strained and weakened and often temporarily unable to function, they were restored to a semblance of normal operation before the end of the war. England, unlike some of the European countries, did not suffer military defeat or occupation by an enemy army. It did not become the center for refugees or hordes of homeless children. As the following chapter will show, some countries virtually lost control of civilian services and experienced a collapse of normal institutions. England illustrates another pattern—the restoration of normal life at the same time that continued inroads on it occurred, to the end that a balance of some sort was maintained. When the pressures and strains of war were ended, restoration of everyday conditions, and indeed improvement of services, could be quickly set into motion.

SINCE WORLD WAR II

Age of delinquents

Official reports from the Commissioner of Police of the Metropolis of London make it possible to sketch a general picture of delinquency by age. The data are for arrests for indictable (serious) offenses for the year 1959, which seems to be "normal" for the postwar years after the immediate effects of World War II had subsided.[9]

Children of eight, nine, and 10 commit few serious offenses. Indictable offenses begin to become numerous at age 12 and continue to increase until age 14, after which they gradually decline, with a slight rise at age 19. As one might expect, the younger the child the less likely he is to have a previous criminal record. Repeated arrests increase regularly from age eight, when less than 1 per cent have a previous arrest to age 20, when 41 per cent have had one or more arrests. These figures suggest that from among a rather large adolescent population of delinquents, a minority build up a criminal pattern of life that for some will continue into adulthood. More will drop out of the ranks of serious delinquents before adulthood. English criminologists regard much adolescent delinquency and minor crime as a "phase" through which young people, and especially boys, pass before they settle down into maturity. These figures tend to confirm this interpretation.

Delinquency varies with age. Crimes that are popular at one age group may be almost unknown at another. Children and young people of all ages steal some means of transportation. With the eight to 13 age group, stealing of pedal cycles ranks high, with only a very few thefts of automobiles. But when all other types of stealing are grouped together, they far outrank the cycle thefts. Breaking into shops, warehouses, and houses account for most crimes in this young age group, with shoplifting not far behind. The indications are that the amounts stolen are small, and almost no crimes of violence are committed.

In the middle-teen or young persons group, 14 to 16, all types of offenses have increased. Many pedal cycles are still stolen, but thefts of automobiles are also frequent. Larcenies are for larger amounts than among young teenagers.

Among late teenagers or young offenders, aged 17 to 20, crime in general has not only increased, but the pattern of crimes is different. This is the age for crimes of violence and thefts of motor vehicles.

---

[9] *Report of the Commissioner of Police of the Metropolis for the Year 1959*, Her Majesty's Stationery Office, London, 1960, pp. 56-64.

The report gives numbers and percentages by age groups of unequal numbers of years, for example, 8-13 or six years, 14-16 or three years, and 17-20 or four years. Above the age 20, the age groups span 10 years. An average per year of the rates has therefore been used here for comparative purposes.

Thefts of pedal cycles have dropped away. Breaking into buildings has decreased, but the value of larcenies has increased.

The crimes as classified in the report used seem relatively innocuous. Most of them are larcenies, that is, taking property, preferably secretly, without threat or harm to a person. This is a "safe" kind of crime. Larceny does not require manhandling the victim, and the risk of injury or death to either the victim or the offender is low. Violence, which does involve personal contact and therefore risk to the offender, rarely occurs except in the young offender age. Violence includes murder, attempts and threats to murder, rape, manslaughter, wounding, robbery, and indecent assault on females. Of violent offenses, only robbery is a type of stealing, and is rare in comparison with larcenies.

Differences between the sexes

The figures given do not differentiate between boys and girls (12, 17, 35). Other sources indicate that the ratio of boys to girls is high. For example, among young offenders serving sentences in Borstal Institutions, there are more than ten boys to one girl. There are only about 200 Borstal girls in all England. These are the serious offenders, guilty primarily of larceny and with four or five previous convictions.

Studies of delinquents tend to concentrate on boys and to ignore, or only incidentally mention girls. Most of the offenses cited above are typically male offenses—breaking into buildings, stealing pedal cycles and automobiles, and sexual assaults.

A study released in 1965 by the Central Council for Health Education, based on interviews with a sample of 1,853 boys and girls between 15 and 19 years old showed a moderate amount of normal sex relationships. According to a London news report, 21 per cent of the boys and 11 per cent of the girls had engaged in sexual intercourse. It was estimated that by the time these young people were 20, a third of the boys and a quarter of the girls will have had sex experience. It is not clear from the news reports whether the sex experiences are casual and occasional, or habitual and if so on a basis of friendship or of prostitution. These conditions are of more importance than the mere percentages of boys and girls who admitted having engaged in intercourse.

According to descriptive accounts of delinquency, young teenage boys habitually spend their free time together, with only the most casual contacts with girls. Older boys have a more general interest in girls and some girls are open to casual sexual approaches. A limited number of girls begin to solicit on the streets and some boys become "ponces" to them, protecting them from unwanted advances from men, living with them, and being supported by them. For many boys, the interest in casual contacts is a passing one and by the end of the teens, they are seeking steady dating with respectable girls, with marriage, a home, and children in view for the future. The girl may pull out of irregular sexual contacts to marry, or become a professional prostitute. Casual sexual experimentation between boys and girls of the working class seems not to damage the girl's reputation, but prostitution sets her apart.

Proportion of children and youth who are delinquent

Although there is great concern over the increase in delinquency since the 1930's and the failure of rates to decline to the pre-war level, actually the proportion of youth that comes before the courts for indictable offenses is slight—about 2 or 3 per cent. Reports often give numbers of delinquents without taking account of increases in the young population. Only when rates are given are comparisons reliable.

Although overall rates are not startling, the concentration of delinquency in certain types or in certain areas sometimes is. A nationwide problem does not exist, but local and temporary problems do.

SPECIFIC TYPES OF CRIMES

Certain offenses are currently of great concern in the United States and certain European countries, for example, thefts of cars and delinquencies by gangs.

Thefts of motor vehicles

Most car thefts are for temporary use; only a minority are resold, stripped of accessories which are sold, or used in further crime (16). Gibbens, an English writer, says that "the theft of cars, and especially 'taking and driving away without the owner's consent' for the sake of joyriding, is a crime of the times and perhaps destined to be one of the most important forms of nuisance."[10]

[10] T. C. N. Gibbens, "Car Thieves," *British Journal of Delinquency,* 8 (1958), pp. 257-65.

The concentration of arrests for car thefts in ages 14 to 20 and especially between 17 and 20 has already been noted. Arrests for larceny of cars does not tell the whole story. Double the number of vehicles recorded as stolen were driven away without the owner's consent and recovered within 48 hours, usually without knowledge of who the thief was. About a fourth of these had had their contents or fittings stolen. Since the thieves were not discovered, the number attributable to young persons and offenders is not known, but it may be presumed that the proportion would be high.

Although few are stolen by youths with the express purpose of using the car in the commission of a crime, the boy with a "borrowed" car may wind up in a criminal act. Gibbens comments on the process by which the "borrowing" of a car leads into a more serious criminal act. A boy may take a van (truck) and then discover that its contents consist of food, which he then distributes to his friends. Or one boy takes a car and invites his friends for a ride. When the gas is used, with the boys some distance from home, they may break into a garage or may steal money to buy gas. The friends who did not participate in the car theft are drawn into this type of stealing—or face walking home.

When Borstal boys who had been involved only in the car thefts were compared with those convicted of other offenses, the car thieves were found to be less likely than the others to have had previous institutionalization in Approved Schools or non-delinquent institutions, and more likely to be living with both parents. However, they are also more likely to have unstable fathers, neurotic symptoms, five or more previous convictions without institutionalizations, and five or more siblings. The presence of neurotic traits leads Gibbens to the conclusion that the use of a stolen car meets certain neurotic needs, such as unconscious sexual motives, the urge to prove masculinity by a daring act, or the desire for independence and a feeling of power. The middle-class boys were more likely to have these psychological traits in the background, the lower-class boys more unfavorable social factors.

The use of some means of transportation for pleasure began long before the invention of the automobile. An account of London from about 1800 describes the "cutter clubs" organized by young apprentices for pleasure outings in the evenings and on Sunday, an imitation of their masters and the journeymen who had the means to buy or rent the small boats. A group of apprentices might pool their money to buy a boat, or, if not able to do that, to hire one. In the boat, they traveled a short distance up the river away from the city where they could find recreation spots, not always reputable, which required additional money. When they did not have enough money—and many did not—for this form of recreation, they stole it, often from their masters. What is new about automobile theft, borrowing, and stripping of saleable objects, especially among young people, seems to be that a new object of pleasure, the automobile, has replaced older objects including the cutter of a century and a half ago.

Gangs

Gangs in England are notable for their absence—"the non-existent gang" is one writer's phrase (11, 29, 33, 36, 37). A third of the serious crimes by persons under 21 are committed by an individual acting alone. Two or more persons are considered a group. Of 3,652 group crimes committed in Metropolitan London, two-thirds of the groups consisted of only two persons and almost another third of three or four persons, leaving only 4 per cent of group crimes committed by five or more persons. Large groups of 12 or more were virtually unknown—only one such group in a year's time was brought to court.

It might be argued that boys might belong to gangs but commit delinquencies individually or by twos or threes. This argument might be a good one, since the most frequent crimes, housebreaking and larceny, are not large-group types of offenses. Also, in English writings, gangs are rigidly defined. They are considered to be groups with a leader, definite membership, continuity through a period of time, a meeting place, initiation ceremonies, and criminal objectives. The failure to find gangs is in part because of the rigidity of this definition.

Small groups of friends who habitually meet at some certain coffee bar or cafe, plan delinquencies, and carry them out are found. One writer speaks of a nucleus of five boys who not only were frequently drunk and disorderly but who planned housebreaking and shoplifting in detail. In time, this group was dispersed by convictions for delinquencies. A "fringe" group surrounded this small nucleus, but seems not to have been involved in the planned delinquent activities. These groups, whether nucleus or fringe, do not meet the

British definition of a structured gang.

A comparison of gang delinquents with other types of delinquents showed that among 320 offenders in London courts, only 11 per cent were in gangs proper.[11] The most serious offenses, however, were committed by the gangs. These gangs consisted of three or four boys, one of whom was the leader.

Adolescent street groups

These groups are at the opposite point from the delinquency-oriented gangs (37) Scott, who used the term, says they consist of five to 30 boys (in some cases girls are tolerated) who congregate in a certain area which, in time, they feel "belongs" to them. They are more interested in companionship with other young people and a search for recreation than in delinquency.

In one account of "unattached" youth, Morse seems to be dealing essentially with the same type as Scott categorized as street groups.[12] The term "unattached" refers simply to young people who are not affiliated with clubs sponsored by some adult organization. They are not social isolates as the word might imply; in fact, they are very group-minded with others of their kind.

The boys described by Morse were employed, lived at home, paid part of their wages to their mothers, and spent the rest freely on amusements, drinking, clothes, and girls. Girls also were employed and spent money freely, often paying for their own amusements, or lending money to the boys, although their wages were less. Their chief interests were social life and parties; they often traveled 20 to 40 miles for a party or dance, or just to meet other young people. They came by bus, motorcycles, old secondhand cars, or by hitch-hiking; "borrowing" cars is not mentioned. Parties were of several kinds. Small ones were held at someone's home, preferably when parents were not at home. If the parents were away for the weekend, the party might stretch out this long. Larger parties were held in a barn or shed. Drink, music, dancing, and some degree of sexual activity were characteristic. Some degree of sexual activity was regarded as natural, although prostitution was frowned upon.

---

[11] Peter Scott, "Gangs and Delinquent Groups in London," *British Journal of Delinquency,* 7 (July, 1956), pp. 8-12.

[12] Mary Morse, *The Unattached,* Penguin Books, 1965.

Loose antisocial groups

Between the small proportion of delinquents in gangs and the many pleasure-seeking adolescent street groups are the loose antisocial groups, the setting for most delinquency (27, 33, 37). These groups are diffuse, unstructured, and without a permanent leader. First one youth, then another, acts as leader. Scott terms this leader a temporary catalyst, who sparks delinquent tendencies already present but does not have the qualities of continued leadership. Among the groups studied, the average number involved in a delinquent act was three and the average age 13. (Scott's study is limited to boys aged eight through 16 and does not cover the young offender group aged 17 to 20.)

In terms of damage done, 42 per cent of offenses were serious; 21 per cent caused considerable damage. However, as many as 37 per cent of offenses were trivial.

Scott also identifies two other types of delinquent association of the same general type as the antisocial groups, in the sense that they are not structured: the fleeting casual delinquent association that develops on the spur of the moment and the groups of friends and siblings who sometimes get into trouble. Offenses tend to be trivial in both types.

A description given by Morse that seems to fit the antisocial street group comes from an industrial city in the north of England. The youths in question habitually gathered in a dockside coffee bar. They ranged in age from about 14 to 20. The older boys formed a small gang of five or 10 members, strongly oriented to crime and with a long history of trouble with the police, court appearances, and time spent in Approved Schools. Poorly educated, they were unstable in job-holding. When they needed money, they planned thefts instead of looking for work. The older teens, 17 and 18 years old, were generally employed but were rebellious and cynical. The younger group, 14 to 16 years old, through associating with the older boys showed tendencies toward duplicating their behavior. The group as a whole is described as dissatisfied, bored, restless; they enjoyed being destructive because there seemed to be nothing constructive to do. Their solution was getting drunk, smashing windows, and fighting. Groups of girls also congregated in the coffee bar, varying from the fairly respectable to those who solicited on the streets. The boys were scornful of the girls but at least some paired off with them.

Sex relations were a normal part of this pairing off.

Teddy Boys, Mods, and Rockers

Professional criminologists have given little direct attention to youths who set themselves apart in appearance—the Teddy Boys of the 1950's and their successors in the 1960's, the Mods and Rockers (14, 21, 38). These groups have provided a heyday for journalists and from time to time a problem for the police. In terms of Scott's categories, they seem to fall primarily into the loose antisocial type of group.

Teddy Boy is a somewhat amusing and derisive diminutive of Edward, based on extreme fashions of clothing that were a caricature of fashionable clothing worn about 1900-1910 in the Edwardian era. One Teddy Boy defended the type of clothing: "Old Edward (King Edward VII) really lived. He drank like a fish, ate like a swine, slept with anything he could get his hands on. Edward revolted against the hypocrisy of his times, and so are we.[13]

The extreme and conspicuous clothing was worn by numerous adolescent boys when they congregated on certain streets and in the amusement places, first in London and then in other cities. The clothing was expensive and hence available only to boys who were employed or had other sources of income. Various references speak of employed working-class boys going home from work, changing into their Teddy Boy clothing and then moving rapidly into the chosen areas where they could mingle with others of their kind. They were not organized into clubs or gangs.

In time this clothing fad died down and was replaced by other extreme styles. The original Teddy Boys had grown up and settled into adult life. Their successors of the early 1960's were the Mods and Rockers. The Mods (from modish or modernist) were middle-class adolescents and youth; their counterpart in a lower social class was the Rocker (from rock-and-roll music). These young people, as those who preceded them, defined life as dull and boring and their parents as old-fashioned. To this view of life was added the clash between Mods and Rockers based on social class differences.

Most of these extremely dressed youth, by whatever name they are called, seem to be less criminal than restless and publicly rude. Small

---

[13] Lloyd Shearer, "Why They Dress That Way," *Parade,* (October 16, 1966), p. 30.

groups among them are seriously delinquent. From time to time, large outbreaks of disorder temporarily erupt and engage the attention of the police. Occasionally during such an outbreak, someone is killed. Some of the youth carry knives or other dangerous weapons, and in a spontaneous uproar, bottles or legs of chairs are used to attack others. However, the usual behavior does not include violence.

Youth riots

It seems probable that youth riots would occur regardless of the type of clothing worn by dissatisfied and socially deviant youth (1, 14, 19, 42). Given a mass of restless and unorganized youth, a precipitating incident may involve first small groups and then larger and more diffuse aggregations. The initial disturbance may be spearheaded by a gang, or may be planned in advance. Active participants are supplied by the fringe adherents. The riots seem to resemble each other in that they arise from some temporary clash or grow out of some long-held prejudice. They are not purposeful in any long-range manner, and are not part of a planned program for social change.

In the 1950's and '60's, small riots occurred in motion picture houses in a spontaneous manner when certain rock-and-roll films were shown: seats were torn up and various persons assaulted while the boys shouted and yelled. Other riots centered on areas in cities into which large numbers of Negro West Indians had moved after World War II. Tension was based on housing, employment, and the association between white girls and Negro men (a result of an unbalanced sex ratio among the Negroes). The first large outbreak came in Nottingham when white and colored youth fought with improvised but dangerous weapons. Thousands of people were drawn into the brawl with many injuries. The crowds were dispersed within a few hours. A week later, when white youth congregated to resume the fight, police succeeded in dispersing them, a move that brought a clash between the white youth and the police. Nine leaders of the original riot were sentenced to prison.

Other brief fights that spread from dances or bars to the streets often arose from antagonism between rival groups or gangs. A few angry words might set off the fight which spread from the original contestants to others already at hand or attracted by the noise.

Another riot that received wide publicity at the time came at

Easter, 1964, when hundreds of Mods and Rockers headed for Claxton for the holiday and came head-on into collision. When the holiday ended and the Mods and Rockers returned to their jobs in London, 170 remained behind in the hands of the police. At their trials, they received sentences of up to three months in jail or fines of from $140 to $210.

Both the sporadic fights between rival gangs and the large unplanned riots occur only occasionally, reach a high pitch of emotion and action, and then subside. As a rule, they last for only a few hours, at the most for a few days. They bring a convergence of police forces from local and nearby stations. In England, more than in some other countries, they are treated with great seriousness, and severe sentences are passed on the leaders.

Riots differ from intergang tussles carried out as a competitive demonstration of strength or to establish the right to monopolize a certain coffee bar or neighborhood. These fights fall into a pattern that may be repeated. The large-scale riot may occur once and never again; the holiday disturbances may be an exception when they tend to become annual events and even part of the fun. Both riots and fights include a certain amount of violence and occasionally unplanned deaths.

Riots and gang fights both differ from the run-of-the-mill delinquencies—usually thefts—that occur from time to time, perhaps when opportunity presents itself, or with previous planning. Among youth, stealing is closely related to the immediate need for money when expenditures outrun wages or when a car is needed for specific and temporary use. Consequently, the amounts stolen are small. The carefully planned thefts that net the thieves huge sums of money are the work of mature and skilled thieves.

ENGLISH EXPLANATIONS OF DELINQUENCY

Studies of delinquency in England have passed beyond the purely descriptive or survey stage and seek explanations for a type of behavior that has been part of the life of English youth for centuries. Sometimes the studies include the testing of theories originating in the United States, which arrived at theorizing in the field of delinquency somewhat earlier than England did. English writers offer a number of explanations, which to date have not been coordinated into a comprehensive explanation of theory, a shortcoming also true in the United States. It is obviously impossible to attempt a coordination here; the various explanations are given below as they have appeared from English criminologists with different interests and backgrounds.

1. During the 1930's and continuing to date, much of the attempt to explain delinquency has centered in psychological studies based on clinical cases.[14] This approach has tended to ignore social factors. For example, Scott, whose interesting classification of groups has been cited above, strongly emphasizes psychological disturbances. He says that gang members who come before the courts usually have gross antisocial character defects and come from a family background where the emotional atmosphere is disturbed and detrimental. In individual cases he speaks of "managing" mothers, inadequate fathers, rejection of the children; he also refers to boys who are antisocial, rigid, insecure, and so on.

Morris, who classifies delinquents as psychiatric or social, estimates that a fifth or a fourth of English delinquents are of the psychiatric type, leaving the great majority as social delinquents whose socialization has been into commonly accepted patterns of delinquency. Psychiatric factors are applicable primarily to a minority of delinquents as the major force toward delinquency.[15] Morris regards the 20 to 25 per cent of psychiatric delinquents as responding primarily to their inner tensions and emotional disturbances and secondarily to cultural patterns of delinquency. The 75 to 80 per cent of social delinquents are the product of social factors, primarily, and secondarily of inner tensions. Morris concluded that normal social delinquents passed through a delinquent phase to emerge as conforming adults, whereas psychiatric delinquents became the hard core of adult criminals.

2. Intergenerational conflicts—bored youth seeking a new way of life versus complacent elders who have accepted their situation in life—provide another explanation. These conflicts are closely related to the concept of a youth culture, a way of life devised and supported by youth who through it seek new outlets, find their own diversions, tolerate their own deviations, and give support and status to youth

---

[14] Howard Jones, *Crime in a Changing Society,* Penguin Books, 1965.

[15] Terence Morris, *The Criminal Area,* Routledge & Kegan Paul, London, 1957.

regardless of the reaction of their elders.[16] The youth culture supersedes the general culture for a period of about six years, after which the adolescent outgrows the subculture and reenters the general adult-dominated culture in which, as adults, they then have a respected place.

Youth culture may be regarded as marginal to both conforming behavior and outright delinquency. Opposing adult pressures toward conformity and yet resisting outright delinquency, youth become overtly hostile and aggressive. When this pattern of life is based on delinquent values and behavior, a delinquent subculture is thought to be prevalent. In England, the antisocial street groups, with the Teddy Boys, Mods and Rockers, and the few gangs give support to this concept.

3. Another approach is based on social class differences. The lower social class contributes heavily to delinquency according to statistics of arrests or court appearances. English data drawn from a National Survey of Health and Development made in 1946 fixes the highest rate of delinquency in the lower manual working class.[17] The rate of delinquency is four times as high in the semi-skilled and unskilled laboring classes as in the salaried and professional classes, the percentages being approximately 20 and 5. Between these extremes are the black-coated workers, 10 per cent of whose sons are delinquent, and the foremen and skilled workers, 15 per cent of whose sons are delinquent. The occupational differences are especially marked for children guilty of indictable (serious) offenses and for repeaters.

Explanation of social class differences takes two forms. One is that certain types of delinquency are imbedded in the normal culture—the values and everyday behavior—of the lower or working class. Delinquency and some forms of crime are in the adult culture and are passed on to children in the normal processes by which parents transmit to their children the values and normal kinds of behavior that they themselves hold to be good. This approach is strongly held by Morris in his study of Croydon, England, and by W. B. Miller in his

[16] John Barron Mays, "Teen-age Culture in Contemporary Britain and Europe," *Annals of the American Academy of Political and Social Science,* 338 (1961), pp. 23-32; *The Young Pretenders,* Schocken Books, 1965.

[17] J. W. B. Douglas and D. G. Mulligan, "Delinquency and Social Class," *British Journal of Criminology,* 6 (1966), pp. 294-302.

study of the United States.[18]

The other explanation that links delinquency with social class emanates from the writings of Cohen in the United States. Cohen's hypothesis is that much lower-class delinquency is a reaction to the frustrated desire of lower-class youth to become upwardly mobile and to share in the advantages of middle-class life. Denied the opportunity to move upward through lack of education and limited social advantages and by rejection by the middle class, these youth develop a specific type of youth culture—the delinquent subculture. The characteristics of the subculture are as follows: formation of gangs that support the subculture; non-utilitarian types of delinquency; hostility and malice; negativism or reversing the value scale of the middle class; versatility in acts of delinquency; short-run hedonism or seeking immediate pleasures; and group autonomy or rejection of outside authority.[19]

Cohen's hypothesis and supporting arguments have been carefully examined by certain English criminologists but not fully accepted. Downes, in particular, has rejected the hypothesis as an explanation of delinquency in two old East London dock communities, Stepney and Poplar.[20] Although there was some feeling of envy and frustration, the norm in the lower class was acceptance of lower-class status. Education that ended for most at the age of 15 and the tradition of class stability motivated against a desire for upward mobility. Full employment and wages that were unusually high for adolescents (although not so for adults) made for acceptance of the working-class status and way of life. Although some parts of Cohen's hypothesis applied to one or the other of the two communities, as a whole, the hypothesis did not fit.

4. Mass communication has been held responsible in part for the growth and temporary fame of the Teddy Boys and similar groups. Publicity in newspapers and on radio and television carried the Teddy Boys to fame. Boys learned of the extravagant dress and the

---

[18] Morris, *op. cit.;* W. B. Miller, "Implications of Urban Lower-Class Culture for Social Work," *Social Service Review,* 33 (1955), pp. 219-36; "Lower-Class Culture as a Generating Milieu of Gang Delinquency," *Journal of Social Issues,* 14, No. 3 (1958), pp. 5-19.

[19] A. K. Cohen, *Delinquent Boys: The Culture of the Gang,* Free Press, 1955.

[20] David M. Downes, *The Delinquent Solution, A Study in Subcultural Theory,* Free Press, 1966.

occasional outbursts of fighting and rioting through the mass media. Dress and behavior, originating in local neighborhoods in London, were imitated in other neighborhoods and other cities. The public reacted with shock and horror to some of the activities, but also with curiosity and excitement. Eccentricity and violence were expected of Teddy Boys, and the Teddy Boys responded by trying to meet these expectations. How far this explanation can be used to account for the swelling, expansion, and decline of Teddy Boyism is not clear, but specific instances in England (and also on the continent) give some credence to the explanation.[21]

In another way, mass communication furthered some incidents of rowdiness and vandalism. Rock-and-roll music, imported from the United States, and certain violent types of motion pictures aroused excited emotional responses and led to some outbursts of vandalism. Not only did initial stimulus come through media of mass communication, but the reports of outbursts through the same kind of media further stimulated violence.

5. Unstructured leisure has long been thought to explain the high rates of delinquency. As the work week has shortened, the hours of leisure have lengthened. The affluence of adolescents and their parents provides money to be spent on leisure, and encourages commercial interests to provide recreation not always of a constructive type. England has established a system of Youth Services which includes youth clubs and centers with salaried leaders.[22] These establishments provide a variety of recreational and cultural experiences. They must compete, however, with nearby commercial institutions—the motion picture theater, dance halls, and coffee bars where young people regularly gather. Various accounts indicate that, in general, it is young people who are not delinquently oriented (the adolescent street groups) or who are only at the threshold of adolescence who make use of the official clubs and centers. The antisocial groups and gangs collect in the coffee bars and commercial amusement centers where they are without supervision and do not need to enter into supervised activities that perhaps demand continued or regular attendance

---

[21] T. R. Fyvel, *Troublemakers, Rebellious Youth in a Affluent Society,* Schocken Books, 1961, p. 70.

[22] John Barron Mays, *On the Threshold of Delinquency,* Liverpool University Press, 1959; *Youth Service in England and Wales,* Her Majesty's Stationery Office, 1960.

to complete some specific project. The clubs and centers fill a need and perhaps prevent a drift toward delinquency, but they do not seem to provide the answer for definite delinquency prevention.[23]

6. Poverty, unemployment, poor housing, slum disorganization, and lack of education form a related time-honored explanation of delinquency, which has had to be modified.

With the many welfare services that prevent or bridge financial crises, poverty and pauperism are very much a thing of the past in England. Employment is full for both adults and adolescents. Adolescents have ample spending money left over after they have paid something to their parents. They do not always manage the spending wisely, and a few do not hold their jobs. But for most adolescents over 15, lack of money is not a major problem. Delinquency continues, with many members of antisocial street groups holding regular jobs. The costly Teddy Boy and other extravagant costumes are possible largely because adolescents and youth have free money of their own.

Much of the oldest and poorest housing has been razed and replaced by housing estates (public housing). Morris found pockets of delinquency in Croydon (a suburban city near London).[24] These pockets were scattered throughout the community in the older housing projects, built between the two world wars. Individual estates tended to have a middle-class section and a lower-class section, differentiated by size, amount of rent, and desirability of location within the estate. The lower-class sections had built up a tradition of lower-class culture, complete with accepted or tolerated delinquent behavior. In addition, an old working-class residential area had the same traditional lower-class culture. The residents of these areas accepted their working-class status, and did not tend to move out. The continuance of delinquency seemed related to the traditional culture, and not to type of housing.

The identification of delinquency as part of lower-class culture led Morris to discard the United States ecological explanation that much delinquency is part of the social disorganization inherent in slum areas—the disorganization related to the process of growth of American cities whereby the transition of land from residential use to business and commercial use leads to neglect and deterioration. In the

[23] Morse, *op. cit.*

[24] Morris, *op. cit.*, Chapters 7 and 11.

United States, these deteriorating areas witnessed for years the passage of immigrants into and through them and out into the city proper, the passage covering often the length of a generation. No matter which ethnic group was in the process of transition, the delinquency rate remained high. It was recognized that the physical deterioration was simply the very observable symbol of the social confusion and conflict that marked the transitional stage between an Old World peasant culture and the unfamiliar United States urban culture. This tying of a high delinquency rate with social disorganization in a given geographical area led to a tripartite ecological theory of delinquency which related physical deterioration on the one hand to the reception of immigrants and their resulting problems of adjustment and, on the other, to the transition in land use. In Croydon, Morris found much greater stability of land use and few transient groups. He therefore replaced the ecological theory with the lower-social-class theory of a permanent strain of delinquency as normal lower-class behavior.

England has sought to open educational opportunities to children of working-class people by channeling children into modern secondary schools that terminate their education at age 15 or into grammar schools that they may attend until age 18 or 19. The compulsory school attendance age is 15. The channeling is made on the basis of an examination taken at age 11. Students in the grammar schools have the further opportunity to apply for entrance at a university. This widening of educational opportunities has not served to lessen delinquency, as some had anticipated. Some children, eligible for the grammar schools, decline to go and others start but drop out. With a working-class background and family tradition, they prefer to remain in the old neighborhood and the familiar types of work. On the other hand, children who fail to pass the test and are assigned to the modern secondary school often feel rejected and hampered—they were not given a chance to go on. The conclusion to be drawn from some writings is that if anything this scheme of education has increased dissatisfaction and added to the restlessness of many adolescents.[25]

Delinquency in England is not a new phenomenon. A glance back through history shows that in many periods of the past, the amount and seriousness of delinquency and crime far surpass anything of the

[25] Downes, *op. cit.*, pp. 259-67.

present. There was an underworld, delinquent subcultures, individual and gang crimes, widespread vice, demoralization of girls and women, and atrocious methods of trying to curb excesses. What is new is different occasions for old disturbances, such as riots growing out of racial tensions, "borrowing" of automobiles, and delinquency among lower-class adolescents who have been relieved of old handicaps of slum housing and poverty. What is new also is the serious research being carried out in the effort to discover the bases of delinquency which seem much more subtle than the old familiar themes of poverty, unemployment, and poor housing.

REFERENCES

1. " 'astings Haint 'ad it so Bad since 1066." *Life,* 57 (September 18, 1964), pp. 61-62.
2. BARRY, SIR JOHN. "The Founding Felons of Australia." *Hartwick Review,* 2 (Fall, 1966), pp. 29-35.
3. BATHURST, M. E. "Juvenile Delinquency in Britain during the War." *Journal of Criminal Law,* 34 (1944), pp. 291-302.
4. BOLL, E. S. "Britain's Experience with Adolescents." *Annals of the American Academy of Political and Social Science,* 236 (1944), pp. 74-82.
5. *British Journal of Criminology,* 6 (April, 1966). Entire issue on White Paper, "The Child, the Family, and the Young Offender."
6. CADOGAN, EDWARD. *Roots of Evil.* John Murray, London, 1937.
7. CARR-SAUNDERS, A. M., HERMANN MANNHEIM, and E. C. RHODES. *Young Offenders, An Inquiry into Juvenile Delinquency.* University Press, Cambridge, England, 1944.
8. CLINARD, MARSHALL B. *Slums and Community Development, Experiments in Self-Help.* Free Press, 1966.
9. COHEN, A. K. *Delinquent Boys: The Culture of the Gang.* Free Press, 1955.
10. DOUGLAS, J. W. B. and D. G. MULLIGAN. "Delinquency and Social Class." *British Journal of Criminology,* 6 (1966), pp. 294-302.
11. DOWNES, DAVID N. *Delinquent Solution, A Study in Subcultural Theory.* Free Press, 1966.
12. EPPS, P. "A Preliminary Survey of 300 Female Delinquents in Borstal Institutions." *British Journal of Delinquency,* 1 (1950-51), pp. 187-97.
13. FOX, LIONEL W. *English Prison and Borstal Systems.* Routledge & Kegan Paul, London, 1952.
14. FYVEL, T. R. *Trouble Makers, Rebellious Youth in an Affluent Society.* Schocken Books, 1962.
15. GEORGE, M. DOROTHY. *London Life in the Eighteenth Century.* Harper and Row, 1964.

16. GIBBENS, T. C. N. "Car Thieves." *British Journal of Delinquency,* 8 (1958), pp. 257-65.
17. GOSLING, JOHN and DOUGLAS WARNER. *Shame of a City, An Inquiry into the Vice of London.* W. H. Allen, London, 1960.
18. GREGG, PAULINE. *Social and Economic History of Britain, 1760-1955.* George C. Harrap and Company, London, 1950, 1956.
19. JEGER, L. M. "After Clacton." *New Statesman,* 67 (May 1, 1964), p. 675.
20. JONES, HOWARD. *Crime in a Changing Society.* Penguin Books, 1965.
21. LAURIE, PETER. "So Young, So Cool, So Misunderstood: Mods and Rockers." *Vogue,* 144 (August 1, 1964), pp. 68-69ff.
22. LIPSET, S. M. *The First New Nation, The United States in Historical and Comparative Perspective.* Basic Books, 1963.
23. LUNDEN, WALTER A. *War and Delinquency.* The Art Press, Ames, Iowa, 1963.
24. MANNHEIM, HERMANN. *Social Aspects of Crime in England between the Wars.* George Allen and Unwin, London, 1940.
25. MANTOUX, PAUL J. *Industrial Revolution in the Eighteenth Century.* J. Cape, London, 1961.
26. MAYS, JOHN BARRON. *On the Threshold of Delinquency.* Liverpool University Press, Liverpool, England, 1959.
27. MAYS, JOHN BARRON. "A Study of a Delinquent Community." *British Journal of Juvenile Delinquency,* 3 (1952-53), pp. 5-19.
28. MAYS, JOHN BARRON. "Teen-age Culture in Contemporary Britain and Europe." *Annals of the American Academy of Political and Social Science,* 338 (1961), pp. 22-32.
29. MAYS, JOHN BARRON. *Young Pretenders.* Schocken Books, 1965.
30. MILLER, W. B. "Implications of Urban Lower-class Culture for Social Work." *Social Service Review,* 33 (1955), pp. 219-36.
31. MILLER, W. B. "Lower-class Culture as a Generating Milieu of Gang Delinquency." *Journal of Social Issues,* 14, No. 3 (1958), pp. 5-19.
32. MORRIS, TERENCE. *Criminal Area, A Study in Social Ecology.* Routledge & Kegan Paul, London, 1957.
33. MORSE, MARY. *The Unattached.* Penguin Books, 1965.
34. PRINGLE, PATRICK. *Hue and Cry, The Story of Henry and John Fielding and their Bow Street Runners.* Wm. Morrow and Co., London, 1955.
35. *Prisons and Borstals, England and Wales.* Her Majesty's Stationery Office, London, 1957.
36. *Report of the Commissioner of Police of the Metropolis for the year 1959.* Her Majesty's Stationery Office, London, 1960.
37. SCOTT, PETER. "Gangs and Delinquent Groups in London." *British Journal of Delinquency,* 7 (1956-57), pp. 4-26.
38. SHEARER, LLOYD. "Why They Dress That Way." *Parade* (October 16, 1966), p. 30.

39. SIMMONS, M. M. *Making Citizens.* His Majesty's Stationery Office, London, 1945.
40. SUSSMAN, F. B. *Juvenile Delinquency.* Oceana Publications, 1959.
41. TEETERS, NEGLEY K. and J. O. REINEMANN. *Challenge of Delinquency.* Prentice-Hall, 1950.
42. WHARTON, K. "Road to Clacton Pier." *Spectator,* 212 (1964), pp. 444-45.
43. *Youth Service in England and Wales.* Report of the Committee Appointed by the Minister of Education in November, 1958. Her Majesty's Stationery Office, London, 1960.

8 / Eight European Countries: Delinquency in Western Societies

This chapter is a supplement to the latter part of the preceding chapter on England. The discussion of World War II demonstrates the delinquent and criminal reactions to the different types of havoc created by war, some of which differed from England's experience. England did not suffer, as some European countries did, from defeat and enemy occupation, nor did it find itself overrun at war's end by hordes of detached children and displaced persons and refugees from other countries whose national affiliation had been changed abruptly.

The latter part of the chapter rounds out the discussion of delinquency in western countries at the present time. Most noticeable are the striking similarities among the countries, including England, in postwar types of delinquency, the frequency and prevalence of different delinquencies, and certain underlying causes. These similarities attest to the comparability of social, economic, and political conditions in the countries, as well as to the speed with which the mass media carry delinquency-stimulating news, fiction, and music from one part of the world to another. Publication of news of atrocious gang fights, magnificent thefts, and outrageous riots bring to each country in turn those crimes and disturbances delinquents in other countries are engaging in and the appropriate behavior for each.

EFFECTS OF WORLD WAR II

Upward trends in frequency of delinquency during and after World War II

Generally speaking, juvenile delinquency increased during the period of actual fighting, not only in the countries that were the sites of battle or subject to occupation, but in countries whose military men traveled overseas to enter the conflict (Canada and the United States), and even in adjacent neutral nations, for example, Sweden and Switzerland (1, 10, 11, 20, 21, 26, 29).

Sometimes the war and its aftermath produced a roller-coaster effect in delinquency rates. In France, which suffered from early involvement in the war, bombing, and occupation by German troops, the number of cases of juveniles under age 18 brought to the attention of authorities almost trebled between 1937 and 1942. The number then declined irregularly to 1954 when it was below that for 1937, after which a slow increase began. The period of great increase was chiefly during the years of German occupation and the early period of liberation.

In some countries record-keeping broke down for a year or more. In the Netherlands convicted juvenile offenders increased markedly between 1940 and 1943, at which time the number was more than double the prewar level. During 1944-45 it was impossible to assemble and keep records. By 1946 the trend was again downward and by 1949 was similar to the prewar levels, though, subsequently, it rose sharply. The Netherlands also had to cope with a large number of youth under age 18 who were guilty of aid to the enemy during the period of German occupation, 1940-45. Those guilty of violence were sentenced to prison; many more were placed in camps from which they could go outside to work. Two-thirds of the total were released by 1947 under certain restraints. Many different factors lay behind these offenses, some of which were the same as for the delinquencies of normal times. Girls, who constituted about a fourth of the offenders, often served as prostitutes to soldiers of the occupation.

For Norway and Denmark, reports refer only to young people over age 14 (Norway) or 15 (Denmark) guilty of serious offenses; all younger children and non-serious older offenders were handled by child welfare councils. In Denmark, rates per 100,000 of the equivalent population for male offenders aged 15 to 20 brought before the courts doubled between 1938 and 1943. By 1958 the rate had declined to about one and a half times the 1938 rate. Later, the trend was upward.

In Norway, from 1940 to 1945, the German military forces administered the police system, courts, and prisons. The statistics no doubt reflect this shift in authority as well as actual trends of delinquency. For the age group, 14 to 17 years, the number of offenders *in prison* reached a peak in 1942; for the age group 18 to 20, the number rose and held to a high level between 1942 and 1944. With the end of the war and restoration of civilian authority, the numbers dropped abruptly, apparently as a result of the release of many of these offenders. However, between 1954 and 1960 the trend turned upward. The offenses for which they had been imprisoned included not only the customary ones but violation of restrictions imposed by the German army, such as possession of radios and firearms, as well as activities in the Norwegian underground movement. It should be noted that the decline after the war was followed by a marked increase in the 1950's.

The pattern of change in Italy was somewhat different from that in other countries. Italy had had a steady decrease in juvenile delinquency from the beginning of the twentieth century, the exceptions being both world wars. World War II showed a decrease during the years of actual combat, perhaps because of diminished supervision by police, a reluctance to report crimes, or disorganized statistical computations. In the postwar years, delinquency increased until conditions became more stable again, when a decrease occurred.

For Germany, from which complete statistics are not available, an American criminologist noted that in 1945-47, immediately after Germany's defeat, the frequency of juvenile delinquency rose above both the prewar and the wartime levels. The currency reform of 1948, with attendant economic stabilization and the establishment of the Federal Republic of West Germany in 1949, was accompanied by a trend toward normal conditions and a decrease in the frequency of delinquency. After a low point in 1954, the trend was again upward.

The situation in Belgium is treated in more detail, based on a special study that traces social changes year by year through the critical period of the war, and subsequent readjustment to normal conditions.

Belgium in World War II

Belgium went through several stages during the extended war period.[1] Military mobilization, beginning September 1, 1939, was a disturbing experience, with the movement of troops, establishment of

[1] The information on Belgium is primarily from Aimée Racine, *La délinquance juvénile en Belgique de 1939 à 1957*. Centre d'Etude de la Délinquance Juvénile, Publication No. 2. Brussels, 1959. This is supplemented from less extensive sources.

defensive positions in the rural areas, and the improvisation of cantonments in cities and villages. From May 10 to 28, 1940, Belgium fought Germany on its own soil, following which the victorious German forces occupied the country. In the autumn of 1944, Belgium was liberated by the Allied forces, after intense fighting against the German forces, until early in 1945. The subsequent occupation by Allied troops was temporary and friendly, but nevertheless disturbing and accompanied by its own special types of delinquency.

Cases of juvenile delinquency increased sharply as soon as Belgium became involved, and especially after the German occupation. The peak year for boys was 1942 and for girls 1943, true both for referrals to juvenile court and for convictions. Younger children, under age 10, were affected earliest and with a greater percentage of increase over 1939. In numbers, however, the age group 13 to 15 inclusive, far exceeded any other three-year age span in the juvenile period, which in Belgium ends with age 18.

For all types of delinquency, the increase from 1939 to 1942 was 239 per cent. Thefts, the most frequent form of delinquency at all times, before, during and after the war, showed next-to-the-highest increase.

Boys experienced an amount of freedom previously unknown. Many joined a movement to reach France. Others followed whatever army currently was in authority in Belgium. In their pillaging forays, they traveled further and further from home. This freedom was made possible in part by the damaging and closing of schools, augmented by the loosening of family controls. The fathers of many had entered the Belgium army in 1939-40 and later were in prison or forced labor camps outside Belgium. With the father (the authoritarian figure) absent from home or dead, the mother found herself unable to exercise control over her adolescent children. Some women became disloyal to their marriage; the number of divorces doubled from 1939 to 1942.

Girls also emerged from the protection of the home, often into some form of prostitution. Soldiers of any country provided a wide market for their services. In some cases, the mothers encouraged their daughters, partly from need for money or food. An increase of venereal disease and illicit pregnancies was noted.

In normal times, there were few beggars in Belgium, but begging by children and adolcscents increased during the war. The closed schools permitted children to beg day and night. Entrances to railway stations and stores were favorite stations for their activities.

The weakening of school and family controls and the resulting freedom of children had other effects than delinquency. Youth were imbued with a spirit of independence and desire for adventure. Some of the delinquent acts were a response to actual shortages of necessities, but others were a response to a frenzy of desire for fun and adventure among both boys and girls. Personal demoralization was apparently part of the result of the disorganization of social institutions and the experience of military dominance during the occupation.

The defeat of Germany freed Belgium from an enemy occupation but brought occupation by the Allied troops. This defeat was obtained only after intense fighting by German and Allied forces with additional physical destruction and hardships for civilians. Temporarily, disorganized behavior increased, and the means of control further declined. The Allied soldiers, well cared for and with an appearance of opulence, caught the imagination of adolescents. Girls, in a sentiment of patriotism or attracted by the uniform, readily made sexual contacts with the soldiers. Their parents imposed little interference, either because of gratitude for their liberation, for financial gain, or in hope of marriage for their daughters. Dance halls, open late or all night, provided a ready meeting place.

Boys also responded to the situation. They roamed the streets in bands or gangs that made their headquarters in unused anti-aircraft shelters. Young boys hung around military camps where they were befriended by indulgent soldiers. Thefts by juveniles continued, as did the black market.

As normal conditions returned, the schools, police, courts, and welfare agencies again gained control of the young, children were brought back into normal social relationships and delinquency decreased, although not to the level of 1939. Among the postwar delinquents were older youth who had collaborated with the Germans; they were placed in special institutions for rehabilitation and later returned to civilian society.

In summarizing their studies of wartime delinquency in Belgium, the Centre d'Etude de la Délinquance Juvénile states that a comparison of Belgium with other European countries involved in World War II showed that Belgium represented a general pattern (19). Both delinquency and adult crime increased, largely in response to the same social situations. The principal causes were the scarcity of consumer goods and the appearance of the black market for easy disposal of illegal merchandise. Added to this was the presence of the army of occupation, against which deception and contempt of authority were not condemned nor considered criminal. War did not render people more bloodthirsty, more sadistic, more shameful, or more crafty. The offenses were primarily against property for use or sale, with a lower increase in crimes against the person. However, this normal predominance of stealing was greatly increased.

The opportunities for delinquency were one part of the situation. The other was the weakening or complete loss of normal institutions of social control—the family, the school, regular employment, and the police.

THE IMMEDIATE POSTWAR YEARS

With the end of the war, delinquencies closely related to the war decreased, but postwar conditions in certain countries brought new problems, marginal deviancy, and offenses, which in turn were also brought under control. One of the most troublesome was juvenile vagrancy.

Certain European countries were flooded with vagrant children and youth who were without means of support from the normal sources of parents or employment. The word vagrant is used both for children who wander about aimlessly, more or less criminally inclined, having no link left with their original home or surroundings, and for children who live at home at least part of the time but spend their days in complete and unregulated freedom. The discussion that follows may be compared with the similar discussion for India in Chapter 4, where the term is used in somewhat the same way.

France

A report for France in the 1940's notes that street children were not a direct result of the war—they existed before and are described as preferring the streets to their homes, which tended to be unstable (33). They divided their time between motion pictures, fairs, swimming pools, and ball games. Poorly educated and unemployed, they pilfered and stole. Sex claimed an undue amount of interest. The war gave indirect support to this way of life. Family instability increased when fathers were deported; family anxieties ran high. Boys stole from the Germans and exchanged the articles for food or sold them on the black market. After the withdrawal of German troops and the return of deported men, many of these manifestations declined, though not without some difficulties, as families attempted to reunite and restore the father's status as head of the family.

Federal Republic of Germany (West Germany)

In West Germany, the situation was quite different (14, 29, 33). In 1945-49 it was estimated that there were 15 million refugees and expellees in Germany, of whom four or five million were children and adolescents. Housing was insufficient. Over two million units had been totally destroyed and an additional two and a half million badly damaged. The refugees and expellees created the need for additional housing at a time when normal needs were far from being met.

Many children became separated from their parents or voluntarily left them. They maintained themselves by various forms of larceny, such as thefts from warehouses and freight cars, trading on the black market, and smuggling metals found in the ruins. They also forged ration cards in their struggle for food and clothing. Some were youth released by the occupation from labor camps, who lacked conventional standards and habits and wandered about the country, stealing, attacking women, and sometimes committing murder.

British zone

The British zone in West Germany had an estimated 40,000 young vagabonds who supported themselves by black marketing, theft, and prostitution (33). If children did not have proper papers, they could not secure food cards and could not obtain permission to live in cities, even if they could get jobs there. The villages, without opportunities for work, were flooded with refugees, a condition still true in 1951. Efforts to gather these uprooted children and youth into homes and schools were impeded by lack of adequate funds and personnel. Although many children were thus restored to normal life, a residue of "true vagrants" remained who resisted incorporation into normal functions of society and eventually turned to a criminal life.

Italy

In Italy, during and after World War II, children swarmed into the cities, where many tried to get along by shining shoes; others robbed military supply dumps, learned to steal expertly from moving trucks, or became small-time retailers in the black market (33). Many children were exploited by adult criminals.

In Genoa, a port city, children who attended half-day schools spent their free time about the ports or climbing through bombed buildings looking for loot. These children might have parents who failed, or were unable, to supervise them. Other children were detached from their parents, many of whom had been repatriated from former Italian colonies in Africa. The parents were uprooted and without work; they operated in the black market, smuggled, and stole; girls and women became prostitutes.

In Milan in the postwar years, it was noted that nearly 2,000 children lived on the fringe of the city without adequate family care. The children took whatever they wanted, without feeling that they were stealing.

In Naples, in southern Italy, 100,000 homes were destroyed by the war. Living conditions, never good, became deplorable, with large numbers of people living without privacy in old storehouses and caves dug into the hillsides, or in the remains of bombed buildings. Some families lived completely on the streets. Children lived by their wits, on the edge of the adult criminal world.

In these various countries, the extreme upheaval of the war and the unusual opportunities for stealing produced many pseudo-vagrants and pseudo-delinquents, who were returned to normal life through the determined efforts of the governments of their countries and with the assistance of other countries, such as the United States. With the end of the war, measures were taken to round up these children and place them in various types of homes and schools. These delinquents of the 1940's and early 1950's would be adults in the late 1960's, and presumably absorbed into various strata of the normal adult world, as failures or successes, as law-abiding citizens, ne'er-do-wells, or outright criminals.

DELINQUENCY IN THE 1950'S AND SINCE

In 1960, the United Nations Congress on the Prevention of Crime and the Treatment of Offenders sought to secure a listing and encourage worldwide discussion of "new forms of delinquency." Whether or not these forms were new or simply current manifestations of old forms, the focus of the Congress brought forth a wealth of material on types of delinquency that were receiving concern and attention in the early 1960's (21). The material in this section is drawn from studies prepared for the Congress, the official Congress reports, and many research publications that appeared during this period. Since not all countries were equally represented, specific delinquencies are discussed in terms of specific countries, but with an attempt to indicate their general occurrence.

Each country has the full range of delinquencies of the Western World — thefts of various sorts, rowdyism, vandalism, sex delinquencies, and, less frequently, aggressions against persons, alcoholism, and drug addiction. Some of these delinquencies have been in existence so long as to be an expected part of a normal deviation from cultural standards, which the society has learned how to suppress or limit. But some new aspects, linked with postwar socioeconomic developments, have aroused apprehension about public safety and the welfare of children. The aspects of delinquency selected for chief discussion are thefts of motor vehicles, gangs, youth riots, shoplifting, vandalism, sex delinquency, and addictions.

Thefts of motor vehicles

Year after year, in war and in peace, thefts of many kinds far outrank any other delinquency. Children of all ages steal, the article stolen differing with the age and with the sex of the offender. A current type of theft, which has not been brought under control, is of motor vehicles, ranging from bicycles with motors attached, through various kinds of two-wheeled motorized vehicles, to automobiles. Which of these is stolen depends upon availability of the vehicle and the age of the thief. Thefts of motor vehicles are closely related to modern technological development and the idea that speedy, individualized transportation is a necessary part of life. Mass transportation for utilitarian purposes has given way to individually owned and operated vehicles that may be used at any hour of the day or night. The use of these vehicles has expanded far beyond utilitarian purposes to include recreation and pleasure. It is the latter usage that appeals especially to the young. Motor vehicles have also been made part of the normal equipment for crime, primarily on the part of adults who plan "quick getaways" by automobile. For the young, motor vehicles, whether two- or four-wheeled, are primarily pleasure vehicles. In Europe, as in the United States, when cars cannot be owned, they will be "borrowed," usually for "joy-riding."

France

In France, a spectacular increase in thefts of motor vehicles began in 1954 (4, 9). Arrests in 1955 were five times those in 1950, and by 1959, the number of 1955 arrests had quadrupled. Thefts of vehicles equalled a fourth of all delinquencies. Most of the thefts are made by adolescents, and in three-fourths of the cases, two-wheeled motor vehicles are involved rather than automobiles, which are taken chiefly by older adolescents.

The vehicles are taken primarily for personal use—they are "borrowed" not stolen. A report from the Prefecture of Police in the Department of the Seine, which includes Paris, shows that only 3 per cent of vehicles were not recovered. Another report states that only 6 per cent of stolen vehicles are sold, and these are of the two-wheeled variety. The vehicles are abandoned on the public highways, or returned to the place from which they were taken. A small percentage have been damaged, and accessories have been removed in 9 per cent of the cases. According to a survey of juvenile courts, the vehicles are used in various ways: usually the youth rides around alone, or with male companions or a girl friend (44 per cent); the second most frequent use is for travel (29 per cent); the third is to run away from home or from a correctional institution (17 per cent). In only 7 per cent of the cases is the vehicle used in the commission of another offense, and in 3 per cent for seduction. Almost no girls steal motor vehicles.

The theft is the first offense for about two-thirds of the offenders but is often followed by a progressive series of offenses. The boy begins by "borrowing" a vehicle for fun or a limited trip, boasting of his exploit; the next step is the theft of anything found loose in the vehicle; finally, with premeditation, he steals the vehicle to sell.

Most of the boys who steal are engaged in the normal activities for their age; they are in school, in apprenticeships, or at work. Different inquiries brought estimates that 55 to 85 per cent came from disorganized families, similar to the families of other types of delinquents. The boys tend to come from middle-class families and according to one report, a third of the families own cars. The boys are not firmly integrated into family or school. The conclusion of one writer, based on a number of reports, is that the thieves are not a special type, but resemble other delinquents in background. Another writer commented that thefts of motor vehicles are not new, but that "what is new is that there is an increasing tendency not to consider these thefts as thefts; the things stolen are simply regarded as 'borrowed.' Cars, and particularly motorcycles, seem to come under semi-collective ownership in the eyes of young people."

Certain practices of vehicle owners contribute to the ease of theft. Cars and other vehicles are parked on the public streets or in large parking lots. The increase of parking lots in France closely parallels the increase in thefts. Cars often are not locked, and the boys know how to start the ignition without a key. They do not know the owners and with the use of cars increasingly becoming an integral part of modern life, they tend to think of the cars as public property along with the streets on which many are parked. The use of the car without any feeling of guilt gives the boys a sense of personality expansion at a time when the youth needs to affirm his individuality.

The Netherlands

The opportunities for stealing or borrowing automobiles are increasing in the Netherlands; the number of private cars doubled between 1957 and 1962 and, no doubt, continues to increase (24, 34). Motorized two-wheeled vehicles are also numerous. In The Hague, in the five year period 1957-62, thefts of motorcycles and autocycles almost trebled, joy-riding as distinct from theft almost doubled, and theft of automobiles increased by 50 per cent. These increases all exceed increases for either aggravated or simple larceny. When age is related to these types of offenses, it appears that juveniles under age 18 are especially active in joy-riding of all types and in thefts of autocycles. A distinction among types of vehicles for joy-riding is not given, and it may be that the younger ages concentrate on the two-wheeled vehicles. Automobile licenses cannot be secured until age 18, a fact that no doubt explains the concentration of car thefts among youth of 18 and over.

Belgium

A report from Belgium states that in reply to a query, half the magistrates think that thefts of motor vehicles are increasing in direct ratio to the increase in traffic (28). In most juvenile cases, the vehicle is "borrowed" for use, rather than stolen. What type of vehicle is taken is directly related to age. When the thieves are ranked from young to older adolescents, the corresponding thefts go from scooters and bicycles to autocycles, motor scooters, motor bicycles, and lastly motor cars. The temptation to take a vehicle from the long lines parked in the streets is overwhelming to youths who understand motor car mechanics and can start a car without the ignition key. Young people between the ages 14 and 18 regard a car as a necessary part of life, for transportation, to startle friends, or make an impression on a girl friend. The urge for self-expression and the exhilaration of driving are regarded as important motives. Rarely are cars taken in the true sense of stealing or for sexual offenses.

Sweden

Sweden has been concerned with the increase in thefts and borrowing of cars, which are chiefly crimes of 17 or 18 year old boys, most of whom have been guilty of earlier delinquencies or crimes and who are likely to become recidivists (21). The increase is related to the increase in the number of automobiles in the country, which rose from 161,000 to 863,000 in the 10 year period 1947-57 and undoubtedly has continued to increase.

A group therapist in penal work makes a distinction between rational and irrational offenders, recognized by the young thieves themselves. Rational car thieves are those who use them to escape from a correctional institution, to get home at night, or to use in connection with another offense or to transport stolen goods. Irrational offenders are those who steal for fun. The relative numbers of the two groups are not given. The therapist suggests that those who steal for fun are inadequate in some ways, perhaps in manliness or social graces, and compensate by taking a car to drive.

Reports from different countries note other offenses and problems associated with joy-riding: drunken driving (Netherlands, Sweden); traffic accidents often with deaths or injuries (Belgium, France, Germany); thefts of articles left in cars (France); escapades with girls (Belgium, Sweden); theft of accessories; and finally, theft of the car itself to sell.

Juvenile gangs

Gangs in Europe are not new (21). Adult and youthful gangs have been active at various times, sometimes politically motivated, sometimes bent on crime. Since World War II, one country after another has become concerned over the prevalence of gangs of juveniles and young adults, whose activities seem only loosely organized and whose motives are unfocused on any specific ideology. But even these latter-day gangs are not new. A French writer cites gangs of the pre-World War I period with picturesque names. He differentiates between these and the current wave of gangs in part by the greater variety of models of activity, spread internationally by motion pictures and journalists' stories.

The gangs of the 1950's and later have caught the interests of police and criminologists and journalists. The names by which the gangs are commonly called have often been the creation of journalists; the gangs themselves seldom use these names. In Belgium and France, they are commonly called *Blousons Noirs* (black jackets); in Germany, *Halbstarke* (half-matured); and in Italy, *vitelloni* (calf).

Gangs are discussed by European writers in three categories: informal peer groups or gangs, organized gangs, and rioting gangs.

French Gangs

A summary of information requested from juvenile court judges and police reveals many characteristics of French gangs (4, 15, 23, 25, 35). They are a boys' activity, centering in the adolescent years. Few members are under 12 years old, few over 18. Within a given gang, the age range usually is not more than three years. Occasionally, a gang has a few young adult members who may provide leadership. Young gang boys are rarely organized; they are fortuitous groups and relatively impermanent. Their chief delinquency is vandalism. Slightly older boys center their delinquency on thefts. Violence is uncommon, but when it does occur, the older boys are usually involved. The older the boys, the more likelihood that the boys will be organized with perhaps some hierarchy of leadership.

Few of the gangs have girls attached to them. One report estimated 20 boys to one girl, as compared with seven boys to one girl in ordinary delinquencies. Eighty per cent of gangs had no girls, 16 per cent one girl, and only 4 per cent two to four girls. Girls may hang around the places where the boys congregate, but the boys pay little attention to them.

Thefts, the typical delinquency of the mid-teens, make up 60 to 80 per cent of the offenses; theft of vehicles is included. The thefts are usually minor in nature. What is stolen belongs to the gang and is stored in their "hideout." It is only when a gang specializes in stealing some readily salable articles, such as records, electric razors, radios, and phonographs, that the value of the thefts is high.

Vandalism ranks next, with aggressions and offenses against morals accounting for very few offenses. Violence rarely appears, but may burst out when one gang encroaches on the territory of another. Occasionally, adult attitudes of hostility call forth brutal attacks. Sexual offenses, while not common, may take the form of rape.

About half of gang boys repeat their delinquent acts, compared with about 30 per cent of non-gang delinquents. Some gangs have only a few repeaters, but others have many. Repeated offenses are most common among older boys and youth and in organized gangs.

Immediately after World War II, gang boys stole things for use, such as food, or articles to resell on the black market. The boys often were out of school and unemployed. Later, thefts became spontaneous and senseless acts. Boys were again in school or employed and the necessities lacking in the postwar period were readily supplied. Delinquencies became wanton; they were hedonistic and seemed to be a means of resolving the uncertain status of the adolescent.

Since most gang boys are in school or employed, their activities are limited to evenings or weekends. The gangs are leisure time or recreational groups. They form without prior planning, when boys come to congregate at some favorite place—a motion picture theater, dance hall, or camp. If a crisis arises, for instance, a boy breaks a window, all the boys rally to his defense. In a short time, the boys are acting as a group instead of as individuals. They respond to hostility by aggression. Soon the gang becomes a closed society.

Only about a third of the gangs have a chief and few are highly structured. The characteristics of the chief are intelligence or personal prestige, sense of organization, physical strength, and age beyond that of the members. The chief is a personage who knows, organizes, and acts. The organized gangs are more likely to have a permanent meeting place than the unorganized, which meet in public places frequented by youths, such as a place where there is a juke box, or on the street corner.

Weapons are of two types: real weapons, such as guns or knives, and articles converted into weapons, such as bicycle chains, belts, clubs, or stones. The latter are more frequent. The weapons are displayed less for aggression than for their symbolic value of status, without close reference to criminal behavior. However, in attacks, the "converted weapon" comes into use.

Without organization, the groups are fluid, and form and dissolve quickly. Few survive the period of compulsory military service, which begins at age 20. When the boys are released, they may temporarily join a gang, but soon jobs and marriage carry most of them into conventional life. Social mobility is not common in France and the gang boys, from the lower class, do not feel frustrated nor aspire to become upwardly mobile. Nor are there many highly organized adult criminal gangs to furnish models or open ready-made opportunities for entrance into an adult criminal career. Gang life in France seems to be an interim occupation or recreational activity between childhood and military service, related to the uncertain status of the boy rather than to deep seated frustrations.

Gangs in Other European Countries

Gangs in other European countries seem to be of much the same type. In Belgium, gangs are not regarded as an acute or major problem (28). However, some delinquent or criminal gangs exist in cities. A gang in Brussels is described as having 17 members aged 14 to 20 years, 11 being under the age of 18. The boys lived in different quarters of the city. They met during the winter in a dance hall of bad repute where they spent much of their leisure. Individually, the members did not have court records, but as a gang, they engaged in acts of bravado and vandalism, such as snatching the ornaments from parked cars. More serious offenses included burglary and the cornering of a homosexual by one boy in a remote part of a park, where an accomplice by agreement discovered them; they beat and robbed the victim, who dared not complain to the authorities. In each case, the personal history of the boy revealed an unfavorable family environment, early withdrawal from school, and a poor work record. Although the gang included some members over age 20, the leader was a boy of 17, who maintained his position through his unusual strength and audacity.

West Germany had a wave of rioting in the late 1950's which will be described in a later section. It also has both marginal groups, called *gammler,* and loosely organized gangs. The *gammler,* according to an article in *Time* (August 5, 1966), are "unwashed, unshaven, unregenerates, clad in turtle-neck sweatshirts, levi's and sandals," and correspond to similar types of youth in other European cities and to the "beatniks" in the United States. Guilty of only a few delinquencies of a minor type, they disturb the German sense of law and order and might be described as a public nuisance.

A full fledged gang active in Dulsberg, Germany, was investigated and reported in 1965 in the *Hamburg Polizei* (12). The gang consisted of 30 boys between the ages of 15 and 20, loosely grouped without leaders, planned corporate action, or gang rules. They met by chance in bars, but had a common background, with 27 of them growing up in the same quarter of the city. Half came from broken homes, some, although still in school, were retarded, 12 had records as behavior problems, only six had learned a trade, and 16 were in unskilled work. Twenty-one had a previous court record at the time of the mass arrest. Many of their group activities were not rationally planned and seemed to be for adventure or bravado. Since they typically needed money, stealing was common. The offenses that could be considered group-motivated numbered 187 at the time of arrest and included breaking into builders' huts, kiosks, stores, workshops, flats when the occupants were absent, and offices. They also broke into vending machines. They looked for cash. They operated only in late evening or at night when buildings would be unoccupied. Their noncriminal activities included use of motorcycles and cars, drinking, smoking, and regular attendance at motion pictures. The stealing was to produce a regular supply of money for these activities. They seemed to want to appear adult but in fact were immature. Until their arrest, their families knew nothing of their criminal activities. Although no one theft may have netted the gang a large amount, the total booty came to about $7,000, and vandalism committed was the equivalent of about $11,000.

Italy, with its generally low rate of juvenile delinquency, was disturbed in the late 1950's by sporadic aggressions of teenagers in gangs. According to newspaper reports, gaudy shirts and blue jeans constituted the favored style of dress, and a motorcycle was necessary equipment, with a tampered muffler to produce the maximum amount of noise. Among the aggressions of these gangs were harassment of motorists with whom they picked fights and whose cars they damaged, and molestation of unescorted women on lonely streets and of couples in lover's lanes. Robberies added to the list. These gangs operated for the most part in the more prosperous cities, for example, Milan and Rome. Boys who were arrested were not limited to the poor, but included the sons of respectable, self-supporting families. In the poorer south, gang activity was at a minimum. Family control is still strong in southern Italy and traditionally crime is not lightly undertaken in the spirit of play, but has such serious motives as personal or family honor, money or passion.

In the Netherlands, disorderly groups of boys, called *nozems,* wear distinctive dress and regard a noisy motor bicycle as a necessary piece of equipment (1, 3). The groups are small, relatively unorganized, and with unstable membership. Their offenses are minor. They do not engage in gang fights nor develop a delinquent subculture that gives support to their misconduct and enables them to defy community norms.

Youth riots

Episodes of limited duration marked by rowdyism and rioting have caused great concern in European countries. Such public disturbances involving 50 or more youths have been widespread and reported from many countries in and outside of Europe. A report of 1962 lists the following: in 1959, Bonn, Nürnberg, Braunschweig, Munich, and in the south of Sweden; in 1960, London, Brighton, Berlin, the United States, South Africa, Zürich, and Dresden; and in 1961, Mannheim, Munich, Copenhagen, and Paris. Historically, many countries have repeatedly experienced riots in protest against oppressions or marked political or economic change. The recent phenomena seem to cause concern because of their appearance in many countries within a short period of time, the youthful age of the participants, and the pointless nature of many of the episodes. They seem to be emotional explosions rather than the expression of social protest.

In the mid-1950's, West Germany experienced a number of riots, attributed to the *Halbstarke* (16, 21). Of 108 riots in West Berlin that were studied, almost two-thirds numbered less than 50 participants, often the same youths appearing in a number of riots. Drunken and quarrelsome, their activities included vandalism, molesting pedestrians, and scuffling and fighting with employees of bars and restaurants. They resisted police who tried to disperse or arrest them. Some riots attracted much larger groups, occasionally as many as 800 to 1,000 participants. These large assemblies usually followed jazz concerts or the attempts of police to break up some favorite sport, such as a motorcycle meet. Often a series of riots lasted for several successive days.

The German study regarded the riots as epidemic in nature. They tended to follow a standard pattern, beginning after the excitement of some crowd event, or frustration of some pleasure—dissatisfaction; loud cat-calls, whistling, and vulgar shouts by individuals; calls, whistling, and shouts in unison. Police efforts to control the crowd were resisted. Finally, the action culminated in wanton destruction, mass rioting, resistance, and marked disorderliness. This sequence of events spread across Germany and then died out.

Their spread and continuance were attributed in part to the effect of mass communication facilities. Certain motion pictures from the United States undoubtedly "set off" many of the episodes, when many youth reacted simultaneously to the same stimuli. The popular press carried exaggerated versions of riots from one city to another, stirred up opposition to the police, and sometimes "manufactured" reports, or reporters eager for a story urged idle youth into disorderly conduct. The newspaper accounts seemed to establish an expectation that youth would riot, and riots accordingly broke out. In time the epidemic ran its course and subsided.

Germany is not the only country to experience excessively aggressive excitement and conduct after motorcycle meets, certain concerts, or the showing of stirring films picturing excessive behavior of youth. In 1957, Denmark had streets blocked by crowds of youth after the showing of exciting American motion pictures that had similarly affected American teenagers. In 1959, according to newspaper reports, a small city in Sweden was overrun by youths and girls clad in black caps and leather jackets, and jeans, who roared into the city by car and motorcycle to watch motorcycle races. Half drunk, they arrogantly pushed civilians around and when opposed by police (and later, troops) turned to vandalism and arson. Twenty persons were hospitalized. Another Swedish city had the same experience in connection with races. Members of the gang said their hero was Marlon Brando who starred in the motion picture *The Wild Ones*.

In summing up European gang activity, whether of the gang type or rioting, reports indicate that gangs usually are loosely organized, and that much of the activity is spontaneous and arises out of immediate lack of money, or in response to random stimuli that may lead the small gang to vandalism and the larger gang to rioting. The center of rioting may be a gang, to which others are temporarily drawn. So loosely structured are many of the gangs that they have been described as conglomerations rather than structured groups.

General explanations for gangs are that the boys come from poorly organized or broken families; have school or employment difficulties; are in transition between childhood and adulthood with low status at the time; or are responding to mass media, often originating in the United States. Little credence is given to the popular American explanation of upward but frustrated aspirations of lower-class boys who wish to climb the social scale; it has also been noted that there are few highly organized adult criminal groups into which the more capable delinquent youth may enter to become full-fledged criminal adults. This statement does not deny that there are many adult criminals in certain cities of Europe but only that, in general, they are less highly organized than in the United States and offer fewer opportunities for the gang boy to progress from his juvenile gang into an adult organized criminal gang.

Shoplifting

Reports from various European countries show an increase in shoplifting, which is linked with the increase in the number of self-service stores that are beginning to replace or supplement the traditional small specialized shops characteristic of most European countries. The increased prosperity calls for the display of many kinds of goods. The open shelves and self-service feature make stealing much easier. The Netherlands reports an increase in shoplifting which is attributed to the above causes.

Belgium has also been concerned with postwar shoplifting by juveniles (7, 28). Boys are the chief offenders, with age 12 being the peak age. Articles stolen are small in value and include many toys. Shoplifting expeditions may be planned by groups as a kind of sport.

The large department stores where much shoplifting takes place are gathering places for truants or children after school and during vacations. The stores are partially responsible for the thefts; they display goods in a tempting fashion on open shelves where they may be touched and handled. The abundance of the goods and the impersonal situation in the large stores foster the idea that stealing may be justified. Although some of the children come from families with adequate income, there is inadequate supervision.

Shoplifting is not by any means confined to children and youth, although they constitute almost 26 per cent according to one West German study of 1,199 cases with 1,321 offenders (17). Among the offenders, 12.8 per cent were children under 14 years, 9.2 per cent were 14 to 17 years, and 3.7 per cent were aged 18 to 21; 74.3 per cent covered all years above age 21. The distribution by sex is not given for the different ages, but among adults, two-thirds were women. In about one-tenth of the cases, two persons were involved and in a few, three or four persons; these were chiefly cases of children or adolescents.

Some of the accounts of gangs indicate that shoplifting may be a gang activity, sometimes becoming a systematic delinquency with specialization in the selection of articles stolen, and reaching a total of many dollars. This purposeful shoplifting is characteristic of older gang boys in contrast to the amateurish thefts of younger children.

Vandalism and other wanton delinquencies

Various reports indicate that vandalism has been increasing (21). There are few definite statistical reports, since vandalism usually is reported under other headings, or is of a minor nature, handled on the spot by the police. Vandalism is defined as wanton destruction of property, such as breaking windows and other meaningless property damage. It also includes the theft of articles which are then broken and abandoned or thrown away. Another type of wanton crime is the unprovoked attacks on people—sometimes never before seen—that result in injuries or death. The amount of damage that can be done in a few minutes by a few boys (rarely girls) is astounding. In France, a group of boys broke 132 windows in 15 minutes in an abandoned military camp (4). A variety of motives are cited in a French study: desire for enjoyment, especially among younger boys; desire for adventure; imaginative activity accompanied by a failure to foresee the damage that may result (for example, a boy of eight may place a stone on a railway track without realizing the result). When drunk, older boys may attack people. Another motive is the desire of a boy to prove his valor to the gang, and another is to defy society and its authorities.

As the above paragraphs indicate, vandalism tends to be a group activity, part of the customary activities of gangs of boys.

The background factors for vandalism resemble those given for a number of other types of delinquency: disorganized families, lack of supervision, irresponsibility of unemployed youth, drinking, nonmembership in organized leisure groups, and so on. Resentments of various sorts are also cited.

Sex delinquency

Sex delinquency is a difficult form of behavior to categorize (21). First, the blanket term refers to vastly different activities: ordinary premarital sex activities of males and females, about which attitudes are most likely to differ from laws; prostitution, legally permitted in most European countries, although sometimes with restrictions to prevent it from becoming publicly offensive; homosexual relationships, which may differ as between voluntary activities of adults and exploitation of young boys by adults—or the reverse; molestation of young children; rape; perversions of various kinds; and incest in various degrees of relationship. All these sexual relationships may involve boys and girls, and several of them may be grouped together under the general title of sexual delinquency. Almost the only generalization that may be made is that there is general disapproval of sexual activity for young children and varying degrees of tolerance for adolescents, but in general a demand for restraint.

Reports on sexual activities of children and youth usually are incomplete. The activities are carried out in secret or within groups that approve or tolerate them. Police may be reluctant to attach the stigma of "sexual delinquent" to young girls so that they record them as involved in some other delinquency, such as disorderly conduct.

When the opinions of officials in different countries were sought for the Second United Nations Congress on the Prevention of Crime and Treatment of Offenders, the following pertinent comments were submitted (21):

France

Offenses against public morals have greatly increased among children under 13 but have decreased to some extent in the adolescent group (9).

Belgium

The various officials who replied to the query seemed to agree that the pattern of sexual behavior was the same as it had been for the past 50 to 100 years (28). However, there was more irregularity at young ages, that is, under 14, whereas formerly puberty introduced a natural interest in sexual relations without personal commitments. The increase was attributed to the "general atmosphere of liberty and enjoyment" in sex relations encouraged by motion pictures, literature, popular songs, and the dance hall atmosphere. Parents were also accused of being apathetic. The rural areas typically have had their own types of irregularities, described as "not only normal relations between lovers, but incest, homosexuality, and even crimes against nature." The writer of the opinion did not believe these lapses from conventional behavior were especially disorganizing—some were infrequent, and the sexual behavior of lovers was accepted as a part of the rural social customs. Recently, an increase in sexual irregularities in some rural areas has been noted. It is regarded as related to the greater ease of contacts and communications of rural young people with cities, and as beyond local control, and, therefore, disorganizing.

Sweden

Prostitution as the main source of income tends to be confined to the later teens. However, sporadic sex relations for gain are widespread among teen girls. Several cases have come to light where teenaged boys have become pimps for young girls, who support them. Homosexual prostitution of young boys has been noted with increased frequency in Stockholm. The comment is made that prostitution is difficult to locate, with the introduction of the call-girl system and the use of cars by prostitutes who drive around and pick up clients.

Italy

The opinion was given that sexual immorality had been increasing among young girls, but accurate information on the exact increase was not available.

West Germany

A study of male juvenile prostitution showed that such cases had almost doubled between 1949 and 1954.

Alcoholism and drug addiction

In European countries, alcoholic beverages are included as part of the everyday diet (18). This usage, governed by custom, is part of the family pattern in all social classes, or is part of certain festive occasions. Children learn the drinking customs at home and tend to follow them as adults. Nevertheless, some countries report they are plagued with excessive use of alcohol and attendant misconduct.

Sweden

Drinking and public drunkenness among young people of both sexes has increased over the past several decades and especially since the end of World War II (21). The comment is made that part of the increase shown in official reports may be due to the tendency of rural youth to seek entertainment in the city, where, if they become drunk, they are likely to be arrested. For the age group 15-17, the rate of convictions per 100,000 for drunkenness had changed from 170 in 1928, to 244 in 1938, to 431 in 1948, to 1,093 in 1957. For ages 18-20, the four rates were 1,126, 1,223, 2,114, and 4,346. Certain changes in the law in 1955 may have contributed to increased use of alcohol at all ages.

Drug addiction among juveniles is not reported by most countries. Sweden noted an increase, but primarily in the use of tranquilizers, with very little use of narcotic drugs.

AFFLUENCE AS A FACTOR IN DELINQUENCY

A standard explanation of delinquency and crime has long been poverty that impelled people to steal from necessity (1). A corollary was an association between unemployment and crime. This explanation was supported by the rise in certain types of offenses during the Great Depression of the 1930's and the more general finding that certain offenses followed the ups and downs of the business cycle. Accordingly, the period of prosperity in Europe since World War II should have witnessed a decline in delinquency; instead, delinquency increased in the most prosperous countries as well as in the poverty-stricken ones in other parts of the world. The following explanations have been offered by different authors.

The increase in income of youth, whether from employment or the indulgence of parents, changes behavior patterns. When the money is not needed for necessities, but may be spent freely by youth, it is often used for luxuries that otherwise would not be considered as within the range of expenditures of a generally low-income stratum of society. Youth who are less well-heeled and cannot keep up with their friends, may fill the gap by stealing either a desired article or the means with which to buy it, for example, a hi-fi set or a motor vehicle of some sort. Even if a motor vehicle is acquired legally, it may lead to deviant types of behavior—speeding, highway accidents from negligence, escape after a theft, or evasion of parental or community supervision especially where drinking or sexual exploits are involved. Self-control and community control for the new freedoms have not yet been established.

Attention is often called to the importance given to materialistic values that seems to increase with increased prosperity. The old family- and church-supported teaching of honesty, thrift, hard work, and sobriety seem disregarded under the impact of money, luxury goods, and exciting commercial recreation now available.

In some countries, delinquency has been attributed to migration for employment; for example, in Belgium, the intrusion of workers from foreign countries who are unfamiliar with local customs. An Italian writer links delinquency in northern Italy with internal migration from the south, which has lagged behind in industrial development (27). Northern Italians discriminate against them and discourage integration. The migrants develop ideas of persecution, and become hostile. They resist authority and engage in such antisocial behavior as thefts, especially of cars; they are also occupationally unstable, which may become a motive in itself for certain crimes.

Another suggested explanation is in the loosening of family controls over children and youth (2). Unstable and broken homes have long been regarded as a major factor in delinquency, and careful studies show a considerable degree of association between the two. Now, some new family factors are drawn into the picture. One relates to the use of motor vehicles which quickly carry young people away from the home neighborhood. Another is the migration of families—or of youth without their families—from rural to urban areas. The closely organized family of many rural communities is unable to function in the city where each person finds employment and recreation individually instead of as a member of the family group. The city provides anonymity that encourages deviant behavior (5). City controls are formal and may be evaded without a sense of guilt. The individual may feel at a loss for companionship and find a substitute for the family or rural neighborhood in the gang of the city streets. Examples of these and other situations are easy to find, but difficult to prove.

REFERENCES

1. Baur, E. Jackson. "Trend of Juvenile Offences in the Netherlands and the United States." *Journal of Criminal Law, Criminology, and Police Science,* 55 (1964), pp. 359-69.
2. Brandt, W. "Changes in Family Structure and Their Relationship to Juvenile Delinquency." *Kiel Recht. d. Jugend,* 1962, 10/14 (pp. 209-12), 10/15 (pp. 231-34).*
3. Buikhuisen, W. "Background to 'Nozem' Behavior." *Med. Inst. voor Praev. Geneesk.,* 1965.*
4. Ceccaldi, M. *Les neuvelles formes de la délinquance juvénile en France.* Report from the Director of l'Education Surveillée to the Ministry of Justice (France) in Connection with the Second Congress of the United Nations, 1960.
5. Christiansen, Karl O. "Industrialization and Urbanization in Relation to Crime and Juvenile Delinquency." *International Review of Criminal Policy,* No. 16 (October, 1960), pp. 3-8.
6. deBray, L. *Deux facteurs de la délinquance de jeunes. Bulletin de l'Administration Penitentiaire,* 1963.
7. Debuyst, Chr., G. Lejour, and A. Racine. *Petits voleurs de grande magazins.* Centre d'Etude de la Délinquance Juvénile, Brussels, Belgium, 1960.
8. Elliott, Mabel A. "Perspective on the American Crime Problem." *Social Problems,* 5 (Winter, 1957-58), pp. 184-93.
9. "Evolution de la délinquance juvénile, periode d'après-guerre." *Annual Report of the Direction de l'Education Surveilleé,* 1959.
10. *Evolution d'une notion de la délinquance juvénile, Colloque de 15 et 16 Mars, 1958.* Centre d'Etude de la Délinquance Juvénile, Brussels, Belgium, 1958.
11. Faustini, G. and Conte, M. T. "Delinquency among Minors in Italy from 1958 till 1963." *Esper. rieduc.,* 1964, 11/12 (pp. 42-83).*

12. FIEDLER, C. "The Dulsberg Gang." *Hamburg Polizei,* 1965, 56/8 (pp. 251-54).*
13. GERMAIN, CHARLES. "Postwar Prison Reform in France." *Annals of the American Academy of Political and Social Science,* 293 (1954), pp. 639-50.
14. HAYNER, NORMAN S. "German Correctional Procedures." *National Probation and Parole Association Journal,* 1 (1955), pp. 167-73.
15. JOUBREL, M. H. "Protection of the Adolescent Threatened by Maladjustment, 1. Adolescent Gangs." *Sauvegard Enf.,* 1962, 17/1-2-3 (pp. 85-99).*
16. KAISER, G. "Rowdyism and Vandalism." *Uns. Jugend,* 2 (1962), p. 664.*
17. LOITZ, R. "Shoplifting." *Kriminalistik,* 1965. 19/10 (pp. 509-12).*
18. LOLLI, G., *et al. Alcohol in Italian Culture.* Free Press, 1958.
19. LOUWAGE, F. E. "Delinquency in Europe after World War II." *Journal of Criminal Law, Criminology, and Police Science,* 42 (1951-52), pp. 53-56.
20. LUNDEN, W. A. *War and Delinquency.* The Art Press, Ames, Iowa, 1963.
21. MIDDENDORFF, WOLF. *New Forms of Juvenile Delinquency: Their Origin, Prevention and Treatment.* Second United Nations Congress on the Prevention of Crime and the Treatment of Offenders, London, 1960. United Nations, Department of Economic and Social Affairs, New York, 1960.
22. NYQUIST, OLA. "How Sweden Handles Its Juvenile and Youth Offenders." *Federal Probation,* 20 (March, 1956), pp. 36-42.
23. OBRAISON, M., J. C. BARREAU, and J. ROCHEFORT, *Les enfants prodigues: problèmes des bandes asociales et essai de solutions.* Librairie Arthème Fayard, Paris, 1962.
24. PEIJSTER, C. N. "Automobile Theft by Minors." Fifth International Criminological Congress, Montreal, 1965. (Mimeographed)
25. PEREZ FERRER, E. E. "Juvenile Delinquency and Gangs." *Rev. Estrud. penitenc.,* 1964 20/165 (pp. 223-314).*
26. PIHLBLAD, C. T. "Juvenile Offenders in Norway." *Journal of Criminal Law, Criminology, and Police Science,* 46 (1955), pp. 500-511.
27. PONTRELLI, E. "Immigration, Anti-social Behavior and Maladjustment." *Esper. rieduc.,* 1965, 12/4 (pp. 29-38).*
28. RACINE, AIMEE. *La délinquance juvénile en Belgique de 1939 à 1957.* Centre d'Etude de la Délinquance Juvénile, Brussels, 1959.
29. REINEMANN, J. O. "Delinquency in Postwar Germany." *National Probation and Parole Association Journal,* 1 (1955), pp. 159-66.
30. SCHNEIDER, H. J. "Motor Vehicles and Juvenile Delinquency." *Acta Criminal. Med. legalis jap.* 1964, 30/4 (pp. 1-11).*
31. SELLIN, T. "Sweden's Substitute for the Juvenile Court." *Annals of the American Academy of Political and Social Science,* 261

(1949), pp. 137-49.
32. SVERI, K. "Criminality and Age." *Acta Social.*, 1961, 5/2 pp. 75-86).*
33. United Nations Educational, Scientific, and Cultural Organization. *Problems in Education,* No. 1., *War-Handicapped Children,* Publication No. 439; No. 3, *Vagrant Children,* Publication No. 644.
34. VAN DE WERK, M. B. "Automobile Theft by Minors." Fifth International Criminological Congress, Montreal, 1965. (Mimeographed.)
35. VAZ, E. W. "Juvenile Gang Delinquency in Paris." *Social Problems,* 10 (1962), pp. 23-31.
36. VEILLARD-CYBULSKY, M. and H. *Les jeunes délinquants dans la monde.* Distributed by Delachaux et Lièstle, Paris, 1963.

* Abstracts of these articles may be found in *Excerpta Criminologica.*

9/ Some Similarities and Contrasts

The emphasis of this entire book has been on social types of delinquency and crime as they appear in relation to social conditions and social changes. Psychiatric crimes, emanating primarily from psychological quirks or abnormalities, and only secondarily affected by social factors, have been passed over. These delinquencies, accounting for a minority of offenses, though often of a bizarre kind, would require a different selection and orientation of materials for their understanding. Rather than complicate the discussion, they are omitted here, and attention is centered on delinquencies where social conditions and normal psychological reactions to them are the dominant factors.

Chapters 2 to 8 encompass 14 societies. When they are classified according to types of social organization within them, 20 units result, which are shown in the following tabulation:

Society	*Primitive village*	*Transitional village*	*City*
Eskimo	x	x	
Mexico	x	x	x
India	x	x	x
Russia			x
Mafia		x	x
England			x
Eight European countries			x

In addition certain special situations closely related to delinquency and crime are included:

Criminal societies: India and Mafia

War: England, eight European countries, Russia
Historical transition: England, Russia, Mafia

The number of societies and social situations is too small a base for sound generalizations. It is possible, however, to make some comparisons, strictly limited to the societies represented.

SOCIAL BACKGROUNDS

The societies were chosen deliberately to represent a variety of backgrounds, in complexity of organization, from primitive villages to modern, complex industrial cities. The range of backgrounds made it possible to look at delinquency and crime in relation to a variety of broad social situations.

Also, the choice was deliberate in including social changes that disturbed, in various degrees, traditional or typical culture, and social institutions and customs; the most radical was the communist takeover in Russia, both in change of values and in its penetration of all aspects of life. War was the most destructive physical change, but did not result in utter destruction of cultural and social elements. Some perspective was attempted by historical summary. Finally, the possibility of the continued existence of an organized criminal segment within a noncriminal society was explored in the criminal societies in India and Sicily.

The situations discussed were varied. Nevertheless, similarities were found to exist.

Basic values

All the societies had basic values that were perpetuated and protected in many ways, from training children to accept those values without question, to fighting the groups inside and outside the society that threatened them. For example, the basic, traditional Eskimo value was physical survival; any threat to this value was severely punished. In Russia the maintenance and further acceptance of the new order and its leaders form a basic value, with severe punishments to those who neglect to support or who oppose it. Communities within a society might have somewhat different values. The criminal tribes in India sought to maintain their tribal culture and to retain traditional rights that they felt were being violated by Hindus and British. Hindus, until recently, sought to retain their caste system intact; now this value is modified and a new one added—to westernize their culture.

More important than the specific value involved is the fact of the existence of values to which individuals committed their loyalties and lives and about which they organized their societies.

Social change

All the societies, and the subgroups within them, had undergone or were currently experiencing social change. The change might be taking place within their own culture, as from rural to urban (in Mexico and India), or might be based on a major ideological change as from monarchy to communism (in Russia). It might be from one culture to another, as from primitive Eskimo to or toward the cultures of the United States and Canada. It might be gradual or catastrophic (as during and following World War II).

In some countries the critical period is already in the past, as in England where the crisis of change in delinquent behavior came with the first stages of the Industrial Revolution, followed by a long, slow process of change in delinquency and attitudes toward it that culminated in the official recognition of juvenile delinquency as independent of crime. Now, changes in England are not crises; they are linked to the continuing process of social change. English writers do not seem to be startled or shocked by changes in delinquency, but attempt to meet them in a rational manner. On the continent, some countries accept the changes in delinquency as typical of a period of general social change—as "of the times"; others seem disturbed by such phenomena as thefts of cars or gang formation.

Changes were accompanied by increased delinquency that seemed to vary in proportion to the abruptness of change and the degree to which change shook or destroyed customary institutions, such as the family, schools, employment, or government. It is not practical to measure change statistically or formally. But descriptive accounts lead to the conclusion that the Communist Revolution in Russia was the beginning of a serious and long drawn-out process of delinquency and crime. Both World War I and World War II broke up customary patterns of behavior and freed people from social controls to act by impulse. In less turbulent periods the rate of change of delinquency is slight but almost never absent.

In none of the countries were the social disruptions of change complete. Individual families and other institutions might disintegrate, but either the preceding social order reasserted itself, or a substitute program was put into operation. For instance, the government reopened schools or built orphanages to replace homes. These readjustments might come from within the society (Russia, Italy, England, Europe except Germany) or be imposed from without (Germany). As order was restored and institutions began to function again, delinquency declined. The later increase in England and Europe seems related to economic and social changes that are within the normal range of change, in contrast to the explosive disruptions of war.

None of the societies, even in the most orderly periods, succeeded in eliminating all delinquency and crime. The closest approach to complete conformity was among children in the primitive tribes and villages. All the societies had adult crime.

Social control

All the societies had some recognized methods of controlling or suppressing delinquency and crime. In the simple villages, misbehavior of children was controlled by families; crimes of adults by community-supported methods. In more highly developed cities, formal agencies were used. Enforcing discipline was part of the role of certain adults—either part of a traditional round of duties or formally assigned to certain officials. The kind of punishment allowed, either in families or by officials, was prescribed, either by custom or in written laws. Punishments were neither haphazard nor at the whim of the disciplinarian.

All societies had customary methods of training children into acceptance of values and conformity to norms of behavior. As a rule, family members had primary responsibility. An exception is Russia during the early period after the Revolution when parents were thought not to be sufficiently indoctrinated into communist ideology to be trusted to so train their children—a variety of formal agencies took over the main responsibilities. In all other societies except the most simple, agencies have long shared the responsibility for training with the family. All societies studied have, at present, organized religious institutions effective in child training, with the possible exception of Russia.

In some societies organized religion had replaced or supplemented earlier indigenous religions that played a similar role (Mexico, Eskimo). In England and the European countries, the transition from indigenous to organized religion came so far in the past that *clear* traces of the original religion are lacking in contemporary practice.

DELINQUENCIES AND CRIME

Kinds of crime

So far as could be determined from available data, stealing was the most prevalent crime in all the societies. Statistics for westernized countries demonstrate this, and descriptions of other countries imply it. What is stolen differs, depending upon what objects are vital to sustain life and are otherwise highly valued in a given society. The object stolen also differs from time to time as necessities or valued objects change. At present, car thefts are widespread in Europe but not in India, where few people have cars to be stolen and the concept of a car as a necessity of life or status symbol is not present.

Violence, injuries, and murder were found in all countries, in the historical periods surveyed and at present. Without any statistical proof, the impression gained was that physical injuries and murders occurred more often, and with less provocation, in the past than at present.

In all the societies where such information was available, stealing was more frequent from strangers, or from any group in which one did not have intimate contacts or look to fellow-members for approval and security, than from one's own group. Criminal tribes in India did not steal with impunity within the tribe; Mafia directed its attacks and thefts against the rich; lower classes stole from the elite; Eskimos stole from non-Eskimos; delinquents shoplifted from large department stores and supermarkets in England and Belgium although they would not steal from the corner shopkeeper in their own neighborhoods. Thefts within the offender's own society were severely punished by that society; outside thefts tended to go unpunished unless the outside group was able to exert control over the thief and his society.

Crimes of violence were similarly categorized. In general, attack against a member of an individual's own society was a crime; against an outsider it was justifiable, or at least was treated more leniently. Killing of outsiders is exaggerated and glorified during times of war.

Boys and girls

The conclusion was drawn that boys and men committed more delinquencies than girls and women. In all the societies with official records, the rate of delinquency and crime is much higher for males than for females at all ages. The inference is made that the same situation exists for the nonliterate societies without records. In descriptive accounts and research reports, offenses by girls and women are almost never mentioned. Moreover, the types of offenses are typically related to the occupations of men or to their social positions.

When a distinction is made between offenses of females and of males, it is in the area of sex offenses. Comparisons are difficult to make, since the definitions of a sex offense differs from one society to another. Among Eskimos, unmarried girls were allowed a certain amount of freedom, but after marriage any extramarital activities were likely to constitute a crime of major importance on the part of her male partner, punishable without ceremony by her husband. Among criminal tribes of India, extramarital sex relations within the tribe were forbidden, but the woman was permitted to prostitute herself outside for the financial gain of the tribe. The Mexican girl was socially disgraced if it was known that she had had sex relations before marriage, but even a brief period of "free union" was regarded as a marriage that entitled the couple to cohabit. None of the societies permitted complete freedom of sex relations at all times for all girls and women. Russia most nearly approached such freedom in the period after the Revolution.

TECHNIQUES TO REDUCE TENSIONS

All the societies had techniques for reducing social and psychological pressures and tensions that might lead to crimes. These techniques differed widely. Some were sponsored by major institutions or the government. Some were simply customary practices. Others verged on deviant behavior but were tolerated.

Festivals

Sponsored outlets for tensions and hostilities included the village dances and song fests of the Eskimos, the fiestas of the Mexicans, religious festivals in India and Sicily, and, both historically and at present, many organized recreational activities in England and Europe. Sometimes special days of license were allowed (Eskimo), although this is not the case for all the societies.

Religion

Belief in a system of supernatural beings also reduced tensions. Social or personal hardships and disasters often were attributed to the spirits or gods. Prayers, sacred rituals, or sacrifices were believed to appease the spirits and bring an end to hardships.

Welfare programs

At present, the most widespread mechanisms for reduction of tensions are the social welfare programs of England and the European countries, including Russia. Financial tensions are reduced to a minimum so far as the necessities of life are concerned. Education and recreation are provided at almost no cost to the individual. The general concept of tension reduction through welfare extends to institutionalized delinquents and criminals. Brutality has disappeared from prisons in most countries. Not only necessities but many amenities are provided for prisoners; a positive effort is made to clear up personal and family problems and to rehabilitate inmates so that they can more readily adapt to the free community when released.

Use of alcohol

Another means of releasing tensions, with or without social patterning, is the use of alcohol. Attempts to completely suppress or eliminate the use of alcohol have been unsuccessful in the countries studied. India's attempt to eliminate it completely has simply opened a lucrative way of making money by illegally making and selling alcoholic beverages. Russia takes an ambivalent attitude; with a state monopoly on the profitable manufacture of alcohol, it nevertheless propagandizes against and punishes excessive usage. Other societies exert some kind of regulation, either through laws or institutional rules.

Freedom of sex relations

A certain amount of freedom of sex experience prior to marriage reduces tensions. Traditionally the Eskimos permitted a limited amount of sexual experimentation prior to settling down to a stable marital relationship; Mexico forbade premarital relations to girls but it was accepted that young men would satisfy sexual urges through association with married women, widows, or prostitutes. India had a similar emphasis on virginity of girls, but at least permitted young men to visit the many prostitutes in cities. Russia, after the long period of almost complete freedom, moved toward prudery; however, intercourse in "meaningful" relationships is tolerated. In Sicily, girls are expected to be virgins. England and the European countries vary in degree of tolerance of premarital sex relations and openness of prostitution, but in no country is there a complete absence of nonmarital sex relations.

Reduction of marital tensions

Ways to reduce or eliminate marital tensions were common: the Eskimos had untrammeled divorce at the wish of either spouse, and several types of wife borrowing or sharing; the free unions of Mexico permitted change of partners without formality; for a long period after the Revolution, Russia permitted a divorce by the simple procedure of either spouse signing a register, and many unions were on a nonlegal basis from the beginning. Mexico also had a widely accepted practice of mistresses for the well-to-do who did not wish to dissolve a legal marriage. India and England historically placed many restrictions on divorce, which is now, however, permitted. Sicily does not allow divorce.

Migration

A number of the communities had paths of partial or complete escape through visits or migration to nearby cities. This was true for Mexican villages—especially the village in transition—for India, and, in recent years, for the Eskimos. Because of the almost total supervision of Russian youth, migration is difficult, which may be one reason for the unruly street behavior of hooligans and for excessive drinking, or even for the secret meetings for listening to forbidden music and writings. England and the European countries have freedom to travel.

Tolerance of crime

Some of the countries ignored or justified petty thefts by the poor.

This was noted for Mexican villages. In Mexico City, such thefts are channeled through the "Thieves' Market." Certain forms of violence (even to the point of homicide) may also be regarded as outlets for tensions.

Social control of mechanisms

None of these or similar tension-reducing mechanisms provided or tolerated by the society were wholly at the will or whim of the individual. Limits were placed upon their use. The mechanisms served as safety valves for pent up emotions; they were checked at the point where they might threaten the security or welfare of the community. For instance, the Eskimo might justifiably kill the seducer of his wife, but a string of murders was a crime not tolerated by the community. In European countries, youth are allowed great freedom on the streets, but a riot or other violence is the signal for police action. The great welfare programs are open only to those who meet broad eligibility requirements.

IMPOSITION OF FOREIGN LAWS

Several of the societies had a radically different set of laws or morals imposed on them by an outside government or by superior administrative agencies. Cooperation by the subject society was not necessarily complete, when the imposed laws ran counter to the traditional laws or customs. A typical reaction was for the subject society or community to continue to follow its own system of approved behavior, apply its own penalties, and conceal from the police or other authorities behavior that violated the imposed laws of the superior group. Eskimos, village Mexicans, tribal or village Indians, Russians, and members of Mafia all are recorded as following this device. During World War II, occupied European countries also failed to cooperate with the occupying forces.

Imposed laws seemed to meet with especially bitter resistance when they struck at "sacred" regulations. In India, for example, the first laws passed by the British against child marriage and *sati* were disregarded for many years; according to some reports, similar laws (as to abolish caste) passed by the Indian government are only superficially obeyed.

If the dominant authority compensates for its disturbance of local customs and laws, and only secular matters are involved, the transition from traditional to foreign regulations seems to meet with less resistance. Among the Eskimos, the destruction of old people and infants who were an impossible burden on the food supply were expedient rather than sacred acts. Government officials and missionaries defined these acts as murder and as immoral. However, welfare payments for dependent children and old age pensions have removed the need for these acts and have made infants and old people an asset instead of a burden.

MASS MEDIA

Several societies placed much responsibility for the extent and vehemence of certain delinquencies on the mass media. Mexico City, Russia, England, Indian cities, and European countries point to exciting rock-and-roll music and films that depict riots and violence, originating in the United States, as stimulating disturbances among youth in their own countries.

FOLK, TRANSITIONAL, AND URBAN SOCIETIES

Turning from specific similarities to a related set of social situations, three types can be distinguished among the societies studied: tribal or folk villages; peasant villages in transition to industrialized urban society; and cities, which may be classified either as overgrown agglomerations of villages or as industrialized urban cities—or somewhere between.

The folk village

The traditional Eskimo village, the Indian-type barrio in Mexico, and the tribes and villages in India are examples of tribal or folk villages. These small communities in different countries had many characteristics in common that were related to misbehavior of children. The details of their similarities differed, since each reflected the larger culture of the total society within which it existed. They were alike in that all secured their own food directly from the land, whether by hunting or fishing, as among the Eskimos, or by tilling the soil, as among the Mexicans and Indians. The general level of living of all three was at or near a subsistence level; even this was maintained only by the unflagging cooperative efforts of the primary group, the smallest effective unit of which was the extended family. The exceptions were well-to-do village families which were few in number and which, among the Eskimos, did not exist. The extended families were part of small villages through which ran a thread of close or remote kinship. Physical survival depended upon cooperation and hard work. This necessity was bulwarked by the feeling of identity within the kin group, which acted as a brake upon misconduct. The most frequent and significant social contacts were encompassed within the kin or village group. Physically, psychologically, and socially, the village turned inward upon itself. Life lay within the folk society, which provided for physical needs, emotional security, pleasures, and social activities.

Children were reared within this self-sufficient folk group by their parents and close relatives. By the available reports, mothers were tender, permissive, and loving during the child's early years, but with an irresistible pressure toward conformity and complete incorporation within the group. Since girls and boys were destined for different adult roles—all within the folk group—the later training of girls fell to the mother and female relatives, that of boys to the father and other adult males. Entrance into adulthood came early in life, usually marked by some formal recognition, such as new adult-type clothing or an advance in occupational responsibility. The age of marriage came early, especially for girls. However, occupational and marital adulthood did not, in any of the societies, bring freedom from the incorporation in the kin group, nor release from the supervision of the elders. In none of the folk societies was there a traditional period of social adolescence—of aimlessness, uncertainty of goals, or freedom from family supervision. Hence, none of the societies had a concept of juvenile delinquency, even if the families occasionally might have to deal with their bad boys and wayward girls. The accounts speak of the close supervision and channeled training of children, of rewards in the way of recognition of development, and of punishment for persistent misconduct. Then, with rather abrupt change of view, the accounts describe adult crime and official punishment.

Villages in transition

Villages in transition from folk to urban pattern were found among the Eskimos, in Mexico (Tepoztlán), and in India. In none of these did the transition come from internal change. In all three cases, it was touched off by contacts with a decidedly more technical, secular, and sophisticated culture. Among the Eskimos, this different culture came from contacts with settlers, villages, or small cities of United States or Canadian origin. In Mexico and India, the contacts were with more urbanized segments of their own culture. The contacts were not all of one kind, but all broke through the wall of traditional culture that for years had shielded the folk community from intrusive cultural elements. Among the Eskimos, the contacts were, and still primarily are, through first-hand interaction. Indian villages found the contacts through periodic migrations of some members to cities, and recently through the introduction of urbanized secondary institutions into the villages, such as schools, courts, and police. In Tepoztlán, the contacts came both through visits of villagers to a nearby small city, migrations to cities, intrusion of outsiders, and the introduction into the village of secondary sources of the outside culture, such as schools and church-sponsored social recreation of a city type.

Stages of transition are clearly seen among the Eskimos. The first stage came when the Eskimos secured from traders and travelers small articles for household use, better weapons for the hunters, and other material objects that could be fitted into their activity patterns. The value system and family patterns were not disturbed. Even the sexual exploits of white men with Eskimo girls and the resulting pregnancies were sufficiently similar to some Eskimo practices to be acceptable.

A second stage of contacts came with the introduction of alien institutions that imposed foreign values on the villagers, sometimes forcefully. Sometimes these could be fitted into the indigenous culture, as the Eskimos added the Christian God to their array of native spirits. Sometimes they brought added benefits to the villagers, such as needed medical care, or a trading post gave an opportunity to trade native products for manufactured equipment.

A third stage came when the villagers began to emulate the outsiders, first in their manner of living—their clothing, forms of recreation, food, and housing—later in their goals and social and personal values. At this stage, conflicts arose between different segments of the village and especially between elders and youth. In all three cultures, schools were an intrusion into the village culture. Teachers were strangers, sometimes from a foreign country, and, even if fellow-countrymen, often were without experience of village living and always with a new range of knowledge. Parents tended to distrust schools, and were indifferent to attendance by their children or refused to send them. When a new religion was introduced, villagers were even more skeptical. The villagers seemed to move from distrust to emulation, and finally to a desire to identify when the outsiders resided in their midst or when the villagers took up residence in or next to settlements with a foreign or more sophisticated cultural level. Eskimos underwent this stage with settlers from the United States or Canada, working-class Mexican villagers with middle-class Mexicans, and Indian villagers with urban Indians. At this stage, the social controls of the family and folk community began to weaken.

Youth who learned of, and wished to follow, the more sophisticated ways found themselves in conflict with the elders in their family and with the ancient values. While still living in the family home in the village, tensions often arose over the disposition of the time of young people and their recreations. A period of social adolescence began to develop. This new stage in the life cycle was not incorporated into the traditional roles and clusters of activities appropriate for different stages of development. Behavior tended to become impulsive and individualized on the part of the young. It was met with old methods of restraint by the elders, who sometimes extended into the middle and even the later teens (formerly the beginning of adulthood) punishments formerly thought appropriate to children. Severe beatings of youth by the father was found in accounts of Mexican and Indian villages.

These new adolescents found several avenues of escape from the binding power of the old ways. One was temporary periodic escape into some nearby city, as when the Tepoztlán youth made visits to the small nearby city, always returning home. Another avenue was migration to a more distant city, with occasional visits to the home village, or a return to the village for marriage and the assumption of adult privileges and responsibilities according to the traditional village pattern. In the transitional stage, youth did not cut themselves off completely from the traditional life, but took a vacation from its restraints. During these periods of vacation, their behavior might deviate markedly from the approved village pattern. Some of it was personally disorganizing, for example, excessive drinking, sexual promiscuity, sometimes actual prostitution by village girls, and a marginal type of crime in the nature of petty thievery or swindling.

Nevertheless, the inroads on the basic personality or character were not deep enough to prevent a return to the village and its ways when the adolescent restlessness had run its course. Those who could not reassume the village ways remained in the city to form a floating delinquent and criminal population or to adjust, in more conforming fashion, to city laws and mores.

The city in process of industrialization

The urban situation breaks into two subtypes. In the first are cities still in the preliminary stage of development into modern urbanization, based on a large-scale money economy. Activities and social control are partially incorporated into secondary organizations instead of remaining in the family, as in the villages. These are the "developing" countries. The outlying areas beyond the cities usually consist of folk villages. The second type of city is typical of the western world where the processes of secondary organization have been going on for long periods of time and have spread from the cities out into the towns and villages. England, Russia, and the other European countries are typical of this stage of urban development. Both types of cities must contend with delinquency and crime.

In the countries under discussion, India and Mexico most nearly approximate the developing countries. In both, cities have been in existence for centuries and an established pattern of urban life prevails. But in both countries, the outlying areas are still essentially of the folk village type, and the migrants who flow into the cities are unacquainted with the demands of city life and preparation needed to meet them. The city is the meeting ground of a long-established urban population, adjusted to the city, and an increasing horde of migrants from folk villages who suddenly find their families, even if present in the city, unable to give them personal or economic security or to supply the social controls and training that had been adequate in the folk village. This situation resembles in some ways the situation in the transitional village, except that the family or individual is now detached from the village and is surrounded by a very different kind of life.

One phase of the new life is the breakdown of family control. The father cannot supply his sons with work nor control their wages and behavior when they secure work. The mother has little opportunity to contribute to the family through minor agricultural tasks and often is drawn into outside employment, leaving younger children unsupervised. The neighbors are less likely to be kin folks who would supplement the family's efforts. Although the city may have, officially or "on paper," a plan for picking up where the family fails—through schools, recreational facilities, juvenile courts, correctional schools, and public welfare—these plans are not fully in operation and are so new and strange to the village migrants that they are sometimes rejected as unneeded or threatening, or are simply ignored. Cities in India and Mexico are both in this stage of development.

A third element in these cities is the prevalence of opportunities for delinquencies and minor crimes by children and youth. A part of the culture of poverty in Mexico City is the incorporation of illegal ways of making ends meet into the daily life of the lower-class people living in the slums. These ways, especially for youth, dovetail into widespread adult criminal patterns on the one hand, and on the other are tolerated by the officials and the middle class as inevitable, or because some profit comes to them for their tolerance.

Industrialized cities

The most serious development of delinquency belongs to the industrialized cities of the West. The most highly developed in technology, based on a massive amount of capital invested in industry, experienced in the secondary life of the city, well-supplied with secondary agencies to supplement the family (schools, social clubs, community houses, public welfare provisions, police, courts, and correctional institutions), they nevertheless have increasing rates of juvenile delinquency and crime. The old formula that poverty breeds crime has broken down in the presence of the post-war increase in affluence and public welfare. When compared with the developing countries there are a number of differences.

The western societies have long since passed through the disorganized city-poverty-crime phase of development. At present, western cities, as compared with the developing countries, have few migrants, and those who come are better prepared for city life since they come not from true folk villages but from villages that are already acquainted with urban patterns of living. Delinquency is more likely to be an indigenous urban growth than a by-product of the maladjustment of folk villagers to urban life that is not prepared to receive them. Not poverty but affluence—an excess of money over what is needed for necessities—seems to be closely related to present types of delinquency, although it is certainly not the root.

In western cities, youth are firmly planted in either school or jobs. Delinquency becomes a leisure time activity, often with many aspects of normal leisure. Money from wages permits a luxurious type of leisure; when wages give out, or are inadequate, the luxuries are secured by theft. Some other person's automobile is "borrowed" for the evening; gas is stolen; money is stolen for an immediate pleasure. These actual crimes shade off into publicly offensive behavior, such as the flamboyant clothing affected by some groups of youth, rudeness to inoffensive citizens on the streets, or the converging bands of youth during holidays at some resort with accompanying wild uncontrolled behavior, often including vandalism and violence.

In the industrialized countries, delinquents seem more prone to cluster in peer groups that sometimes take the form of structured gangs, although the apex of this degree of organization of delinquent behavior seems to be reserved to the United States. To the extent that bands form and establish some continuity, the way is open for the development of a delinquent subculture which gives security and status to its members with little regard for outside disapproval or legal prohibitions.

Communism

Russia provides an interesting case of a country that for almost a half century has been pushing its way, under official pressure, from the older combination, of nonindustrialized cities plus folk villages, into full industrialization. No country has gone as far as Russia in conceiving a plan for complete satisfaction of needs, channeling of behavior into conformity to stated standards, and attempting to suppress delinquency and crime. According to the ideals of communism, delinquency and crime should have no place in a socialist society. However, they continue to exist.

Criminal societies

Mafia and the criminal tribes of India demonstrate the takeover by crime of the central position in an autonomous sub-society within a larger society when the government of the larger society is weak and timid. These criminal societies have values to justify crime. They perpetuate the society through training children to accept the values and to learn the skills of the specific kinds of crime practiced.

WAR

From time to time, societies experience violent upheavals that radically change or virtually destroy the social organization. In the twentieth century, among the societies covered, examples are the Russian Revolution, the Mexican Revolution, the independence of India, and the First and Second World Wars. Such struggles and wars generate violence of many types that are not likely to occur in times of peace. The offenders often are motivated by high ideals of patriotism and, when peace is restored, may be honored by their own society. Wars also disturb the normal patterns of behavior and agencies of social control. People who have not strongly internalized the customary values seize the opportunity to act, impulsively or in a deliberate manner, to secure objects or wealth previously denied to them or to vent suppressed hostilities through unaccustomed violence.

World War II is used as a recent example of violent disturbances. The discussion is limited to the second type of delinquency and crime. War crimes are not included, nor is the disaster to Germany fully explored. The delinquencies are treated in connection with the breakdown of family and community controls and the temporary presence of enemy armies of occupation. Of great significance is the speed with which normal and sometimes improved agencies of organization and control were put into working operation after peace was declared, civilian efforts were transferred to peacetime pursuits, returned military forces absorbed into civilian life, and youth corralled into normal activities. The immediate effects of war seemed violent but short-lived.

Index of Names

Index of Subjects